CULTURE SHOCK!

Paris
At your Door

Frances Gendlin

Graphic Arts Center Publishing Company
Portland, Oregon

In the same series

Australia	Hong Kong	Philippines	London at Your Door
Bolivia	India	Singapore	Rome at Your Door
Borneo	Indonesia	South Africa	
Britain	Ireland	Spain	A Globe-Trotter's Guide
Burma	Israel	Sri Lanka	A Parent's Guide
California	Italy	Sweden	A Student's Guide
Canada	Japan	Switzerland	A Traveller's Medical Guide
Chile	Korea	Syria	A Wife's Guide
China	Laos	Taiwan	Living and Working Abroad
Cuba	Malaysia	Thailand	Working Holidays Abroad
Czech	Mauritius	Turkey	
Republic	Mexico	UAE	
Denmark	Morocco	USA	
Egypt	Nepal	USA—The	
France	Netherlands	South	
Germany	Norway	Vietnam	
Greece	Pakistan		

Illustrations by TRIGG

This book is published by special
arrangement with Times Editions Pte Ltd
Times Centre, 1 New Industrial Road, Singapore 536196
International Standard Book Number 1-55868-405-0
Library of Congress Catalog Number 97-74481
Graphic Arts Center Publishing Company
P.O. Box 10306 • Portland, Oregon 97296-0306 • (503) 226-2402

Printed in Singapore

CONTENTS

7-2015

La Palette is a well-known café in Paris. Parisians flock to outdoor cafés as soon as the spring weather permits.

ACKNOWLEDGMENTS

I am extremely grateful to Colette and Claude Samama, who read every word of the manuscript and who saw me through the project from beginning to end. I value your friendship and support. *Je vous en suis très reconnaissante*. And to my stalwart friend Jean Coyner, whose help throughout was invaluable and whose humor was often sorely needed.

For having read and commented on drafts of the manuscript, thanks especially to Jean and Warren Trabant, who feel the same about Paris as the day they arrived almost fifty years ago; to Fenn Troller, Sally Leabhart, Judith Oringer, Jaem Heath-O'Ryan, and John Zaugg, who also created the elegant maps in Chapter One.

Doctor Francis Bolgert, Mary Briaud, Mme. Henriette Chaibriant (l'Assistance Publique), Rabbi Tom Cohen, Robert Cole, Véronique Gaboriau, Géorges Gross, Drew Harré, Juan Sanchez, and Mme. Michele Simonin (Chambre de Commerce et Industrie de Paris) all read parts of the manuscript and made valuable suggestions, as did Bill Benoit, Ann Overton, James Keough, and Linda Sparrowe. Legal and cultural consultant Jean Taquet read and commented extensively on sections concerning permits. I thank you all for your kindness, and if there are any mistakes herein, they are mine.

Thanks also to Jessica Dempsey, C.J. Maupin, Susannah Patton, Alison Benney, and Laura Steinberger for conversations about living in Paris. And my appreciation for their encouragement over the past few years to Arlette, Eliane, Elsa, and Thierry Samama, and Roland Gozland, Virginia Crosby, and Tom Leabhart. And never least, thanks to my family, for their patience.

A NOTE ON FOREIGN WORDS

Throughout the book, French words are shown in *italics*. If they are words that have exactly the same spelling and meaning in English, italics appear only for the first use. Places, organizations, and other entities are shown in **bold face** the first time they are used, except in Chapter One.

Note that the French call native English-speakers *Anglophones* (as opposed to *Francophones*) and that the word Anglophone is used here in appropriate places. Where nearby services or shops may be needed (e.g. bakeries), they are listed by *arrondissement*; where the services might be needed no matter where they happen to be (e.g. churches), they are listed alphabetically. Where full addresses are given in the text, including the entire number of the *arrondissement* (e.g. 75012), the word Paris has been omitted; if writing to these addresses, be sure to include the city name.

It should also be noted that the French are enthusiastic users of initials and acronyms, so the many Parisian organizations and other entities that are commonly referred to thus appear so here. When looking in the telephone book for a number, if you can't find a listing under its full name, try its initials (RATP, SNCF, FUAJ, etc.).

INTRODUCTION

Fluctuat nec mergitur—It tosses on the waves but does not sink.
—ancient Paris motto

PARIS: MORE THAN THE LOUVRE

Imagine having the Louvre at your doorstep every day of the year and the world's finest temples of gastronomy available to your every culinary whim. Tourists fantasize about how wonderful it would be to live in Paris, but of course few residents of any city go to museums every day or—if they are at all concerned about their budgets—frequent expensive restaurants on a daily basis. Yet Paris truly is a city in which ultimately it is better to live than to visit—somewhat for the reasons above, to be sure, but more for deeper, more lasting reasons that you will discover as your life in Paris continually unfolds. Immersion into any new culture takes some effort, but this is *Paris*, after all, the most entrancing—and yes, romantic—city in the world and worth whatever effort it takes.

Many famous cities have ardent admirers, but there is something unique, something almost palpable, about Paris that inspires true love. It is not about you or me, this love, nor about anyone else—it is about the city itself and how being part of it makes us feel about our own lives. But why Paris? Certainly its charms are not unique. Rome is as historic and Venice as beautiful. Hong Kong is as bold and Marrakesh as exotic. Yet none save Paris has it all. None save Paris combines the best of what has been with a vision of the best to come. None save Paris has the ability to insinuate itself into our daily lives and to demand so much of us. And none save Paris gives so much in return. But the spirit of Paris is hard to convey: its impressions are so personal and its offerings so varied that each new resident ultimately seems to discover it anew.

How many of the thousands who have come before you can you name, people who have made the city their muse? Look at the commemorative plaques on buildings as you pass by. Pablo Picasso painted his masterpiece *Guernica* while living on rue des Grands-Augustins, around the corner from rue Christine, where poet Gertrude Stein lived for a time. Farther north, at Square d'Orléans, the Polish composer Frédéric Chopin settled in near his lover, writer George Sand. Amadeo Modigliani, the "king of Montparnasse," unfortunately died there young and broke, but composer Virgil Thompson (who claimed that if he had to starve to death, he preferred to do it where the food was so good) found fame in time. Ultimately it was writer Katherine Anne Porter who expressed what so many people feel: "Oh God … I'll never leave Paris again, I promise, if you'll let me just get there this once more. If every soul left it one day and grass grew in the pavements, it would still be Paris to me, I'd want to live there."

Parisians have long felt that they have mastered *l'art de vivre*, the art of living well. Tourists who stroll the length of the beautiful Champs-Elysées may sense the enveloping French traditions of elegance, of culture and poise, but it is the total absorption with *l'art de vivre* that truly enriches the soul. It is the habits of everyday life—walking down the city's beautifully designed, historic streets on your way to work, passing graceful apartment buildings and fountained squares, shopping in the exquisitely arranged markets, or lingering in the spring sunshine at a sidewalk café—that continually remind you how gracious Parisian life can be. Or watching a film under the summer stars at La Villette, hearing organ music soar to the high reaches of the Cathedral of Notre-Dame, or gathering with Parisian friends at a neighborhood *bistrot* where you are known as an *habitué* (regular customer)—that will remind you of its fullness as well. Make no mistake: appreciation of experience is what Paris is about.

Much about living in Paris is easy. It is easy to get around and to find out what is going on, no matter how deplorable your spoken French. The city has one of the most efficient public transportation systems in the world, reaching into every hidden nook you would want to explore. Everything you need or want is available somewhere within the city's confines. City Hall provides more information for its residents than you would think possible—from brochures picturing current street repair projects, to a booklet listing all municipal sports facilities, to every detail parents might need to educate their children, to an explanation of why the city's water is so good. Descriptions of public gardens, suggested walks through historic neighborhoods, and schedules for museums and cultural events are produced for residents, not just for visitors. Shops sell guides, histories, restaurant critiques (from the wonderful to the interesting, down to the weird and cheap), directions to intriguing shops, and compendiums of helpful advice from what is open on Sunday to what can be delivered to your door. And locally produced English-language publications are current on the area's events; this includes the indispensable *FUSAC*, described in Chapter Two. Actually Paris may well be the best-explained city in the world.

So what takes the effort? Moving, of course, settling in, getting used to maneuvering and finding the things you need as you descend upon a city not yet your own. Don't underestimate the time required to get your bearings, much less to cram the furniture you had shipped into a space that turns out to be too small. Or to deal with the fact that there is no hot water tap to hook up to the washing machine you brought from home. Or that the documents you were told to bring were not the right ones after all. Or that your three-pronged plug does not fit into the two-slotted transformer. Or that you cannot get a bank account without proof of domicile, but without a bank account cannot get an apartment. These difficulties are wearying to be sure, but can be overcome with dispatch — we hope — by using the information in this book.

The first guidebook to Paris was published in 1685. Ever since, tourist guides have put forth the city's history and described its remarkable sights and sensations. In varying detail, they review restaurants and suggest hotels of all categories. Each tries to present the material in a more eye-catching manner than the others, and each has its own approach to capturing the glory of the *Ville Lumière*, the City of Light. All, however, have one thing in common: they are designed for people visiting for a short while, those tourists who think that what they see in a week is what they would get every day of the year.

This book, different in approach, starts where tourism ends, and it is designed to offer specific advice and assistance about daily life in Paris, including a representative variety of services and shops. Whether your *séjour* is for a month or two or a year or two, the type of information you need for a successful stay is different — deeper and more detailed than that found in tourist guides: where and how to look for appropriate housing, how to manage finances, how to stay healthy and where to get fit, how to access the Internet and where to buy a computer so you can, and where to find a hamburger for your kids are just a few examples of basic information that should help you move comfortably onto the Parisian scene.

VIVE LA DIFFERENCE

Yet, there is a difference between learning how a city works and adapting yourself to its cultural rules. In Paris, this is what takes the effort, requiring more adjustment than you might suspect. How much you want to adapt is up to you, for Paris is flexible above all. You can spend all your time with English speakers—some 100,000 live in the Greater Paris area—and learn just enough French to ask a grocer if the melons are ripe. Many foreign residents do, feeling as much at home and just as content about their Parisian adventures as those who plunge in head first, immersing themselves immediately into what they think is the culture of their Parisian neighbors, intent on figuring it out.

In either case, your success will depend on your expectations. Preconceived ideas may not always prove true. It is best not to assume that life in Paris is more or less like life at home, except for the language. It isn't. Every culture has its own characteristics and attitudes; each populace has its particular approach to life. Start from scratch and take Paris as it is. Appreciate its remarkable beauty, explore its delicious novelty, enjoy its agreeable differences, cope with its difficulties, and try to laugh (if only to yourself) when your own cultural assumptions collide head on with the differing assumptions of the French.

Or when their assumptions collide with yours. "We never talk about money the way you Americans do," an elegant *Parisienne* once said to me, explaining what she thought an important difference between her culture and mine. "We would never ask how much your furniture cost or how high your salary is." I tried to assure her (without success) that never in my life had any American asked me such questions, but her assumptions of my culture were no more developed than mine of hers.

11

LEGENDARY RUDENESS DISMISSED

Here we should talk about these Parisians, for figuring them out is an ongoing subject for articles and books. Talk about *Culture Shock!* Parisians are a constant topic of conversation among newcomers, at least until they think (they think!) they have finally understood the French. Two books—both informative and witty—tell what it is *really* like to feel like an extraterrestrial on this Parisian planet. In *French or Foe* by Polly Platt and *French Toast* by Harriet Welty Rochefort, foreign women married to French men recount their experiences—both amusing and trying—and give advice to newcomers striving for acceptance into Parisian life.

Tourists have so long complained about the rudeness of Parisians—providing many pithy anecdotes—that it has become legendary. Even the famous French guide, *Le Guide du Routard*, warns French travelers coming to Paris not to expect much service or hospitality, saying *"Paris n'est pas la France."* Paris is not France. We all have our stories of how we were ill-treated by someone, sometime, but the best are those that draw a laugh, perhaps a laugh at ourselves for having gotten it all wrong (whatever it was on a particular day) or at how we were, yet again, misunderstood.

Yet all these stories concern Parisians we do not know personally—shopkeepers, bureaucrats in offices, reservationists at train stations. They are all people from whom something is needed, and needed *now*, people whose first answer to your request many be a terse *"non."* (We are not talking about Parisian friends here, who are like friends anywhere—although even here the list of what is done or not done can make a newcomer's head spin.) Residents—as opposed to tourists—who must deal with cultural differences on a daily basis, come to understand that rudeness plays only a small part and that actually the problem—if it is one—is something slightly different. It is this difference that needs to be understood.

Photo: Zeny Cieslikowski

Paris the beautiful: Notre Dame and the Seine, which winds leisurely through Paris.

THE TOURISTS ARE WRONG

In this case the tourists are wrong—dead wrong. The truth is that Parisians, especially those you do not know, are meticulously, if superficially, polite. Immediately upon seeing you they say *"bonjour madame"* or *"bonjour monsieur;"* they express thanks at the end of a transaction, and they wish you a *bonne journée* (a good day) when you depart. But this is where it ends. They do not volunteer advice that would help with a decision, they do not automatically proffer their expert opinions in a given situation where you know nothing, and they do not chat with you while you choose between a yellow or blue tie. In short, they do not help you out. And many do not smile. Yet their formality and strict manners are pleasant,

13

even a relief, if you come from a society where shopkeepers and clerks do not distinguish between friendliness and familiarity. Formality has its place, and its place is Paris.

Most Parisians are not rude, they are just the way they were taught to be. As children their upbringing was strict and unwavering, with expectations for proper behavior, their schooling rigid and competitive. They were taught to get things exactly right, to be direct and to the point. Even their handwriting was controlled, and as adults their handwriting is still scrutinized when they apply for a job. But their cultural indoctrination did not include the welcoming smile or small talk. If a clerk's reply is *"non,"* it may well be that he does not want to risk being blamed or to bear the responsibility for having made an error.

As art critic John Russell once commented, "It must seem that in Paris every door is marked 'private,' every notice means 'keep out' (even if it doesn't actually say it) and all information is classified." So do not take it personally that the French are not like you. They're French. But don't give up, for there are ways to be successful in getting what you need, and this is what you need to know.

BREAKING DOWN THEIR RESERVE

Some foreigners have never met their neighbors, some have become fast friends with the person across the courtyard. Somehow, Paris brings out who you are and responds in kind. If you are someone who is irritated easily by small problems, Paris will no doubt irritate you much of the time. If you see little problems as challenges, you will meet them successfully more than many others do. And if you are a person who makes friends easily, you will eventually break down some of the barriers of Parisian reserve. But if you are too reserved in outlook, you will wind up not knowing the person next door. It's tricky. A simple *"bonjour madame/monsieur"* in the elevator is acceptable (although more than many Parisians are used to), but if you add "how was your vacation?" you may well be going too far. Some people joke, however, that if you want to make friends in animal-loving Paris, just walk a dog.

If it takes time to make Parisian friends, once you have made them, they will be loyal for life, going out of their way for you, including you in family gatherings at a *bistrot*, in their walks in the Bois de Boulogne, or at their evenings at the Opéra Bastille. This does not mean that you may use the familiar *tu* to address each other or that you can drop in unannounced. It does not mean that any of the social rules may be broken (even if you do not know what they are until you have broken them). It does not mean that they will think your joke is funny, if in their culture it is not. And it does not mean you can be overly intimate, which is worse than not being friendly enough. The French in general tend to guard their privacy, so they are astounded when foreigners — especially the open, gregarious Americans — divulge too early in a budding relationship aspects of their lives that the French tell only their oldest friends.

Yet, this reserve is slowing giving way, especially among the young. Young Parisians who have grown up with international films, with English-language television dubbed into French, with performances by international rock groups, and who wear Adidas sports shoes and Levi's jeans are more relaxed in their approach to life — in their opinion, keeping the best of French culture while moving onto the international scene. These are the ambitious and well-educated young professionals who speak other languages, travel more widely than their parents ever did, and who will eventually bring about change to the hierarchical, top-down structure of French life. These are the young shopkeepers and clerks who are eager to try out their English (which may be no better than your French) and boldly ask you questions about your own culture, so different from their own. In the meantime, their parents complain that Paris is *trop américanisé*, concerned that foreign (i.e., inferior) cultures, especially American commercialism, are infiltrating their own. Afraid of globalization but knowing it is coming, and even knowing that in many ways they are benefiting from the availability of inexpensive, good-quality products, does not mean they like it one whit.

Actually, this is a time of some confusion as Paris strives to maintain its ancient traditions while adapting to conditions unforeseen. An old saying, *plus ça change, plus c'est la même chose* ("the more things change, the more they stay the same"), may no longer be so apt. And a culture that believes in rational solutions to most problems is at a loss when they do not appear. Is France becoming less French, and if so, what, if anything, is there to do? How many McDonald's should be allowed in Paris? There are more than 100 so far. How many poor immigrants from Arab nations should the country admit, and how many jobs will they take from the French? Unemployment remains high at 12 percent. And to what degree should the beautiful French language be infiltrated by foreign words? Parisians feeling *le stress* of modern life often go out to the countryside for a *long week-end*.

Other world capitals are dealing with problems of the same sort. Yet the marvel of Paris, what brings such richness to its life, is that the city is holding tightly to its most appreciated traditions while meeting the future head on. Old, wood-paneled and mirrored restaurants serve elegantly presented plates of low-fat foods. Airy, high-ceilinged apartments in seventeenth-century *hôtels particuliers* now have hookups for washer-dryers. Narrow, medieval streets are refurbished rather than widened. And even most of the exquisitely landscaped, aristocratic gardens have begun to let people walk on the grass.

THE PARIS RULES

Fortunately, as your Paris life unfolds and you come to know which neighborhood *fromagerie* (cheese store) is your favorite or which teller at the *banque* goes a little out of the way for you, you will be dealing less with strangers and more with people you know. You will walk down the streets and suddenly realize that the city's by-ways and hidden nooks are your own. The essence of your life will seem more vibrant, your conversation more animated, your days more full. Now you will be developing your own *art de vivre*, keeping your own culture and traditions while taking on those of the French. This is the beginning of *la belle vie*, the good life you had originally imagined, but come true in ways you had not expected. What can you do to help it along?

- Learn French. Do the best you can even if at first it is not very good. If you don't, you will always remain an outsider, even in the shops near your home. Pronunciation is the key, even though your French accent may be more reminiscent of Dracula than of Yves Montand. With just the slightest mistake, you may be looked at as though you were from another planet. Pronunciation does make a difference: *salut* (pronounced "saloo") means "hello," for example, but *salaud* (pronounced "saloh") is a word not used in polite society. Some people think it does not matter *what* you say as long as you say it correctly.

- Let nothing faze you. Be cordial at all times. Before you have even entered all the way into a shop, say *"bonjour madame"* to the *vendeuse*, ask to look around, and say *"merci,"* and *"au revoir"* when you leave. If you need to get someone's attention—a person who for whatever reason has not looked up from a desk or counter as you approached—manners will do the trick. Say, *"Excusez-moi de vous déranger, monsieur, mais..."* ("Excuse me for bothering you, sir, but...") and then ask for what you need. The French, whether they like it or not, will respond to manners. If someone seems unkind, do not take it personally and don't overreact. With cordiality you at least stand a chance of an easy transaction; without it, you do not.

- Look good and act in control. Appearances and confidence count. Parisians respond to people who look well put together and who come across as poised, with some dignity of spirit. Even if you are a student who has arrived in Paris *sans soucis et sans les sous* (without a care and dead broke), make an effort to portray yourself as worthy of note. A confident attitude conveys that you will not accept inferior service, and this is something the French respect.

- Pay attention. Read the books mentioned above and listen carefully to the stories of friends who have already been through the acclimatization process. Read also Sally Adamson Taylor's *Culture Shock! France*. Pay attention to each situation for they are not all the same. If you are a boss going to an employee's home for dinner, your approach will be different than if you are the employee going to the home of your boss. Learn how late you should arrive for dinner (variable, but *never* on time). Learn which flowers are taboo (chrysan-themums, which are for funerals, or carnations, which are depressing) and that generally you do not bring wine, which may insult the host, who has probably selected something special from his *cave*. On the other hand, some people say that a man may bring flowers and a woman may bring wine. It takes some figuring out. When you have doubts, just ask a Parisian, who will no doubt be pleased that you are making an effort to understand how Paris works.

- Ply *le système D*. Parisians too make train reservations and need help from clerks, and they too get the answer *"non."* Literally, *le système débrouillard* means being resourceful on your own, getting by, muddling through. Basically it means finagling any way you can, within socially acceptable and legal parameters, to get what you want, whether it is a connection through a friend of a friend or using every persuasive charm you have to convince an office clerk to bend a rule just a little (that truthfully might not be a rule at all). In short, the ability to *séduire* or charm someone who is brusque and unhelpful is *le système D*. Play on their sympathy. Rely on their expertise. Be helpful but persistent. Don't take *"non"* for an answer. Ply *le système D*.

- Love Paris every minute, for it deserves to be loved, and it responds in kind. The more you partake of its resources, the more you participate in its traditions, the more you take on its pace, the more you will get in return. As Ernest Hemingway wrote about his life in Paris when he was young and poor: "There is never any ending to Paris and the memory of each person who has lived in it differs from that of any other ... Paris was always worth it and you received return for whatever you brought to it."

Parisians know they live in the most fascinating city in the world and with a peculiar "pride of place" believe that it is theirs and theirs alone. No matter how excellent your French, no matter how many years you have spent in Paris, you will never know Paris as well as they. So they think, and it is up to you to prove them wrong. But wouldn't it be nice if they—who are so sure their culture is superior to everyone else's—displayed genuine curiosity about your own? Some do, of course, and these are the people most likely to become your friends, comparing customs, laughing with you at differences, and generally taking you under their French wings to help you along. It is up to you to find them, and eventually you will if you look in the right places— your church, your workplace, your gym, or your professional and social clubs. Be open to what this glorious City of Light has to offer, for everything is ultimately here for you to find. *Bienvenue à Paris*. Welcome home.

CHAPTER ONE

THE CITY OF LIGHT

PAST AND PRESENT ENTWINED

Paris is without a doubt the most beautiful of the world's capital cities, and well it should be. For more than a millennium, kings, emperors, and presidents have devoted their patriotic, religious, and imaginative energies to creating their capital, and the result is Paris, a city of splendor unmatched on the world's stage. Yet it is a city designed to be lived in as well as admired, and it is the almost seamless weaving of the city's intricate history into today's everyday life that makes the experience of Paris so deeply rich.

It is hard not to think about Paris' history wherever you go. Every street name is a voice from the past, from rue Vercingétorix, recalling the Celtic warrior who rebelled against the conquering Romans in 52 B.C., to boulevard Haussmann, named for the man who 150 years ago designed much of the structure of Paris today.

If you are stuck in traffic on the fume-ridden, 36-kilometer beltline highway, the *périphérique*, remember that your slow path is following the city's final fortress walls of almost 200 years ago. Wherever you are, the saga of Paris is in plain view.

Of course, Paris is more than its streets. Over a thousand-year period, almost every French monarch left his mark on the city, as Parisians are taught in school. Most evident today, though, is the legacy of two men, Georges Haussmann and François Mitterrand, neither of them kings. Under Napoleon III, Baron Haussmann refurbished (and strengthened the security of) a city that had declined under revolution, overcrowding, and epidemics of disease. He demolished the slums and replaced them with straight streets and broad avenues (that police could control), spectacular squares, landscaped parks, an efficient sewer system and reservoirs, and apartment buildings that remain gracious abodes today. President Mitterrand's *Grands Projets* envisioned the Paris of tomorrow — urban revival and an architectural entry into modernity — for a city whose cultural and economic position would be solidified in the European Union and beyond.

At the end of this millennium, Parisians grumble about the state of their city. Talk about the traffic and the smog! Nonetheless, they are proud of how the history of Paris melds into their comfortable, modern surroundings, and they basically know how fortunate they are. Foreigners have to work for this understanding, learning where the past shows through and how the city's modernity takes its shape from history. Keep some reference books handy. *Around and About Paris* by Thirza Vallois is a three-volume description of every district. In French, try the *Guides du Promeneur*. Both describe detailed walks through each area that show how the city has evolved. *A Traveller's History of Paris* by Robert Cole is concise and well presented. And *Le Dictionnaire Historique des Rues de Paris* is a two-volume etymology in French of every street name in the city. All are available in bookshops.

THE PHYSICAL PLANT

A small city, Paris encompasses no more than 80 square kilometers and is only about 12 kilometers across. It was built on a low, marshy plain with its highest point, 148 meters above sea level, at its northeastern edge. The city lies on both sides of the river Seine, toward the center of what is known as the Paris Basin. Thirty-six bridges span the river, bringing the Seine and its banks into the daily life of the city. The river rises in Burgundy and wends its way for more than 600 kilometers to the sea. Thirteen of those kilometers run gently through the city from east to west, taking a long curve through the middle and flowing around two islands, one of which since ancient times has done its part to make the city what it now is. Although officially Paris is *intra-muros* (within the old city walls), Greater Paris today includes the outlying towns that border the *périphérique*. About two million people live *intra-muros*. Ten million more live in the suburbs, giving the metropolis a population of over twelve million.

Dense and compact, Paris nonetheless retains a sense of human scale. Buildings are low, few neighborhood streets run straight, and there is always something unexpected, often charming, to catch the eye. Despite its warrens of narrow, medieval streets, Paris is an open city, characterized by ornate, spectacular squares that celebrate its history and by wide boulevards that converge at open junctions where residents do their shopping or sit at sidewalk cafés. Formally planned gardens and parks and casual, leafy squares dot the landscape. One hundred thousand trees line both narrow streets and wide boulevards. Two beautiful wooded parks, the Bois de Boulogne to the west and the Bois de Vincennes to the east, provide respite at Paris' flanks. The Seine, too, opens the city as it flows through, and it is joined from the northeast by the canal Saint-Martin, itself crossed at intervals by little metallic bridges and lined in places by pleasant rows of trees.

Photo: Zeny Cieslikowski

Spring blooms in Paris.

Although the climate is fairly mild overall, and Paris often shines gloriously in the sun, the city's uneven weather can bring problems in any season. In winter, the temperature may hover below freezing for weeks, with the wind howling down the wide boulevards and nipping at narrow corners. Rains make the river rise, and occasionally there is snow. The spring, even well into the supposedly romantic April is often unpleasantly grey and wet, but there are also splendid, almost-warm, sunny days. True spring begins in May—the first signs are newly planted flower boxes on windowsills and the tables that begin to reappear outside cafés. By the time summer is in full swing, however, late in July and into August, the often sweltering temperatures and high pollution drive Parisians out of town until the beginning of September, when they return in a burst of energy known as the *rentrée*. September and October can be the best months, pleasantly sunny and warm.

23

THE LAYOUT

Since the time of Napoleon in the early nineteenth century, Paris has been divided into administrative zones called *arrondissements*. Originally there were twelve, but in 1860 Napoleon III annexed outlying villages, doubling the population and creating more *arrondissements*, finally reaching the current twenty. Each *arrondissement* has its *mairie* (town hall), its mayor, and its *conseil d'administration d'arrondissement* (district council), which elects the mayor of Paris. Most of the bureaucratic business for residents is done at their local *mairie,* and the *mairie* is the best source for information about all public functions in the city.

The *arrondissements* begin at the core of Paris, the Ile de la Cité, and move in an outward spiral, with the areas becoming larger toward the periphery. City maps are arranged and numbered by *arrondissement*, from the 1*er* (*le premier*) to the 20*e* (*le vingtième*). Historically, the eastern parts of Paris were the factories and the workers' neighborhoods, shabby and dense. The western parts—upwind from the unsanitary conditions and stench of industry—were the most aristocratic. Thus it was to the west that the nobles removed themselves after the 1789 Revolution, and the west remains the most luxurious today. The ambitious *Grands Projets* of President Mitterrand have upgraded the eastern *arrondissements*, however, with imaginative, modern public buildings, miles of planted walkways, old buildings refurbished and new ones built, and neighborhoods now trendy rather than squat.

Within the *arrondissements* are the *quartiers* (neighborhoods) with their individual characters and traditions. Although in times past Parisians could be categorized by their *arrondissement,* this is less true today as rising housing costs are forcing them to make their homes wherever prices are reasonable. Many older neighborhoods are being gentrified, sometimes to the dismay of long-time residents who bemoan the loss of their area's traditional character in the process of its becoming a more agreeable place to live.

Parisians have also identified themselves by which side of the river was their home. In fact, the city has historically characterized itself in relation to the Seine. From the Middle Ages, the Right Bank (*Rive Droite*) was the mercantile focus of the city, servicing the aristocrats who had settled near the Marais and the Louvre. The Left Bank (*Rive Gauche*), home to the Sorbonne and other institutions of learning and the arts, was inhabited by artists and intellectuals. Even today, the modern city continues to divide itself thus, with headquarters of banks, the largest department stores, and much of the city's commerce clustered on the Right Bank, while the Left Bank has the universities, the artists' galleries, and the vibrant atmosphere of creativity and ideas.

THINKING ABOUT PLACE

Parisians live in every habitable square meter of space in their city, in spacious apartments overlooking leafy boulevards and in tiny walk-up flats above neighborhood stores. The *quartiers* can be airy and open, crowded and dense, or a succession of commercial streets that seem not to be a neighborhood at all. Apartment buildings range from the graceful and traditional to the modern and faceless, down to the dilapidated and cheap. Some tranquil side streets have charming little houses, and many large buildings look inward onto quiet courts, but some apartments must have windows with *double vitrage* (double panes) to keep out the noise of the street. Parisians live in them all.

If an area seems strictly for business, just look up and you will see a flowerpot on a ledge and a curtain waving in the breeze of an open window. If an area seems so noisy you could not understand anyone possibly living there, just wait until you see someone coming home from work with a briefcase in one hand and the evening's *baguette* in the other. And if an area seems absolutely perfect, be prepared to pay handsomely for the perfection, so rarely achieved.

25

The neighborhood you choose for yourself will, of course, depend on your circumstances and your purse. Much will depend on the length of your stay, whether six months or a year, or perhaps permanent, with family in tow. A residential neighborhood may not be important if you are single and your *séjour* is only a few months, but a workplace close by may not be important if you are married and your children need a park and proximity to a bilingual school. Much will also depend on your personal preferences: will you prefer living in the *banlieue* (suburbs) even if it requires the use of an automobile? Or would you prefer a lively area in the *centre ville*, even if you have to drive your children to school? Or is living in a dense *quartier* acceptable if it is close to restaurants and exciting cultural activities? Remember that not all areas look residential, but Parisians and newcomers alike live in them all.

After deciding on your priorities, given the ever-present need for compromise, look carefully at each *quartier* you are considering. Are there open spaces in which to stroll, sidewalk cafés in which to relax, the kinds of shops you use, a park in which children are playing? Is there a *métro* stop nearby, and even better, a *correspondance*, meaning a junction of two different lines? Is there a major street artery nearby, but not too near? If you look at an apartment on a weekend, come back during a rush hour and realistically gauge the traffic and the noise. Look at the mix of people walking on the street, do some window shopping, and do everything you can to understand if this is the best place for you.

The River Islands

The Ile de la Cité, the oldest part of Paris, remains the sentimental heart of the city. *Kilomètre zéro*, the point from which French distances are measured, is a dial embedded in the square in front of the Cathedral of Notre-Dame. From its beginnings 2,000 years ago as home to a Celtic tribe called the Parisii, the island has been an area of constant activity. Today, tourists congregate at Notre-

Dame and Sainte-Chapelle, the Conciergerie, and at a memorial to the deported Jews of World War II. Parisians come to the Préfecture de Police, the Hôpital Hôtel Dieu, and the Palais de Justice, built on the site where Roman governors once resided and later the kings of France. Hardly a residential neighborhood, there are nonetheless pockets of elegant apartments, especially north of Notre-Dame, along the *quais*, and around the intimate Place Dauphine, an enchanting, tranquil triangle of leaves and brick and white stone dating from 1607.

Both the grandeur of the island and its apparent lack of neighborhood character are owing to the redevelopment by Baron Haussmann, who demolished a warren of narrow streets and dilapidated buildings, and who brought order to the island while dispossessing its 20,000 residents. It is this centrality that makes the Ile de la Cité convenient, especially for a short stay. Bridges go directly into the 5e and 6e on the Left Bank and into the 1er and the 4e on the Right Bank. Even the métro stop on the island opens onto Place Lépine, the popular market for flowers and birds.

Just to the east is the Ile St-Louis. Despite tourists who stroll down its main street, rue St-Louis-en-l'Ile, the island remains peaceful and gracious. Although bridges connect it to both river banks and to the Ile de la Cité, the feeling of remove from modern life reminds one of how Paris must have looked 300 years ago. Poplar trees shade the streets, and the views of Paris from the *quais* are exceptional. Since development began only in the seventeenth century under Louis XIII, there is a unified architectural feel to the island, its harmonious, gracious buildings of approximately the same width and height. The old *hôtels particuliers* (townhouses) and the large restored apartments still house affluent Parisians, and some foreigners have bought apartments to rent them to tourists for a well-deserved, often hefty price. Unfortunately, few long-term apartments come available, and when they do, their prices are steep, but the residents think the Ile St-Louis worth the price.

27

Map: John Zaugg

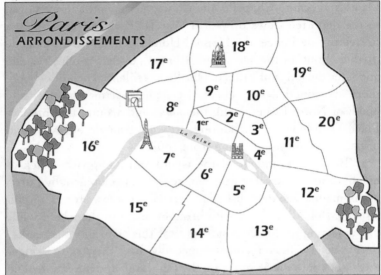

The twenty arrondissements of Paris.

First Arrondissement (1*er*)

Encompassing many of the attractions tourists come to see, such as the Louvre, the Tuileries gardens, and the long rue de Rivoli, along with some of the city's most fashionable hotels, the **First Arrondissement** is populated day and night, but not particularly by residents. From its beginnings, this has been among the most commercial areas of the city, and even now, just a few streets away from the tourists, financial and administrative offices continue to rule.

The atmosphere of the 1*er* is, in a sense, determined by the Louvre. To its east are the busy traffic junction of Châtelet, the former site of a dreaded prison, but now home to several popular theaters, and Les Halles, for hundreds of years the city's marketplace and now site of an enormous shopping complex, Forum des Halles. Les Halles has lovely gardens, a cultural pavilion, and a popular play facility for children, but its periphery is a hangout for young tourists and street entertainers. La Samaritaine department store draws shoppers, and commerce dominates this eastern edge.

Yet, as is so typical of Paris, tucked in a few streets away is one of the more peaceful oases in the city, the quiet and romantic Jardins du Palais-Royal. Spacious old apartments nestle amidst discreet offices, and residents can still have the feeling of gentle separation from modernity while deep in its heart. An interesting neighbor is the lovely, circular Place des Victoires, home to fashion designers who occupy the harmonious seventeenth-century buildings. This may not be what one considers a real neighborhood, but it has its attractions, including a variety of restaurants.

West of the Louvre, the area still benefits from its royal heritage, when kings lived at the Tuileries in a palace destroyed toward the end of the last century during the protests of the Paris Commune. What remains are the Jardins des Tuileries, a landscaped greensward that is one of Paris' most beautiful parks. Across the rue de Rivoli are both tourist shops and high-class enterprises of the type that once tended to the aristocrats who lived in the shadow of the king. Bordered on the west by the imposing Place de la Concorde, the size of a small town in itself, the area culminates nearby in the spectacular, grey granite Place Vendôme, a royal square begun by Louis XIV in 1686, and now home to exclusive banking establishments, jewelers, offices, a few plush apartments, and the Ritz Hotel. This remains the upscale end of the *arrondissement*, and the apartments in the side streets and above the shops along rue du Rivoli can be comfortable and gracious. Much depends on the shops below and where the tour buses stop. The parallel street above, rue St-Honoré, is lined with shops and restaurants. Although none of this area is much of a residential neighborhood, for a short stay it might be fun.

Second Arrondissement (2e)

Continuing the commercial center of Paris, the tiny **Second Arrondissement** contains *La Bourse* (Stock Exchange), financial offices of every type and nationality, airline offices, travel agencies, and insurance companies. Cafés, cinemas, and theaters keep the western edge alive well into the night. This is not really a residential area although, of course, there are apartments here and there, and some rundown areas are being revitalized by a younger set of Parisians.

Toward the east are the hundreds of factories and warehouses of Paris' clothing industry, the "rag trade," which centers at cart- and traffic-jammed Sentier and Place du Caire. Except for streets near the fashion-designer enclave of rue Etienne-Marcel and Place des Victoires and a few streets toward the east, there are only a few areas one would consider for a residence. Away from Place de l'Opéra, much of the area is deserted at night and on weekends, except for the large avenues and the eastern boundary of boulevard Sébastopol. There is little open space, and this is the least green area of the city.

The 2e, however, is the site of some *passages*, covered shopping arcades dating from the last century. Several are beautifully restored for upscale shopping and dining, while others remain full of jumbled stores. Also here is one of Paris' important market streets, the pedestrian-only rue Montorgueil, an attractive combination of food emporiums, *traiteurs*, and terraced cafés. People come here to do their shopping, but although refurbishment is now beginning to spruce up the area and prices are fairly reasonable, most still head somewhere else to home.

The Marais (3e and 4e)

The **Third** and **Fourth arrondissements** are collectively known as the *Marais*, ancient swampland that once was part of the riverbed of the Seine. Although not all parts of the Marais conform to the trendy image the name now evokes, many streets have a feeling of historical delight, of being transported back to the Paris of 300 years ago.

The 4e, as noted, is the oldest part of the city, encompassing as it does half of the Ile de la Cité; this also was the first part of the Right Bank to be settled—around the present rues des Blancs-Manteaux and Vieille-du-Temple—more than 1,000 years ago.

The Marais became popular with royalty and aristocrats about 400 years ago. The Place des Vosges was the first royal square to be built in the city and has been authentically restored to look much the same as it did in 1612: a square of almost identical, warm brick and stone townhouses with steep, pitched roofs, surrounding an exquisitely sculptured, symmetrical garden. In fact, the southern part of the Marais had from the sixteenth century seen the building of *hôtels particuliers* for nobles and aristocrats, especially near Place des Vosges, then called Place Royale. In the eighteenth century, the area was abandoned when the court moved west toward Versailles. Sadly, with the vicissitudes of time and politics, the Marais declined.

How it has changed! Now one of the city's most colorful districts, the Marais benefited from the 1962 *loi Malraux,* which mandated preservation of historic districts. Decrepit medieval streets and once-stately *hôtels particuliers* were refurbished without succumbing to the faceless modernization that other parts of the city were suffering at the time. Now this area is an unexpected delight of still-narrow, angled streets without a major artery to confront pedestrians, low-rise buildings, and not a métro station in sight. Art galleries, fashion shops, nightspots, and restaurants enliven this good-natured district that is more in demand every day.

Although a Jewish community lived here until its expulsion from France in 1394, it is since the last century that the influx of Eastern European Jews has given the quarter much of its character. Focused at the thirteenth-century rue des Rosiers and rue des Ecouffes, kosher restaurants, bakeries, delicatessens, and groceries abound. That they draw crowds on Sunday, when the rest of the city is closed, has encouraged neighboring boutiques and galleries to stay open as well, making this a lively area every day, although many of the Jewish shops are shut on Saturday.

The Marais has also become the major focus of the Parisian gay community. Starting near Châtelet and moving east, gay nightspots and restaurants contribute to the area's eclectic 24-hour atmosphere. The bookshop, Les Mots à la Bouche, in rue Ste-Croix-de-la-Bretonnerie is a central information point for this increasingly open and accepted community.

All in all, the part of the Marais that stretches west from Place de la Bastille to rue des Archives is a fun and somewhat affordable area in which to live. Comfortable apartments can be found in a range of prices, but parking in the crowded streets is scarce. The residential area includes the small *quartier* below rue St-Antoine. Buildings of homogeneous architecture line its sides, and most are well maintained. Just a few museums, some antique shops at Village St-Paul, and the remnants of the medieval city wall draw visitors. Convenient shopping for both areas stretches along the rue de Rivoli, where it takes over from rue St-Antoine.

Above the fashionable rue des Francs-Bourgeois, once the northern perimeter of the city walls, the *3e* begins, although here it is indistinguishable from the *4e*. On lovely rue Payenne, the Museum of the History of Paris was, in the seventeenth century, the *hôtel particulier* of the literary Marquise de Sévigné, who enjoyed its proximity to aristocratic neighbors in rue du Parc-Royal and Place Royale. This area declined when the nobles moved on, melding in dilapidated spirit with the *quartier* farther north, toward what is now the gritty Place de la République.

This northeastern corner (known as *Temple*) is where the Knights Templar in the twelfth century settled after their return from the Crusades. Their Enclos du Temple was a powerful, fortified city, containing a palace, a church, and commerce, and it provided safety for workers and artisans within its walls. It is all long gone, even the tower in which Louis XVI was kept prisoner until his execution in 1793. When it was finally torn down by Napoleon, all that remained were the workers and tradesmen, and the area took on a rather shabby character, which it still has today.

It was precisely the inexpensive aspects of this sector that drew its present population. The post-World War I influx of Asians made the 3e the first Chinese community in Paris, and there is still an Asian presence around rues des Gravilliers and au Maire. At rue de Nazareth there is an important Jewish synagogue, as this was the community's center before it moved south toward rue des Rosiers.

Much of this northern border remains dull, with unreconstructed housing in drab streets, although this means that rents are not high. The rag trade continues: a cheap clothing market is always on the verge of being shut down, and some factories employ the immigrants who continue to come. Nonetheless, gentrification is slowly moving north, up rue Charlot and around the pretty little Square du Temple. As the feeling of the Marais expands and housing becomes scarce, this area is sure to benefit.

The Latin Quarter and St-Germain
Encompassing the **Fifth Arrondissement (5e)** and by extension some of the **Sixth (6e)**, the *Quartier Latin* is where many romantic images of Paris come true. This can be one of Paris' most exciting areas in which to live. Judging from the numbers of people — French and foreign alike — who day and night stroll the boulevards, explore the medieval streets, browse in the bookshops, or frequent the cafés or cinemas, this ancient part of Paris is a most intriguing place to be.

Although the *5e* is named for the medieval scholars who were required to speak to each other in Latin, the part of the *6e* that borders on the crowded boulevard St-Michel qualifies as well, for it was all one *quartier* until Baron Haussmann widened the ancient Roman road and distanced an integral part of the quarter to the west.

Famous first for the Sorbonne, founded in 1230 by Robert de Sorbon, the Latin Quarter is today an area of diverse intellectual endeavors. Even the Sorbonne is just one part of the seventeen-school University of Paris system, much of which is still centered here. This *arrondissement* contains the Collège de France, a humanist institution founded in the sixteenth century, several of the prestigious *Grandes Ecoles*, the famous *lycées* Louis-Le-Grand and Henri-IV and the Institut du Monde Arabe, plus other institutions, a government ministry, museums, the impressive Islamic mosque, the Val-de-Grâce hospital, a botanical garden with zoo, the oceanographic institute, and an aquarium. Here too are important historical churches and, imposing itself on the area's village-like streets, the grand Panthéon.

Fortunately for those who live in the area, the Latin Quarter remains agreeably residential. Its low, stucco or stone buildings nestle securely amid the massive institutions that dominate its core. Along the narrow, medieval streets on both sides of the bisecting boulevard St-Germain, apartments of all types can be found: large and small, long-term and short-term rentals, for this is an area that caters to faculty and students, a population that comes and goes.

Rents may be high, especially for the larger apartments in the narrow streets north of St-Germain, heading toward the *quais*. South of the boulevard, going up into the winding hilly streets, the residential area is more affordable. Of course there are tourists here, particularly on the charming rue Mouffetard and at Place de la Contrescarpe, but somehow they do not intrude. The area that borders the 13e is fairly inexpensive and lively and popular as a result. Just about any street will do nicely here, but do not look for apartments in October, when the students return and are looking for their own.

What draws tourists as well as locals are the international book stores and music shops, offbeat boutiques, world-renowned jazz clubs and cabarets, theaters, an inviting mix of restaurants and cafés, and a large selection of foreign film houses. Tourists congregate around Place St-Michel, where shops are downscale and restaurants overpriced. Nonetheless, this all contributes to the exuberant, youthful atmosphere that pervades the *Quartier Latin*.

The intellectual and artistic focus of the 5e becomes more sophisticated as one moves west toward Place St-Germain-des-Prés. Here, where the Romans dedicated a temple to the goddess Isis, is the heart of the 6e, the 1,500-year-old site of Paris' first Christian church, now the Eglise St-Germain-des-Prés. This square is one of the most picturesque in Paris, and the crowds who come here every day of the year, whether to visit the ancient church or to sip a coffee across the street, know it full well.

For centuries this area was an extension of the Latin Quarter but is now known for the period after World War II, when existentialism and a liberated, intellectual life unfolded at those now-famous cafés—the Deux Magots and the Café de Flore, at the Brasserie Lipp and at the bookshop, La Hune—when Simone de Beauvoir and Jean Paul Sartre came here after the Vavin métro station at Montparnasse was closed. Jazz had long been hot nearby on rue St-Benoît. Today the cafés are the province of tourists, of the chic set from the *arrondissement* to the west coming to see and be seen, and of a few writers trying to soak up the atmosphere of the past.

This part of the *arrondissement* has it all. Starting near Place de l'Odéon and stretching past Mabillon, the well-trod streets off the boulevard have antique shops and art galleries, cinemas and theaters, some of the city's trendiest restaurants and cafés, upscale boutiques, and markets at rue de Buci and near rue Mabillon. Toward the Seine, in the *quartier* Beaux-Arts, named for its prestigious arts school, the narrow, angled streets have low-rise seventeenth- and eighteenth-century buildings, their apartments rented by both Parisians and foreigners.

This is certainly one of the most agreeable *quartiers* in the city. Between the relaxed 5*e* on the east and the reserved 7*e* on the west, housing here shares the character of its neighbors. It starts at a reasonable price along the east and gradually becomes more expensive the farther west one goes, particularly between boulevard St-Germain and the Seine. The atmosphere is unique, and it is one Parisians are fighting to preserve, although the battle seems lost. Local shops are moving out as rents rise and impersonal giants, such as Armani, Louis Vuitton, and Cartier, are moving in.

Although the atmosphere may change from street to street, it doesn't change for the worse. Around Place St-Sulpice, with its fountained square and fashionable surrounds, and along such streets as the classy rue de Tournon, rue de l'Odéon, the wide boulevard Raspail, and rue Notre-Dame-des-Champs, the apartments are large, airy, and often expensive. This holds true especially for buildings overlooking the spectacular Jardin du Luxembourg, one of the nation's most beloved public gardens and once the exquisite palace grounds of Marie de Médicis. This residential part of the *quartier* may be more quiet in spots, but it picks up once again as the busy rue de Rennes reaches Montparnasse, where the atmosphere of quiet sophistication begins to disappear.

Seventh Arrondissement (7*e*)

Despite the tourists that stream constantly to the Eiffel Tower, the **Seventh Arrondissement** is one of the most luxurious and tranquil areas of the city. The broad, leafy streets provide a haven for residents, for the government ministries and embassies that have moved into the eighteenth-century mansions of the aristocracy, and for some erstwhile nobles who still live in their ancestral homes. This is "old money" Paris. The presence of the Assemblée Nationale, of UNESCO, and of the area's most famous official resident, the French prime minister, at the Hôtel Matignon, brings security to the area, and this is the safest *arrondissement* in the city.

Living here is extremely agreeable, almost a suburb in the city center. Although there are discreet commercial areas and some restaurants, there is little evening activity. Yet the 7e is situated between the vibrant 6e and the middle-class 15e, both of which offer every service that the 7e might not. Apartments are large, gracious, and well maintained. In general this is an open and airy *arrondissement,* its widest border along the Seine, and it has several long green stretches that bolster the feeling of luxury. The Champ-de-Mars, the longest grassy promenade in Paris, is a charming park stretching from the Ecole Militaire to the Eiffel Tower, and the Esplanade des Invalides has a welcome green strip down to the river. A popular area for families with children, there are several small playgrounds and a hidden park at Square Récamier.

Antique shops and galleries thrive in the compact area known as *Le Carré Rive Gauche*. Especially popular with foreigners are the chic rue du Bac area and other small streets throughout the *arrondissement*. Many provide commercial services, and on rue de Sèvres is the famous department store and food hall, Le Bon Marché. The charming market street, rue Cler, is convenient to the old townhouses and modern apartments of rues Bosquet and de Grenelle.

Map: John Zaugg

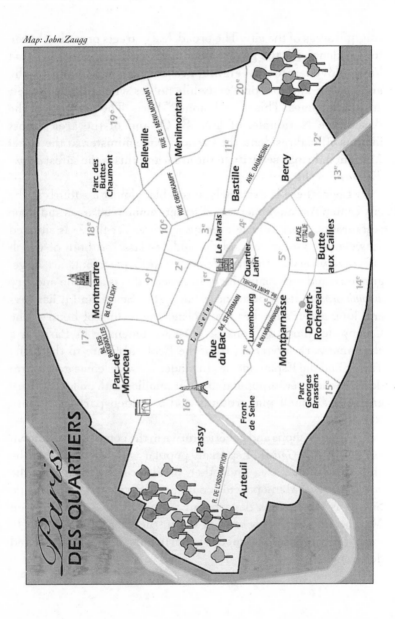

Eighth Arrondissement (8e)

The spectacular avenue des Champs-Elysées and the tourists who have taken it over dominate much of the **Eighth Arrondissement**. Although a major overhaul of this seventeenth-century aristocratic promenade brought back a touch of its distinction after years of decline, its high rents are now afforded primarily by international chains such as Virgin Megastore and the hotels and restaurants that cater to the ubiquitous tourists. Despite the persistence of such traditional institutions as Fouquet's restaurant and the Lido Cabaret, this is one of the least Parisian parts of Paris.

This was not always the case. When the Tuileries Palace burned down during the uprising of the Paris Commune in 1871 and the 1er lost its aristocratic favor, this adjacent area took its place. Preferred by the upper classes since the area was laid out by the famous Le Nôtre during the time of Louis XIV, the rue du Faubourg-St-Honoré was then a street of eighteenth-century townhouses of wealthy Parisians, their gardens overlooking the still-bucolic Champs-Elysées. But not today! The old mansions are now occupied by embassies and offices, and the Palais de l'Elysée is the official residence of the president of France. Few of the old gems of apartments still exist, so when the corporate types go home for the evening, the side streets are left empty and dull. Contributing both to the commercialization and elegance of this eastern edge is the Golden Triangle of the *haute couture* salons of famous French and international designers, high-class shops of other sorts, and some of Paris' finest restaurants, which peek out amidst flowery gardens.

Nonetheless, people live here and live very well. Around Place François-1er, tucked quietly toward the Seine, and farther west at avenue George-V, graceful buildings house a privileged few, primarily older, wealthy Parisians. The apartments are large and comfortable, but rarely available. These areas are fairly quiet, with high-class *traiteurs* and a few services catering to the rather sedate population.

Fortunately, the 8e offers much more. The lovely and formal Parc Monceau at its western edge, dating from the late eighteenth century, is one of the more desirable districts of Paris and popular both with Parisians and newcomers. Here are wide streets, including avenue Hoche, rue de Monceau, and the residential end of the long boulevard Malesherbes, plus small, charming side streets abutting the park. Apartments are plush and airy, with high ceilings, floor-to-ceiling windows, and upmarket prices. In general, the elegant atmosphere of the Parc Monceau area and its proximity to the markets and services of the 17e make it a lovely place to live.

Ninth Arrondissement (9e)

The dense, southwestern edge of the **Ninth Arrondissement** is home to the famous Opéra Garnier, department stores, shops, cinemas, theaters, banks, and the American Express office. It is always crowded and always on the go. Restaurants of all levels line the broad boulevards that were built by Louis XIV three centuries ago to replace the old city ramparts. These wide boulevards even today manage to convey some slight feeling of openness to one of the few areas of the city that has limited residential desirability and few green, open spaces to provide relief from the stress of urban life.

To the east and just out of the tourists' line of sight, the *arrondissement* continues with a fitful character. A Jewish community lives around rue Richer, its Sephardic kosher restaurants and Middle Eastern shops incongruously situated near the famous Folies Bergères. Rue Cadet is the area's market street, and the only bit of green in this otherwise colorless commercial area is the small Square Montholon.

Farther north, however, the atmosphere becomes more agreeable, although it can change in character from street to street. Winding up toward the Place St-Georges is a long-time artists' quarter that once bridged sophisticated Paris below to the village of Montmartre above. Here also is a section built around 1820, known as the *Nouvelle Athènes*, which became fashionable after the construction of the church of Notre-Dame-de-Lorette. Today one still finds pleasant streets amid the uninspired, and although many of the old buildings have been taken over by offices, others offer agreeable rental apartments. Place Gustave-Toudouze and a triangular space on rue Henri-Monnier are little oases lined with small shops and cafés, and the Square Alex Biscarre is a hidden touch of green. At the northwest is Place Adolphe-Max, a charming square surrounding a small park and playground, but just beyond is boulevard de Clichy, which can be somewhat seedy.

In the 9e are some of the lowest rents and purchase prices in the city. If you are attracted by the reasonable rents, the interesting nightlife toward the northern edges, or even by the international mix of population that is creeping down from Montmartre, choose carefully, as almost every street has its own atmosphere.

Tenth Arrondissement (10e)

Much of the **Tenth Arrondissement** is truly drab. Unfortunately close together and dominating most of the area, the Gare du Nord and the Gare de l'Est exist in the atmosphere that train stations create, and their railroad yards cut through the entire northern part of the district. Much of the housing is working-class and uninspired. People come to several important hospitals, some theaters and museums, and to the rue de Paradis (known for its china shops), but they do not come for the neighborhood. This holds true all the way to Place de la République.

Toward the busy rue du Faubourg-Poissonnière, however, is an area that once was home to prosperous Parisians who wanted

41

to live north of the city in homes with gardens and fresh air. Now some of the old buildings are being restored, and some reasonable rents can be found. Close to rue d'Enghien there are still areas to avoid at night, but this should gradually change.

Toward the east, however, is where the *arrondissement* deserves increasing respect. The Canal Saint-Martin opens up the area, and refurbishment is making the quai de Valmy area one to consider for housing. The cobblestoned strip is shaded by plane trees, arched footbridges cross at intervals, and the *quais* are lined with graceful, nineteenth-century apartment buildings, trendy cafés, and shops. Nearby, the eastern surrounds of the lovely Jardin Villemin are agreeable, despite their proximity to Gare de l'Est. This area is sought out by young Parisians, who are attracted to its vibrant atmosphere, openness, and reasonable prices.

Bastille to Nation (11*e* and 12*e*)

One of the most up-and-coming areas of eastern Paris, the southern strip of the **Eleventh Arrondissement** and the adjacent northern area of the **Twelfth** are much in demand. Starting at Place de la Bastille and stretching to the enormous Place de la Nation, this former furniture craftsmen's suburb of Faubourg St-Antoine is being completely revitalized. Rents are still moderate in areas, although they are rising as formerly shabby neighborhoods are spruced up. Only pockets of the old proletarian atmosphere can still be found, distressing those who fear that the area is becoming too homogeneous and losing its village feel. Most people seem to agree, however, that the youthful, electric atmosphere is bringing a new energy to eastern Paris.

It begins at Place de la Bastille, which from July 14, 1789 (Bastille Day) to the mid-twentieth century (site of the student uprising of 1968) was known for protest and resistance. Now, however, it is an engaging, open area that is dominated on the east by the Opéra Bastille, one of Mitterrand's *Grands Projets*.

On the south reappears the Canal St-Martin, which went underground at rue du Faubourg-du-Temple, flowing below the broad, green boulevard Richard-Lenoir. In summer, sunbathers on the canal's landscaped and cobblestoned banks watch boats slowly pass through the locks to the Seine. The rest of the square is taken by trendy, terraced cafés — a taste of what is to come directly to the east.

Actually the area is mixed in spirit, partly by habit, partly by design. Some established artisans and furniture makers still inhabit the *cours* and *passages* to the sides of the picturesque, vibrant rue du Faubourg-St-Antoine. Although some workshops will stay, others will slowly disappear as redevelopment raises rents and forces them out, allowing room for new, more upscale entities to move in, including younger artists and artisans. Here are the majority of the *bistrots*, cafés, and shops that draw the crowds, as well as new businesses, galleries, and the consulting and high-tech firms that are drawing young professionals. The major streets of rue de Charonne and rue de la Roquette are connected by the trendy, cobblestoned rue de Lappe (once known for prostitutes and pimps), rue des Taillandiers, and rue Keller, a center for the gay community.

Old warehouses converted into lofts, restored buildings, and new apartment blocks make an eclectic mix. There is an interesting market and a park-like setting on the wide boulevard Richard Lenoir. As in the Marais, gentrification is expanding north as older buildings are restored and retail activities expanded. Although the recently trendy rue Oberkampf is upgrading its character, the renewed atmosphere does not yet extend to Place de la République or to the northeastern border with the 20e at Belleville.

To the south of rue du Faubourg-St-Antoine, in the 12e, the life of the *cours* and *passages* continues. Just a few streets away, however, at Place d'Aligre, an atmosphere of bustling crowds and exotic aromas takes hold. The covered Marché Beauvau gives over to an inexpensive, international extravaganza that spills out into rue d'Aligre and down to rue de Charenton. Owing to its proximity to Gare de Lyon, which opened Paris to southern Europe and then to Africa, this has long been a varied area, changing again with the influx of young, professional Parisians. Although housing blocks intrude on the otherwise low-rise residential *quartier*, the neighborhood spirit persists.

Almost a secret in the eastern area of the *arrondissement* is the Allée Vivaldi, a hidden greensward surrounded by modern offices and residences. Across an arched footbridge, the open Jardin de Reuilly has gardens, playgrounds filled with children, and a grassy expanse, and it too is surrounded by pleasant, unobtrusive, modern housing. To the northwest of the garden, and also connected by a footbridge, is the bucolic Promenade Plantée, a landscaped, 4.5 km path on a former elevated railroad bed. How welcome is this bucolic promenade that originates at the Bastille and how interesting the arched vaults below, now called the Viaduc des Arts. Its galleries and artisans' *ateliers* draw visitors into what is becoming a lively, upscale area, despite its proximity to the Gare de Lyon.

Yet at avenue de St-Mandé and below, there has long been a solid, unpretentious, residential district in the *quartiers* of Picpus, Bel-Air, and Daumesnil. Increasingly as this area is revitalized with new shops, offices, and housing, it will be even more in demand.

To the south, train yards from the Gare de Lyon unfortunately isolate the former wine warehouse district of Bercy. Part of the revitalizing *Grands Projets,* Bercy now includes the huge, ultra-modern Ministère des Finances, the Palais Omnisports de Paris-Bercy, and Parc de Bercy, a *jardin de mémoire* incorporating neighborhood landmarks, ruins, and old plane trees. In Bercy are a newly designed commercial area, modern housing blocks, artists' studios, and some large hotels, but this long strip that borders the Seine is only beginning to develop the ambience predicted and so far bears little relation to the quarter above. Nonetheless, the new Météor line of the métro stops here on its way to the Bibliothèque Nationale François Mitterrand directly across the bridge, and, given the thousands of people who now work in this area, it should quickly develop a personality of its own.

Thirteenth Arrondissement (13*e*)

Connecting the 12*e* to the **Thirteenth Arrondissement** is Paris' newest bridge, the Pont Charles-de-Gaulle. Parisians call it the "bridge to nowhere," as its construction anticipated a residential revival and commercial expansion of the two *arrondissements* it connects, a development only slowly taking shape. Yet the large 13*e*, along the city's southern edge, is already one of the more interesting districts of Paris, known primarily as home to some 30,000 of the city's Asian population.

It's hard to remember how this area must have looked centuries ago — an area of sweet pastures and vineyards, of the little hamlets of St-Marcel and Gentilly and the river Bièvre, all now long gone. First the butchers, then the tanners of hides, and finally the factories for textiles and dyes all threw their waste into the Bièvre. Along its banks were workers' housing, cheap shops, squalid nightspots — and crime. If Parisians today complain of the area's homogeneous atmosphere and its impersonal apartment blocks, they have forgotten the cholera epidemics of the mid-1800s and the open sewer that the Bièvre had become, finally covered over only around 1910.

The *arrondissement's* eastern edge flows along with the Seine, across from Bercy, and here several imposing edifices control a rather colorless area. There is the ultra-modern four-building library complex, the Hôpital Pitié-Salpêtrière, and the busy Gare d'Austerlitz. With new housing being built and planned, this will over time become a new *quartier*, the *Seine-Rive-Gauche*, and galleries are already starting to move in. Currently, however, as one heads into the *arrondissement*, it is the broad avenue des

Gobelins that has the lively atmosphere and residential popularity of the 5e, its neighbor to the north.

Along with the seemingly ubiquitous apartment towers built in the 1970s are hidden enclaves of the old, charming Paris. Unassuming private homes are next to faceless apartment projects, and traditional Parisians live side-by-side with Asian immigrants. It was these immigrants who descended on Paris in the seventies and who did not mind the apartment blocks that had been built to replace old slums.

To the south of the enormous, commercial Place d'Italie is what makes the 13e so famous: its Asian population, which lives in an area known as the Triangle de Choisy. Between the avenues d'Ivry and de Choisy, a dense international community has enlivened the new blocks and renovated older buildings. Here are several large Asian supermarkets, many small groceries and shops, and dozens of Asian restaurants, creating an atmosphere unlike any other in Paris. Yet even here are surprises more traditional: just a few streets west, by the placid, unassuming Place de l'Abbe Henocque, are little streets of private houses and gardens, and the Cité Floréale, to the south, is a triangular, flowery nook just off Place de Rungis.

To the northwest is one of Paris' few remaining true villages, la Butte aux Cailles, an intricate set of hilly streets with old-world charm and small town flavor. Low, five-story houses, local shops, and narrow streets characterize the area. The small steep park, almost hidden on its northern edge, is used by locals, as is the large market on boulevard Auguste-Blanqui.

Montparnasse and Beyond (14e)

Legendary for the bohemian Montparnasse, the **Fourteenth Arrondissement** includes so much more that its residents often consider it to be the best-kept secret in Paris. In fact, despite the ongoing attractions of Montparnasse, despite the hospital complexes that dot the area, and despite the broad avenues that cut the *arrondissement* into a pie, the 14e has as many residential attractions as any other area in the city.

Montparnasse sits at the northwest corner of the *arrondissement* and encompasses small edges of the 15e and 6e. It stretches east to the Observatoire built under Louis XIV and south to the pleasant junction of Denfert-Rochereau. But Montparnasse is identified properly not for its geography but for its intriguing atmosphere. It was a hangout in the eighteenth century for students venturing away from the Latin Quarter, and since then it has been known for its bohemian and intellectual life.

Imagine the intensity of this area less than a century ago — a workers' district, cheap rents for their studios and cheap booze drew poverty-stricken artists, descending from the increasingly expensive Montmartre. Famous now — Amadeo Modigliani, Marc Chagall, and Pablo Picasso — were unknown then, and Modigliani, tubercular and drug-addicted, became "king of Montparnasse." Eastern European Jews without a franc to their names came to escape pogroms, and Russians such as Lenin and Trotsky considered revolution. In the twenties, after World War I, came the Americans: writers and artists and their patrons. Paris was a playground for those with American dollars, and unlike in the United States, the alcohol flowed until all hours in cafés such as Le Dôme, La Coupole, and La Closerie de Lilas. Unfortunately in 1929, the stock markets crashed, pockets were emptied, and the Americans went home. But not, of course, the French. It was about this time that a new breed of intellectual came to the area around Carrefour Vavin — people such as Sartre and Beauvoir — but when World War II came, and the Germans took over the cafés of Montparnasse and closed the nearest métro station, the crowd moved up to St-Germain.

Now Montparnasse strives to hold on, and legends die hard. The commercial area and cinemas are always crowded, and the old cafés, exciting cabarets, and nightspots hum into the morning hours. But the sterile Gare Montparnasse, the 59-floor Tour Montparnasse, its adjacent shopping mall, and several concrete apartment blocks do nothing to remind us of what once was.

The residential secret begins around the expansive Place Denfert-Rochereau. Although the *quartier* has changed and high-rise development tries to encroach, much of the area remains reminiscent of a Paris that has disappeared in other places. Broad streets close to the square, such as rue Froidevaux and boulevard St-Jacques, have stately buildings and an open atmosphere. The massive, concrete Place de Catalogne, part residential, part offices, dominates toward the west, but it gives way to the long rue Vercingétorix, its top portion now a neighborhood promenade and park. Renovated studios and apartments with quiet courtyards nestle in some of the short streets (the *impasses, cités,* and *villas*), and artists' *ateliers* still dot the entire area. Off the busy avenue du Général-Leclerc, and just a few steps from the market street, rue Daguerre, is the astoundingly beautiful villa Adrienne, a community of gracious apartments overlooking a lovely little park.

From Plaisance to Alesia is a lively area, both commercial and residential, with interesting little streets mixed in with some that will, no doubt, soon be renewed. Rue d'Alesia is known for its discount clothing shops, but it is also the commercial artery in this agreeable part of the *arrondissement*.

Yet it is the southern area that has it all. Parc Montsouris has beautiful gardens, a charming, terraced restaurant where bands perform nearby, a puppet theater for the children, and a good-sized lake that is home to graceful aquatic birds. Overlooking this wonder are the apartments on rue Nansouty. Adjacent—and throughout this area—the *villas* of private homes are exceptional. And just across Boulevard Jourdan, in another green expanse, is the Cité Universitaire, a student city since the

Photo: Zeny Cieslikowski

The café Deux Magots at Place St-Germain des Pres.

1920s, with 37 international residences providing the residents with an eclectic atmosphere. This greensward stretches west to the Porte de Vanves, the scene of one of Paris' most popular weekend flea markets.

Fifteenth Arrondissement (15*e*)

The largest *arrondissement* with the highest population in Paris, the **Fifteenth Arrondissement** is a comfortable middle-class community. Sitting to the southwest, it stretches north to the subdued 7*e*, east to Montparnasse, and south to the *périphérique*. Until recently the province of chemical factories, metallurgies, and gasworks, the 15*e* has few tourist attractions, save perhaps for some offbeat museums and the lovely, futuristic Parc André-Citroën. It is the locals who dominate: young Parisian families, middle-level professionals, and retired persons, many of whom came for the reasonable rents and the uncomplicated atmosphere. Prices here are moderate in comparison to other areas on the Left Bank or in the 16e, just across the Seine.

Apartment blocks built in the sixties and seventies impose along the river in an area called Front de Seine, with an elevated, landscaped walkway connecting the buildings. Here children play in the evenings, their parents chatting on benches close by. On rue Linois is the multi-level Centre Beaugrenelle, but just a few streets away, at Place St-Charles, this modernity gives way to graceful *Belle Epoque* buildings and the services that a middle-class French population expect.

Still along the river, the 14-hectare Parc André-Citroën, a beautifully designed green space built imaginatively on the site of a former automobile plant, lends its character to an area that is being totally revitalized. Citroën-Cévennes is a new residential *quartier* around the revamped rue Balard, with both modern housing and refurbished old apartments.

Elsewhere, little communities hold their own. The commercial rue du Commerce, with its shuttered houses, looks much as it might have fifty years ago, especially around Place Etienne-Pernet. Here are inexpensive restaurants, neighborhood shops, and the Place du Commerce, a pleasant, leafy square. Past rue Lecourbe, the streets around rue de Vaugirard and rue de la Convention are popular for their comfortable, middle-class focus.

Another park surrounded by a residential area is the southeastern Parc Georges-Brassens, built on the site of a former slaughterhouse. With grassy areas, a small lake, and a carousel for children, this bucolic park breaks the monotony created by the modern apartment blocks that impose over older, routine buildings. Nearby, however, in Passage de Dantzig is La Ruche, the famous beehive building of artists' studios used by Chagall, Modigliani, Soutine, and Léger, among others of Montparnasse fame, and which still provides studios today.

Montparnasse, where the northeastern corner abuts on the 14e, is perhaps the 15e at its most interesting. Despite the district's commercial nature and the domination by Tour Montparnasse, the streets off rue de Vaugirard and rue Pasteur are residential, with proximity to a market, supermarkets, and the Maine-Montparnasse shopping complex. Hidden above the railroad station is the Jardin Atlantique, a landscaped roof garden with fountains, play areas, and tennis courts. Close by are the large Hôpital Necker and the famous Institut Pasteur, around which are agreeable little residential nuggets, benefiting from their proximity to the elegant 7e, to oases such as Place de Breteuil, and to the elegant market at avenue de Saxe.

Sixteenth Arrondissement (16e)

The most aristocratic of Paris' *arrondissements*, this large area at the western edge of the city was among the last to be incorporated into the city system. Its two main *quartiers*, Auteuil and Passy, were small villages amidst farmland and a forest stretching west, which was the hunting ground of the French kings. Underground mineral springs turned the area into an aristocratic spa in the seventeenth century, and it was to this area of rural elegance that the nobility retreated during the Revolution.

Today the **Sixteenth Arrondissement** still enjoys a small-town atmosphere. Just past the western edge is the Bois de Boulogne, what is left in Paris of those royal woods. Some Parisians claim the 16e is boring, for there is little nightlife, and in the summer many of its residents close their homes and depart until the *rentrée*. Whether this is a detriment is moot, for the *arrondissement* is known for its tranquility, for its graceful mid-rise buildings with spacious, costly apartments, and for its little *villas* and *hameaux*—leafy lanes with a country feel. Indeed, this is one of the areas extremely suitable for families with children.

51

Starting from what was once the hill of Chaillot and is now Place Charles-de-Gaulle, the streets around the spectacular avenue Foch are residential. Avenue Foch itself, the broadest in Paris, has traditionally been home to Parisian wealth, although in recent years some dubious elements walk the streets under the luxurious apartments at night. Close by, avenue Victor-Hugo is also chic and expensive, as one would expect from these avenues that radiate out from l'Etoile.

Toward the Porte de la Muette is the Organization for Economic Cooperation and Development (OECD), its surrounding streets home to many of its diplomats and to old Parisian wealth. Starting at the Place du Trocadéro and cutting across the *arrondissement* to the Porte de la Muette, the wide avenue Georges-Mandel continues as avenue Henri-Martin. Buildings are set back from the double boulevard, whose trees provide shade and cushioning from noise. Somewhat south is the Villa Beauséjour, with some surprising old Russian-style cottages. Families like this area that is close to the charming Jardins du Ranelagh and to the Bois de Boulogne.

Past the Trocadéro gardens, Passy takes hold. Here one enters the village: a residential neighborhood, a church square, several commercial streets, including rue Bois-le-Vent and the main street, rue de Passy, with its high-quality shops and services. Much of the prized residential district lies between avenue Mozart on the north and the long rue Raynouard, although areas around Square Charles-Dickens and rue des Eaux are well worth exploring.

South of Passy, the village and vineyards of Auteuil were among the last areas to become urbanized, and Auteuil remains a small town with a church square. Rue d'Auteuil, the main street, formed this picturesque village along with still-welcoming streets, such as rue Boileau and rue La Fontaine, the extension of Passy's rue Raynouard. Even in this area of quiet certitude there are surprises: the gated community of Villa Montmorency holds 80 private houses in curved, leafy streets—an almost rural setting. Just north, closer to the Jardins du Ranelagh, the buildings in the short Place du Docteur-Blanche are strikingly Art Nouveau. Housing anywhere in this area is generally expensive, often interesting, and it is a popular area for foreign residents.

Seventeenth Arrondissement (17e)

Encompassing the farming areas of Monceau and Ternes on the west and the workers' villages of Batignolles and Epinettes on the east, the **Seventeenth Arrondissement** today is largely residential, but the area has several moods. Cut neatly in two by railroad tracks heading out from Gare St-Lazare, the western area is open and up-market, but the east is distinctly working-class and crowded.

On its southern and eastern edges and above the stately Parc de Monceau, the 17e has the atmosphere of its affluent neighbors near l'Etoile. What was once the Plaine de Monceau continues with broad avenues and a feeling of openness for the gracious apartments that were, a hundred years ago, the most modern in the city. The avenue de Wagram heads into the heart of the district from l'Etoile, opening up at Place des Ternes, with its charming flower market. Off boulevard de Courcelles and rue de Prony is a residential district only somewhat less aristocratic than the 16e. Particularly toward l'Etoile there are extremely genteel places in which to live.

The area is convenient to the markets at rue de Lévis and rue Poncelet, both holding fast to an atmosphere that is too quickly disappearing. Radiating to its west on streets such as rues Lebon, Bayen, and Guersant, is a solid *quartier* leading to the boulevard Pereire, flanking a grassy esplanade that covers the railroad tracks. Just beyond is Villa des Ternes, leafy and comfortable.

The area northeast of the railroad yards is a solid workers' *quartier*, with a few pleasant residential streets amid many others with little distinction. Two parallel streets typify this dichotomy:

the long rue des Moines is working-class, with rather drab five-story buildings, neighborhood markets, shops and cafés; only a few streets away, the Cité des Fleurs is a quiet pedestrian zone with single-family, gardened homes. Backing on the railroad yards, the Square des Batignolles with its rolling lawns and little lake relieves the congestion and enlivens this area. Unfortunately, it is one of the few green oases in this part of town.

Eighteenth Arrondissement (18e)

Known now for the tourists who swarm each day up the *butte* (hill) to the Basilique du Sacré-Coeur or for others who hang out at seedy nightspots on the southern edge, Montmartre nonetheless manages in places to retain some of its old-time character and can be an extremely agreeable place to live. Ranging from lovely to shabby and from enclaves of traditional Parisians to those of recent immigrants, the **Eighteenth Arrondissement** moves up winding picturesque streets from the boulevards de Clichy and de Rochechouart, around the Butte Montmartre, and out to the *périphérique*. It is probably one of the most unpretentious areas of the city, with few historic monuments and little modern development. Some areas are well worth considering and some are definitely not recommended.

Montmartre is named for the martyr Saint Denis, who was decapitated for promoting Christianity to the Gauls, and it was from ancient times a place of pilgrimage. Yet it is more recently that Montmartre has accumulated the reputation that follows it still. An area of fields, vineyards, and gypsum mines until the early twentieth century, the hilly area with winding roads and fresh breezes was outside the city's toll walls and became known for low rents and cheap nightlife. Workers descended here from the countryside during the Industrial Revolution, as did artisans, struggling artists, political protesters during the Paris Commune, and anarchists. Today, however, the southern edge teems with tourists who savor the artificial bohemian atmosphere created by shopkeepers on their behalf.

Nonetheless, at the western side of Butte Montmartre, between Sacré-Coeur and the Montmartre cemetery, there are some wonderful residential nooks, charming squares, winding narrow streets with both older and modernized homes, some with gardens. Real estate prices here can be high, but lower than in more trendy areas. The views and atmosphere may be worth the price. Look above rue des Abbesses, intersecting with rue Lépic, the famous market street, or west, near rue Damrémont. Farther up the hill, rue Caulaincourt is interesting, and avenue Junot has been nicely restored. Although people walk through here, the tourist atmosphere is at a distance. The small, green Place Casadesus is frequented by locals, and Villa Léandre, one of a few charming alleys of small houses, seems to be a quiet country lane, as does the nearby Hameau des Artistes.

Unfortunately, claiming the southeastern edge of the *arrondissement* are Pigalle and Barbès, home to both dubious nightlife and trendy clubs. An unsettled feeling stretches to rue de la Goutte-d'Or, just off boulevard Barbès, long a poor, cramped workers' *quartier* and now an area of immigrants. The crowded, bargain department store Tati can be fun, as can the exotic shops and inexpensive markets and restaurants. But this area has had the worst crime rate in the city and is not an area to be frequented at night.

On the back slope of Sacré-Coeur is the rest of the 18*e*, on the east deeply cut into by railroad yards coming up from the 10*e*. Rue du Poteau, north of the *butte* is a good market street, and there are some oases around Square de Clignancourt. Nonetheless, along its top the *arrondissement* is fairly charmless and drab, despite the presence of Paris' most famous flea market, jammed every weekend with bargain hunters.

Belleville and Ménilmontant

The **Nineteenth Arrondissement (19e)** is the 1860 amalgam into the city system of the slaughterhouse town of La Villette and a part of Belleville, an industrial, working-class city of more than 60,000 people. The rest of Belleville sits to the south in the **Twentieth Arrondissement (20e)**, entwined with its neighbor Ménilmontant. Once a slum of radical politics and protest, Belleville was split apart in the final expansion of the *arrondissements*, with the belief of the government that the zone's rebellious spirit would lose its focus. But these areas, along with the former villages of Bagnolet and Charonne, remain inextricably linked, with a mood of their own.

At the northeastern tip, above avenue Jean-Jaurès, is the ultra-modern La Villette, a 55-hectare green expanse, science museum, and entertainment complex. It begins alongside Canal St-Denis and straddles the Canal de l'Ourcq that cuts across the top of the area, ending at the impressive Bassin de la Villette. In the daytime families come for the museum, children's programs, the theme gardens, the canal-side promenades, and bicycle paths. In the evening, entertainment takes over and all Paris comes. As interesting as this all is, it is currently not much of a residential district, although some old warehouses are being converted into studios and apartments.

When Baron Haussmann cleared Paris' slums, many lower-class Parisians migrated to Belleville. Cottages went up willy-nilly on small, hastily carved roads that are often today, after sprucing up, the charming *culs-de-sac, impasses,* and *villas* of a large district that remains mixed in population, mixed in atmosphere, and also mixed in price.

From Buttes-Chaumont to Place du Rhin-et-Danube, the *quartier* is most agreeable, benefiting from its proximity to the beautiful, hilly Parc des Buttes-Chaumont. How amazing that while forcing the poor to these already overcrowded reaches, Baron Haussmann created nearby one of the city's loveliest outlooks! Around the park's perimeter are the broad residential rues Manin and Botzaris. Off rue Mouzaïa and rue du Géneral-Brunet remain the *villas* of private houses, coveted places to live. So are some parts of rue de Belleville, still the high street of a small town. But these and other nooks strewn across the southern part of the *arrondissement* compete with others of dilapidated housing and even more with faceless high-rises designed to replace them, especially surrounding Place des Fêtes, once the village square.

It should be no surprise that this area drew a population looking for work and cheap housing. Immigrants came, some legal, some not: Eastern European Jews sought refuge first from pogroms and then the Nazis, and there were Greeks, Armenians, and Turks. Most recently have come the Asians, Arabs, and Africans—again some with legal papers, some without—bringing a visible instability and some anger to the area as the French debate how to handle the large immigrant influx. Today this population congregates to the sides of the boulevard de Belleville at the Arab and Asian shops, Muslim and Jewish establishments, and the crowded, inexpensive market. Much of this western side where the 20e and the 11e abut is rundown and looks it, but parts see the mixed results of urban renewal.

If in the sixties the 20e began to experience the same faceless development as parts of the 13e and 15e, the outcry of the residents, *les Bellevillois,* caused at least some areas to be preserved. Thus this hilly northern part of the *arrondissement* sees apartment blocks, charming cottages, and dismal slums. Coming up is the area immediately above the steep Parc de Belleville, with new cafés and bars beginning to enliven the area. Down the hill, though, it approaches boulevard de Belleville and the unsettled area described above. The commercial rue de Ménilmontant cuts across the multiracial area, separating it from the *quartiers* below.

West of the cemetery Père-Lachaise—the largest garden in Paris—and toward Porte de Bagnolet, lie the old hamlets of Charonne and Bagnolet. In this generally residential area around Place Chanute and Square Séverine are small cottages in hilly, flowery side streets, such as rue Paul Strauss. There are also interesting niches off rue St-Blaise. Of course, these are all nestled amid apartment blocks or adjacent to areas that are still waiting to be refurbished. It just depends on where you look.

La Défense and the Western Suburbs

Just beyond Paris' western suburb of Neuilly-sur-Seine rise 2,000 acres of modern skyscrapers, high-rise residential blocks, France's largest shopping mall, and miles of landscaped, connecting walkways. This is La Défense, a multi-use business/residential complex planned in the 1930s, realized in the sixties and seventies, and topped off in 1989 by the construction of La Grande Arche, a 400-meter-high arch of two hollow towers, connected at the top and larger than the Cathedral of Notre-Dame.

Some 100,000 people work at La Défense, in the offices of 800 international corporations such as IBM, FIAT, British Airways, and ELF. Thirty thousand people live here, in a pleasant, homogeneous area close to some of the international schools. Housing is modern and affordable, agreeably built around landscaped squares and elevated walkways that hide the public transportation systems below. The Quatre-Temps shopping center holds hundreds of shops and restaurants and the *hypermarché* Auchan. In fact, all conveniences are here, including a variety of cultural attractions, and central Paris is no farther than a métro or RER (commuter railway) ride away. Yet, if La Défense does not encompass the traditional charms of the city center, it has its own reasons for existence, and for people who work here, these may be worth considering.

Many foreign residents, especially those with families, commute into the city or to La Défense from the *banlieue* (suburbs), which offer a tranquil lifestyle, spacious gardened homes, and proximity to many of the international schools. The suburbs are categorized by those that are near (*la proche banlieue*) and served by métro from Paris and those farther out (*les banlieues plus éloignées*), reachable by RER. *La banlieue ouest* (western suburbs) are most in demand, especially by new arrivals to Paris. The standard of living is high, and housing affords more space for the same prices as in the city center. Having a car is essential, however, as not all services or shopping needs can be found in every small town.

Although the suburbs are beyond the province of this book, they should be considered, for many are extremely popular with the international community. Look at elegant **Neuilly-sur-Seine** and its neighbor **Levallois-Perret**, at the western edges of the city. Try **Boulogne-Billancourt** and its neighbor across the Seine, the charming, affluent hill town of **Saint-Cloud**. **Suresnes** and **Puteaux** are also home to many Anglophones, as is **Courbevoie,** beyond La Defénse.

If the south interests you, look at **Issy-les Moulineaux**, a town of winding streets, its own town square, and an atmosphere more casual than some of its neighbors. Just beyond, look also at **Meudon**, accessible by RER, prized both by commuters into Paris and those who work in the industries that border the Paris side of the Seine.

Of the outer reaches, **St-Germain-en-Laye** is probably the most well-known. A charming, affluent, country town, it has provided upscale services to Anglophone residents since the seventeenth century, when the English James III and his retinue were in exile here. All conveniences that residents could want are here, which also benefits its less-famous neighbor **Le Vésinet**. The gentle lifestyle of these areas makes them extremely popular for the Anglophone community. Check them out.

CHAPTER TWO

HOUSING AND SETTLING IN

BEFORE YOU LEAVE

It is said that there are more than 100,000 vacant apartments in Paris, but this does not mean that satisfactory housing will be easy to find. Apartments in Paris, despite a reputed depressed market, remain expensive both to rent and buy, and some *propriétaires* (landlords) will not rent if it means lowering the price. This has the consequence of turning some heretofore less desirable parts of town into trendy, gentrified areas and makes just about any area worth considering. Ultimately Paris rental apartments are available in any price range, if you are willing to search widely and compromise. Apartments currently average 100F per square meter (m²), depending on the neighborhood and amenities of the building. A basic 80-m², two-bedroom, *non-meublé/vide* (unfurnished) apartment might rent for about 8,000F per month. A *meublé* (furnished), short-term apartment costs more, but one offering at least a year's lease may sometimes cost about the same as an un-furnished apartment.

As soon as you know your departure date, start thinking about housing. If your company is sending you to Paris, discuss its relocation procedures. On your own, plan to begin making contacts well in advance of your departure. Three months in advance is not too long to begin inquiries, to place ads, or to commit yourself with a deposit. If you plan to deal with real estate agencies, you will need time and *patience*. Call weekdays, for many agencies are closed weekends, and in August many landlords and agents are away on holiday. If you plan to commit to an apartment, make sure you have seen recent photos of the apartment before you sign a lease, or ask someone you know in Paris to check it out.

APARTMENT HOTELS

For short-term stays, *résidences hôtelières* combine the comforts of an apartment with the amenities of a hotel. Suites are of various sizes and include cooking facilities. If regular cleaning services and a concierge are important to you, consider a *résidence*, although, of course, they are more expensive than apartments. In Paris there are many reasonably priced, short-term, rental apartments, and finding someone to perform household services is not difficult. Yet an apartment hotel can be an easy way to spend a month or so, especially while searching for long-term lodgings. If you know where you want to live, try a residence nearby to get a feel for that area. The **Paris Tourist Office** at 127, avenue des Champs-Elysées 75008 may have *Les Résidences de Tourisme* (tel: 01.49.52.53.54). See *Résidences Hôtelières* in *Les Pages Jaune* (Yellow Pages, described in Chapter Ten).

- **Citadines Apparthôtels**: Chain of upscale apartment hotels. Call for brochure (tel: 01.43.45.83.69; fax: 01.47.59.02.33; US tel: 800/332-5332).

61

- **Orion Apartment Hotels**: Apartment hotels at La Défense, Les Halles, Bastille, and place d'Italie (info. tel: 01.40.78.54.66). Apartment sizes and prices vary. In the United States: B&V Associates, 140 East 56th Street, New York NY 10022 (tels: 800/755-8266; 212/688-9526; fax: 212/688-9467).
- 1er — **Hôtel Résidence des Halles**: 4, rue des Halles (tel: 01.40.13.85.80; fax: 01.40.13.85.78). Small, basic but well-maintained residence near Châtelet. Good prices for longer stays. Laundry on premises.
- 5e — **Hôtel Résidence Henri-IV**: 50, rue des Bernardins (tel: 01.44.41.31.81; fax: 01.46.33.93.22; US tel: 800/528-3549). Small residence with well-appointed apartments rented by the day, week, or month. Tranquilly located on a cul-de-sac, yet near the métro and shopping streets.
- 15e — **Flatotel Tour Eiffel**: 14, rue du Théâtre (tel: 01.45.75.62.20; fax: 01.45.79.73.30). Well-maintained, studio-to three-bedroom suites, fully equipped. In a residential area near the Eiffel Tower.

THE INDISPENSABLE *FUSAC*

An excellent resource for *locations* (rentals) is *FUSAC (France USA Contacts)*, a biweekly English-language advertising publication that lists both short- and long-term apartments. Many are listed by the owners themselves. Real estate agents who specialize in working with international clients and who have English-speaking personnel advertise their services in *FUSAC*, as do relocation agencies. Consider subscribing before departure, either to select an agent or to rent a short-term apartment while looking for permanent housing. *FUSAC* in Paris: 3, rue Larochelle 75014 (tel: 01.45.38.56.57; fax: 01.45.38.98.94). In the United States: PO Box 115, Cooper Station, New York NY 10276 (tel: 212/929-2929; fax: 212/255-5555). Price: US$90 annually. In Paris, it is free in Anglophone book shops, stores, pubs, and restaurants.

AGENCE IMMOBILIERE

To look for a long-term apartment, it is best to work with an *agent immobilièr* (real estate agent) or relocation service and to start the process about three months in advance. Some agents work on exclusive contracts, but smaller agents generally specialize in their own districts, so you may have to work with several agents in order to see apartments in different *arrondissements*. Some agencies, however, have relationships with others in different areas. Agents in each *arrondissement* display in their windows descriptions of their most desirable listings, usually pinpointed by the closest métro stop. In choosing an agent, note that all reputable agencies are licensed; their documents show their financial guarantor, insurance company, and other references. Also be aware that agents represent the interests of the landlord, not the renter.

When contacting an agent, be as clear as you can about your requirements, although these might change as you start viewing what is available. Specifying your budget, location preferences, and special needs can help an agent best target apartments. Fax an agent several months in advance and follow up by telephone. Ask the agent about financial documents you will need to show in order to be accepted by a landlord.

Commissions generally run 10–15 percent of a year's rent but are not regulated. Most often the commission is shared by the landlord and the tenant. Inquire of agents as to their commissions and the services included. Sometimes they include drawing up the lease and making an inventory of the apartment. There may be a separate charge for drawing up the lease, but the real estate agent pays a part. For furnished apartments, however, the tenant pays the entire fee.

In addition to looking in *FUSAC* for bilingual agencies, see *Agences Immobilières* in the Yellow Pages and *Paris Anglophone*, a directory of services for English speakers in Paris that is available in book shops in Paris and abroad.

A Paris neighborhood in the autumn.

RELOCATION SERVICES

Relocation agencies provide personalized services for the new resident in Paris, and they are helpful when contracted with several months before arrival; their services can be crucial, however, for people who do not have much advance notice of their move, for they can step in quickly with good results. Initially, they work with real estate agencies to find appropriate housing, and they are expert in negotiating prices. They are also helpful in dealing with bureaucratic requirements and formalities, such as the complicated tangles of work and resident permits, car registration, and insurance. They provide valuable information on schools, household insurance, and getting utilities hooked up. Some offer cross-cultural meetings to help acclimatization. Staff members speak English and are used to dealing with the concerns of newcomers.

Relocation agencies charge a flat fee for all services. They are expensive, but depending on your circumstances and the extent of your needs, well worth the price. Often the services work with companies that are transferring their employees. See if your company works with a particular relocation service and if they pay all fees.

- 11e—**At Home Abroad**: 28, rue Basfroi (tel: 01.40.09.08.37; fax: 01.40.09.98.16)
- 16e—**Executive Relocations**: 30, rue de Lubeck (tel: 01.47.55.60.29; fax: 01.47.55.60.86)
- 17e—**Cosmopolitan Services Unlimited**: 113, boulevard Pereire (tel: 01.55.65.11.65; fax: 01.55.65.11.69)
- **Corporate Relocations**: 15, rue Croix-Castel 78600 Maisons-Laffitte (tel: 01.39.12.00.60; fax: 01.39.12.36.00)
- **Entrée into Paris**: 184, avenue Charles-de-Gaulle 92200 Neuilly-sur-Seine (tel: 01.40.88.39.40; fax: 01.46.37.22.09)

LOOKING AFTER ARRIVAL

Occasionally good *appartements* (apartments) are found by referrals from friends or by scanning *les petites annonces* (classified ads) placed in newspapers by the owners themselves, who hope to avoid paying the landlord's share of the real estate commission. These ads often say *propriet. loue.* Some landlords advertise privately in order to escape signing a lease, to avoid taxes, or perhaps because the apartment is not up to standard. Although the price might seem reasonable, do not accept substandard facilities or fail to be protected by a written contract. Ultimately, there are few bargains.

If an apartment appeals to you, call right away to set up an appointment. Some properties will have open houses, listed as *ce jour*, giving the time of the open house and the address. Bring your passport and proof of financial means in case you decide to take the apartment. Landlords may insist that income be at least three times the amount of the rent. References from previous landlords, even from your home country, a bank, and employers are usually required, as are parental guarantees for students. Because the rare, desirable, reasonably priced apartments go quickly, make a commitment as soon as you can. If you do not speak French fluently, bring someone with you who does.

Newspaper Advertisements

De Particulier à Particulier is a popular and extensive real-estate tabloid issued each Thursday. It lists sales and rentals offered privately plus a description of recent sales for price comparisons. Get it early on Thursday morning and start looking. The Tuesday issue of *Le Figaro* is known for its rental listings, and many other papers have listings as well. Other good days to look are Friday and Saturday. *La Semaine Immobilière* is a tabloid also issued on Thursday, and *J'annonce* comes out on Wednesday morning.

Organizational Help

The Paris Tourist Office should have a copy of *Short Term Renting Apartments*, a resource for stays under 90 days. **Allô Logement Temporaire** at 64, rue du Temple 75003 (tel: 01.42.72.00.06; fax: 01.42.72.03.11) is a non-profit membership association that helps find furnished, short-term apartments.

Understanding the Ads

To decipher advertisements, start with the building itself. Its location in the *quartier* is given as the closest métro stop. *Standing* means it is a high-class building, as does *bel immeuble*. Apartments are advertised by *pièce* (room), excluding bathroom and kitchen. They are also advertised by the square meter, and some ads will specify *F1* or *F2*, indicating the number of main rooms. An apartment of *deux pièces* has two rooms, a kitchen, and bath. A *studio* is one room, and a *studette* may be as small as 18m². A *chambre* may be as small as a *studette*, but without cooking facilities or a shower. *Mezzanine* means there is a loft for a bed. Pay attention to size, for an apartment of 55m², despite the number of rooms, might be too small for your needs. On the other hand, most apartments — except for the old, elegant, and extremely expensive — tend to be small, and kitchens and bathrooms especially may not be as large as you are used to.

Some ads will mention *wc séparé* (separate room for the toilet) plus a *salle de bains* (a room with sink plus bathtub) or *salle de douche* (with a shower). Unfurnished apartments may have no built-in *placards* (closets) and free-standing *armoires* must then be purchased. *La cuisine* (the kitchen) may be equipped only with cupboards, a sink, and outlets for you to install your own appliances, unless the ad says *cuisine équipée* or *cuisine aménagée*. A *cuisine américaine* means that the kitchen is separated from the living room only by a bar. An apartment on the *RdeC (Rez-de-Chaussée)* is at street level, and an apartment on the 1er *étage* means it is one level

67

above. Ads for apartments higher up usually indicate whether or not there is an *ascenseur* (elevator). *Cave* indicates a storage area in the basement. *Parking* indicates a garage space, and *box* means the space has a lockable door.

Considerations

Do not dismiss lightly a building that seems untended on the outside. Many buildings are built around center courts and on the inside may be pleasant and quiet. Many apartments in older buildings have been modernized as well. Yet, make sure to open the windows to gauge the amount of noise from the street, no matter how high up the apartment. Some relatively quiet streets become extremely noisy between 6:30 pm and 8:30 pm and others may be noisy if there is a late-running bus line or late-night bar. In this regard, do not inspect apartments in August or on weekends, when traffic is light and all of Paris seems calm. But if the apartment has *double vitrage* windows, much of the street noise will be filtered out when windows are closed.

Not all buildings have elevators. Think twice about renting an apartment above the third floor of a building without one. Although the view may be lovely and the breeze cooling, it can get tedious climbing the stairs day after day, especially carrying groceries, and the charm quickly fades. If you wouldn't live in such a building at home, don't rent it in Paris.

Decide whether having an onsite *concierge/gardien* is important, as increasing numbers of buildings have replaced them with a *digicode* (key panel) or *interphone* system for secure entering. In this case, inquire as to how packages are received, how garbage is removed, and how maintenance of the building is performed. In addition to the code number to enter, many buildings require pressing a *porte* button to exit, and have a *minuterie/lumière* button that lights the stairwell or corridor for a few minutes until you get to your floor.

Inspect the appliances, if there are any. Some people negotiate the purchase of kitchen appliances and cupboards from the former tenant. Otherwise, expect to purchase them for yourself, either new or used through ads in *FUSAC*.

Check the electrical wiring and voltage. All apartments in Paris should have 220V, 50Hz electricity, and outlets for major appliances should be grounded. Some older apartments may not have enough kilowatts coming into the apartment to use a washer and dryer at the same time. Inquire about heating and test the hot water for temperature and pressure.

Ask whether the heating is *chauffage par l'immeuble*, meaning that the heat is paid by the building and included in the building *charges*, or *chauffage individuel*, meaning that the tenant pays directly for the heat. In this regard, look carefully at how well the windows close, for Paris is cold in winter and hot in summer. As most buildings have no air conditioning, see if there is more than one exposure, as cross ventilation can at least bring a welcome breeze.

Inspect the facilities in the basement, including your *cave*. Newer buildings may have underground parking, but the older ones do not, and street parking is difficult. If there is no *parking*, inquire about garage possibilities in the neighborhood. In this case, visit the garage to see how cars are parked and to determine hours when the car is retrievable.

Furnished Apartments

Furnished apartments rented by the week or month are more expensive than those leased for a year, and studios and one-bedroom apartments are popular and thus proportionately more expensive than large ones. There is a great deal of turnover in short-term apartments, and reasonably priced, furnished lodgings can be found with some effort.

Most people coming to Paris for periods under a year rent under short-term arrangements. These rentals are not strictly regulated, and contracts (*bail à usage d'habitation en meublé*) are most often negotiated. Real estate agents' commissions are paid by the renter. Generally the rent includes the habitation taxes, building charges, and insurance. All people residing in an apartment or house must be covered for property damage and personal liability. Minimum insurance does not cover any damage done by the tenant to the furniture, to the building, or even to a neighbor's apartment: for example, by neglect of the plumbing. A comprehensive homeowner's policy is necessary even when renting a furnished apartment for one year.

No laws apply as to what constitutes a furnished apartment, so you should inquire specifically about the items you require, such as a desk, a microwave, or toaster. Ask the landlord for an *inventaire détaillé* (detailed inventory) and make sure it matches what is actually there. Check and report in writing any irregularities in the apartment, so that upon leaving you will not be charged for damage. Do not hesitate to specify every furniture scratch and stain. When vacating the apartment, check the inventory once again.

Unfurnished Apartments

Unfurnished long-term apartments are usually offered in three-year leases (*bail de location* or *bail de trois ans*). Leases are renewed automatically lacking notice from the tenant. When giving up the apartment, three months notice is required (less if the tenant is being transferred abroad), and the letter sent to the landlord must be sent *en recommandée avec accusé de réception* (registered mail with notice of receipt). A tenant, however, may be evicted only with six months notice for non-payment or if the apartment is to be sold or occupied by the owner. A tenant may not be evicted between October and April for any reason. Annual rent increases are regulated by law and are no more than about 5 percent. The landlord will require a *caution* (deposit) of up to two months rent, plus the first month's rent in advance; more than this is illegal. You can pay your rent by check or have it deducted from your bank account. In either case, you should receive a *quittance de loyer* (receipt) from the landlord each month.

Discuss who pays the *charges* (miscellaneous expenses) for services shared by all building residents: garbage pickup, maintenance of the common areas and elevator, landscaping, etc. Also pay attention to the *taxe d'habitation* (habitation tax) paid by all people resident on January 1. This tax is assessed according to the value of the property, so the more expensive apartments and *arrondissements* have higher taxes.

Renters with a lease are required to have property insurance. Inquire in advance as to your carrier's requirements to ensure that the locks and shutters conform to specifications. The most common policy is *assurance multirisques habitation* (multi-risk insurance), covering theft and water and fire damage, as well as third-party liability. Make sure to get a *constat a l'amiable* from your agent, so you can file a claim within the required three days after damage occurs. See Chapter Seven for insurance agencies.

A *huissier* (bailiff) may be asked to certify the condition of the apartment, both upon rental and termination of the lease. In any case, make sure when signing the *état des lieux* (inventory of the property) that all damage is noted, no matter how minute. The landlord will charge for damages at termination of the lease. If you do need to make some repairs or adjustments, get a written *devis* (estimate of charges) from the contractor before starting any work.

Utilities (except water) must be registered in the tenant's name. Call **EDF/GDF (Electricité de France/Gaz de France)** to inquire as to the procedure (tel: 01.49.02.80.80). Make a record of the meter reading, so that you pay only for usage after you move in. Telephone service, handled by **France Télécom**, takes just a few days to get hooked up (tel: 1014). For all utilities, it helps if you know the previous tenant's name. For telephone options and services, see Chapter Ten.

Each French *département* has an office that offers information on tenants' rights. In Paris, the *mairie* has a booklet, *La Protection des Locataires*, which gives appropriate contacts to call concerning tenants' rights.

PURCHASING AN APARTMENT

Apartments in Paris are generally *en copropriété* (condominiums), in which the resident owns outright the apartment and, jointly with the others in the building, the common areas. The apartment building is managed by an outside *syndic* (a company specializing in building management), and the efficiency of the building depends on the particular *syndic*.

If you are considering buying property in order to resell after a short time, understand that France taxes the worldwide income of its residents. This includes the sale of a residence in the former country of residence once the French residence permit has been obtained. If buying property as a speculative investment, note that property transfer taxes of up to 20 percent are paid by the seller, and this affects the price of the property, both upon buying and later resale. In addition, if the resale is under two years, the transaction may be deemed as speculation, with a capital gains tax of about 50 percent. Thus, if you are considering the purchase of a property with the intention of selling it again, make sure to understand the tax ramifications both in France and in your home country.

Upon deciding on a property, the buyer signs a *compromis de vente* (contract) and makes a down payment of about 10 percent, which commits both buyer and seller. The *promesse de vente* allows the buyer three months to confirm the purchase and find a loan. Do not sign an *offre d'achat*, which commits the buyer but not the seller. Closing costs can add about 10 percent to the purchase price.

All transactions are completed by a *notaire*, a member of the legal profession who deals with real estate and family law. Acting on behalf of both parties (although sometimes each party is represented by a *notaire*), the *notaire* researches, prepares, and signs all documents. The *notaire* can be crucial to the successful completion of a business transaction. The number of *notaires* in each district is limited, and their fees are fixed by law. No matter how well you speak French, choose a bilingual notary. Ask friends who have bought property, at the bank where you are considering taking out a mortgage, or call the **Centre d'Informations de la Chambre des Notaires de Paris** at 12, avenue Victoria 75001, which also has some helpful brochures (tel: 01.44.82.24.00). See *Notaires* in the Yellow Pages.

Borrowing Money

Many French banks have mortgage plans for foreign buyers, some lending money in whatever currency is required. See Chapter Nine for banks that cater specifically to Anglophones. The British banks below specialize in mortgages and offer information in English. Mortgages can be at fixed or variable rates and usually run from 15 to 20 years. The amount of down payment varies considerably.

- **Banque Woolwich**: 9, rue Boudreau 75009 (tel: 01.42.68.42.68; fax: 01.47.42.72.72)
- **Abbey National:** 163, boulevard Haussmann 75008 (toll free tel: 08.00.10.10.11)

MOVING YOUR BELONGINGS

Anyone who has lived the previous year outside France may transfer personal belongings without customs charges; this includes personal vehicles. EU (European Union) citizens do not need to go through customs formalities but must have an inventory of the goods.

Non-EU citizens may import household goods duty free within twelve months of taking up residence in France. There must be a complete inventory in French of the goods, including the value of each object; this, along with the certificate mentioned below, must be stamped at the nearest French consulate before departure for France. A sworn statement must declare that the articles have been owned and used by the importer for at least six months. Sometimes sales receipts showing ownership of the item are requested. (These are also helpful in case of burglary, as insurance companies often demand proof of value.) The items must be for personal use and may not be sold within a year. The **Office des Migrations Internationales (OMI)** application must be completed, translated into French by a translator (*traducteur assermenté*), and certified by the nearest French consulate. Non-EU citizens must also, before departure, obtain at their nearest French consulate a stamped *Certificat de Changement de Domicile* (Certificate of Residence Change), which gives the date of change of residence.

One television may be imported duty free. Consider buying a television set in Paris, as converting a set to the French SECAM operating system may be more expensive than buying a new set.

Inquire well in advance of shipping about all requirements and adhere to them exactly. In addition to checking with your French consulate, information in English can be had in Paris from the **Centre de Renseignements Douaniers** at 238, quai de Bercy 75012 (tel: 01.55.04.65.10).

Check carefully the charges for shipping your belongings, for the process can be quite costly. Sometimes it is cheaper to buy some items in France. If you are thinking of sending some small items to yourself through the mail, think again. The post office charges duty on all items coming into France through the mail, even used, personal effects.

Inquire of a mover in your area about its international procedures and affiliates in France and how it can help with bureaucratic requirements. International carriers can ship and pack almost any item, including automobiles, and they will provide free estimates. Some will split shipments between the cheaper sea carriers and the more expensive, but faster, air carriers. Prices and services vary, so shop around. Ensure that the service on both sides is door-to-door and ask how long it will take and for an expected delivery date. Insurance should cover full value of the belongings. Generally, it takes up to about a month for shipments from within Europe and about two months from the United States. See *FUSAC* for ads of movers (most of whom generally display the symbols of their international affiliates) and *Déménagement* in the Yellow Pages.

To take household possessions out of France, residents must prove that all tax statements have been filed. Upon clearance, a *quitus fiscal* will be issued, allowing the goods to leave France.

Self-Storage

If your apartment does not hold all your household items, consider renting a self-storage locker. Units, clean and dry, come in various sizes. The renter keeps the key and has sole access to the locker. Check to see hours of access; some are closed on Sunday.

- 3*e*, 13*e*, 17*e*, and 19*e*—**Access**: (toll free tel: 08.00.51.85.39). Several addresses: 74, rue Vieille-du-Temple; 181, avenue de Clichy; 20, rue Barrault; 221, boulevard Macdonald.
- 12*e* and La Défense—**Abacus**: 20, boulevard Poniatowski (tel: 01.53.33.88.88); 235, rue de la Garenne 92000 Nanterre (tel: 01.41.19.49.49).

Femme de Ménage/Household Help

Ask the *gardien* of your building or a neighbor for recommendations concerning occasional house cleaning. For full-time or regular part-time household help, relocation services can assist in the search and with the paperwork.

A *femme de ménage* must have valid working papers (although some do not), and the employer must register her with the authorities and pay into the *Sécurité Sociale* (Social Security). The authorities must be notified every three months of the hours worked and the salary paid. The salary may be paid with a *chèque emploi-service*, a paycheck booklet available at post offices and banks. Inquire at the **Paris Famille Service** of the *marie* (tel: 01.42.28.92.43); ask also for the brochure, *Les Emplois Familiaux*.

The cost of domestic help is partly deductible from French taxes in order to encourage at-home help. Full-time domestics generally work 40 hours per week. Additional hours are paid at a higher rate, and 50 hours is the maximum allowed. If the employee works less than 18 hours per week, it is not necessary to give notice for dismissal. For work of more than 18 hours, a week's notice must be given to an employee of under six months and a month's notice for those over six months. Paid vacation time is also based on a percentage of time worked.

• *7e* — **Maid in Paris**: 36, rue Fabert (tel: 01.47.05.16.90). A cleaning service geared to the English-speaking community. Personalized service.

MAKING FRIENDS

The large international community in Paris offers a variety of support and welcome groups, both formal and informal. The American, British, and Irish embassies have community liaison offices which may have answers to specific questions, and **SOS Help** can answer questions and make referrals on a wealth of issues of concern to the newcomer (tel: 01.47.23.80.80).

The **American Church in Paris** at 65, quai d'Orsay 75007 is a social gathering place for the English-speaking community (tel: 01.40.62.05.00). Each October the **Women of the American Church** sponsor an excellent *Bloom Where You Are Planted* acclimatization program for newcomers, accompanied by a helpful booklet on living in Paris. And the **British Consulate** and **St-Michael's Church** have a booklet, *Digest of British Societies in Paris*.

WICE (WICE Institute of Continuing Education) at 20, boulevard du Montparnasse 75015, a wide-ranging organization, offers a variety of courses on living in France, French culture, and politics (tel: 01.45.66.75.50; fax: 01.40.65.96.53). The groups below can be helpful; as most are run by volunteers, hours may vary. See also Chapter Eight for business networking.

- **Accueil de France**: (tel: 01.47.27.45.62). Information on French life for new arrivals.
- **Association of American Wives of Europeans**: (tel: 01.47.28.46.39). Activities for American women.
- **Association of Irish Women in France**: 24, rue de Grenelle 75007 (tel: 01.42.22.51.08). Social, cultural, and networking events for Irish women.
- **American Women's Group**: 22 bis, rue Pétrarque 75116 (tel: 01.47.55.87.50; fax: 01.47.55.87.51). Social group to help Anglophones make friends and adapt to French culture. Regular newsletter.
- **British and Commonwealth Women's Association**: 8, rue Belloy 75016 (tel: 01.47.20.50.91). Clubrooms and a library, social and cultural activities, "at-homes," and a monthly newsletter.
- **Canadian Club of Paris**: 29, rue de la Parcheminerie 75005 (tel: 01.46.33.16.24; fax: 01.46.33.03.33). Canadian book shop sponsors events, lectures, social outings.
- **Canadian Women's Association**: 5, rue de Constantine 75006 (tel: 01.44.43.21.03). Events and networking for Canadian women.
- **Royal Society of St. George**: (tels: 01.45.01.57.50; 01.60.02.24.58). Activities for English people.

CHAPTER THREE

FORMALITIES FOR RESIDENCE

VISAS

To stay in France more than three months continuously, non-EU citizens need the *visa de long séjour* (long-stay visa), which must be obtained before departure for France. Go to the French consulate with jurisdiction over your location to determine the current requirements and to get the forms. The French government requires the application to be made from your country of citizenship, unless you are a resident of a different country. Processing the visa may take up to four months once the forms have been filled out and translated into French by a consulate-approved translator. It is rarely possible for a non-EU citizen to enter France as a tourist and then change status. (For student permits, see Chapter Five.)

FRENCH EMBASSIES AND CONSULATES

In most countries, the French Embassy is located in the capital city. In large countries, France also has consulates that are responsible for wide geographic regions.

- **Australia**: Canberra: 6 Perth Avenue, Yarralulma ACT 2600 (tel: 06/216 01 00; fax: 06/216 01 27); 31 Market Street, Sydney NSW 2000 (tel: 02/92 61 57 79; fax: 02/42 83 12 10); 492 St. Kilda Road, Melbourne Vic. 3004 (tel: 03/98 20 09 21; fax: 03/98 20 93 63).

- **Canada**: 42, Promenade Sussex, Ottowa (tel: 613/232-1795) Consulate General: 2, Elysée, Place Bonaventure, BP 202 Montréal, Qué. H5A 1B1 (tel: 514/878-4381); 130 Bloor St. W., Suite 400, Toronto, Ont. M5S1N5 (tel: 416/925-8041); 1201-736 Granville St, Vancouver BCV6Z1H9 (tel: 604/681-2301).

- **Ireland**: 36 Ailesbury Road, Ballsbridge, Dublin 4 (tel: 1/260-1666; fax: 1/283-0178).

- **New Zealand**: 1, Wileston Street, Wellington (tel: 64/4 4720 200).

- **South Africa**: Carlton Centre, 35th floor, Commissioner St, PO Box 11278, Johannesburg 2000 (tel: 11/331-3460; fax: 11/331-3497); 1003 Main Tower Standard Bank Center, Cape Town 8001 (tel: 21/215-617).

- **United Kingdom**: 21 Cromwell Road, London SW7 2EW (tel: 171/838-2000; fax: 171/838-2001); 58 Knightsbridge, London SW1; 11 Randolph Crescent, Edinburgh EH3 7TT (tel: 0131/225-7954). Offices also in Belfast, Cardiff, Liverpool, and St. Helier.

- **United States**: 4101 Reservoir Road, N.W., Washington D.C. 20007 (tel: 202/944-6195; fax: 202/944-6138); 934 Fifth Avenue, New York NY 10021 (tel: 212/606-3689; fax: 212/

606-3620); 31 James Avenue, Park Square Building, #750 Boston MA 02116 (tel: 617/542-7374; fax: 617/542-8054); Marquis 2 Tower, Suite 2800, 285 Peach Tree Center Avenue, Atlanta GA 30303 (tel: 404/522-4226; fax: 404/880-9408); 737 North Michigan Avenue, Chicago IL 60611 (tel: 312/787-5359; fax: 312/664-4196); 10990 Wiltshire Boulevard, Suite 300, Los Angeles, CA 90024 (tel: 310/235-3200; fax: 213/312-0704); 540 Bush Street, San Francisco, CA 94108 (tel: 415/397-4330; fax: 415/433-8357). Also in Miami, New Orleans, Honolulu, Houston, and San Juan.

Carte de Séjour

Within a week of arrival in Paris, non-EU nationals with a *visa de long séjour* must register at the **Hôtel de Police, Centre d'Accueil des Etrangers**, according to *arrondissement*:

- 1-3*e*, 10*e*, 19*e*: 90 boulevard de Sébastopol 75003.
- 4-7*e*, 13-16*e*: 114, avenue du Maine 75014.
- 8-9*e*, 17-18*e*: 19, rue Truffaut 75017.
- 11-12*e*, 20*e*: rue de Charenton 75012.

To obtain the *carte de séjour*, fill out the questionnaire and make an appointment with the **Préfecture de Police,** which will be between two and twelve weeks later, depending on the number of pending applications. For information and general inquiries, try:

- **Préfecture de Police, Service des Etrangers:** 7, boulevard du Palais 75001 (tel: 01.53.71.51.68). Information in person only.
- **Centre Interministériel de Renseignements Administratifs (CIRA):** 21, square St-Charles 75012 (tel: 01.40.01.11.01). Referral and information service on all French administrative requirements and procedures.

You must present a passport, a valid *visa de long séjour*, and three black and white passport photos, as well as proof of an address in France, financial resources, medical insurance, and a health certificate from a consulate-approved physician. Other requirements (e.g. student identification card or work contract) depend on the purpose of the stay. The *carte de séjour* is issued for one to ten years and is in itself a work permit. Depending on the situation, it may be renewed in one-year increments for three years, after which consideration is given for a ten-year permit. Dependents accompanying a person who is to work in France follow the same procedure.

Carte de Résident

EU nationals have the right to decide where in the EU they want to reside and work. (Not all categories of British nationality qualify; check with the French Embassy before departure.) To stay more than three months, however, you must have a French residence permit and should apply for it before the three months are up. Issuance of the *carte de séjour de ressortissant d'un état membre de la CEE* (*carte de séjour*/residence permit) is usually automatic but sometimes dependent on evidence of sufficient financial means.

To reside in France permanently and to receive the *carte de résident*, almost everyone else must have held the *carte de séjour.* (A foreigner who has been married to and living with a French citizen for more than one year is generally awarded the *carte de résident*.) Non-EU nationals with the *carte de séjour* who have resided in France for three consecutive years may apply for the *carte de résident*. It is valid for ten years and is renewable with proof of employment or sufficient financial means for self-maintenance in France. For information, inquire at the *Préfecture*.

DOCUMENTS TO BRING

Bring as many of the following documents as possible for the entire family; in fact, bring anything you might think pertinent. Documents that may need to be translated into French by an approved *traducteur assermenté* are marked with an asterisk. The *fiche d'état civil*, a formal attestation of the civil status of the person, is often required, especially when married persons use two different surnames. Keep photocopies of every document and form and keep them separate from the originals.

When you go to the *Préfecture*, take as many documents with you as possible. You will not always be told which documents are required, and if you do not have your complete folder with you, you may have to come back again with other papers. You also may need to bring a stamped, self-addressed envelope, depending on current procedures.

Do not expect everything to go smoothly. When dealing with *l'administration* (the bureaucracy), adhere strictly to the rules. If a form says to bring three black and white photos of a certain size, do not vary from the requirements. Never lose your temper, be sarcastic, or raise your voice, despite unhelpful personnel and brusque service.

- *Visa de long séjour*
- *Certificat de changement de domicile*
- *Carte de long séjour,* work permits (as required)
- *Fiche d'état civil*
- Passports for the whole family
- Photocopies of the first pages of your passports
- Extra passport photos
- Visa (as required)
- Birth certificates*
- Marriage certificate*
- Divorce certificate*
- Medical records*
- Proof of medical insurance, if you are not covered in France*
- Work contract or proof of financial means
- Proof of ownership or insurance for jewelry and automobiles*
- Valuations of goods to be brought into France
- Inventory of furniture and other personal items*
- Driver's license*

- Car registration and ownership documentation
- Proof that all taxes are paid, especially on automobiles*
- Insurance papers
- Certificate of Change of Residence*

ANGLOPHONE EMBASSIES

Foreign embassies are most helpful to their citizens during times of crisis. They replace lost passports and help in medical or legal emergencies by making referrals to appropriate doctors, dentists, or lawyers. They do not, however, help people get out of jail. Yet in all emergencies, embassies act as liaison between the family at home and the person in France. It's a good idea to carry the telephone number of the consulate in your wallet.

Always carry your passport or residence permit with you, as the police have the right to ask anyone to show their identity papers. Any time your residence changes, you must show evidence of the new address to the *Préfecture*: lease, rental receipt, telephone bill, etc). If your *carte de séjour* is lost or stolen, make a *déclaration de perte (de vol)* at your local *commissariat de police*. Make a copy of your *carte de séjour* as soon as you receive it.

Report lost passports at the appropriate *commissariat* and take the report and two passport photos of the exact size specified to your consulate. It is always helpful to bring extra photos with you, and this is when having a photocopy of the first pages of your passport will be most helpful. Each country has different requirements for such replacement, and Canadians especially should be aware of the need for a guarantor/*répondant*.

For non-emergencies, embassies renew passports, record births, marriages, and deaths, notarize documents, and provide advice on matters such as absentee voting and filing taxes. Sometimes they offer information on local services, including lists of English-speaking doctors and attorneys, translators, and international schools. Some have community liaison offices (of varying

83

responsiveness). Embassies with the most residents in Paris provide the most information, but basic services are the same.

Some countries allow their citizens to register their address in Paris, making it easier to replace lost passports and to be contacted in case of emergency. Information is confidential and not released without permission. Inquire of your embassy.

Most embassies are open for consular affairs in the mornings only. Find out when your embassy is open before going. On the national holidays of France and of your own country, the embassy will no doubt be closed. At larger embassies, it is the consulate that aids its citizens. See *Ambassades, Consulats et Autres Représentations* in the Yellow Pages.

- **Australia**: 4, rue Jean-Rey 75015 (tel: 01.40.59.33.00; fax: 01.40.59.33.10).
- **Britain**: Embassy: 35, rue du Faubourg-St-Honoré 75008. Consulate at 16, rue d'Anjou 75008 (tel: 01.44.51.31.00; consulate fax: 01.44.51.31.27; embassy fax: 01.44.51.32.88).
- **Canada**: 35, avenue Montaigne 75008 (tel: 01.44.43.29.00; consular services: 01.44.43.29.02; fax: 01.44.43.29.99; fax for Canadians resident in France: 01.44.43.29.86).
- **Ireland**: Embassy: 12, avenue Foch 75016; consulate: 4, rue Rude 75016 (tel: 01.44.17.67.00; fax: 01.45.00.84.17).
- **New Zealand**: 7 ter, rue Léonard-de-Vinci 75016 (tel: 01.45.00.24.11; fax: 01.45.01.26.39).
- **South Africa**: 59, quai d'Orsay 75007 (tel: 01.53.59.23.23; fax: 01.47.53.99.70).
- **United States**: Embassy: 2, avenue Gabriel 75008; Consulate: **Office of American Services:** 2, rue St-Florentin 75001 (24-hour tel: 01.43.12.22.22; fax: 01.42.66.91.83, attn. Office of American Services). For passports, call from 3 pm to 6 pm (tel: 01.43.12.49.42). State Department's emergency number (US tel: 202/647-5226); say it is an emergency and ask for the duty officer.

CHAPTER FOUR

THE JOB HUNT

THE JOB OUTLOOK

Foreigners hoping to work in Paris should take into consideration that salaried jobs are hard to find. The continuing unemployment rate of over 12 percent has resulted in the tightening of
regulations for hiring foreigners and made it more difficult for a
non-EU citizen to find employment. In addition, the government
policy of decentralization of French industries has reduced jobs
in the Paris area by about 200,000 positions. Fluent French is
almost always a requirement, and without it job possibilities are
minimal. For non-EU citizens, with certain exceptions as noted
below, the appropriate working papers must be obtained before a

85

position may be offered. It is true that non-French companies hire some of their country's citizens for assignment abroad, but generally overseas operations hire locally. Nonetheless, libraries in your home country should have resource materials on international companies and about recruitment fairs for overseas positions. It is not a good idea to come to France as a tourist, hoping to find employment and obtain residence status.

Work for EU Nationals

EU nationals may work in France without serious restrictions. You have three months in which to find a job, but the time may be extended if you can prove that you are genuinely looking and have a real chance of finding one. Once you have found a job, you must obtain a *Sécurité Sociale* number and a residence permit.

Full British citizens may work without restriction in France. Information about the national vacancy bank (NATVACS) should be available at your local job center. It may take your application and send it to the **Agence Nationale pour l'Emploi (ANPE)**, the French national employment service (see below). Register with the ANPE upon arrival in France. The **Franco-British Chamber of Commerce** at 31, rue Boissy d'Anglas 75008 accepts classified advertisements for its monthly publication, keeps resumés for job applicants for three months, and maintains a job offer file open for viewing (tel: 01.01.53.30.81.30).

Work Permits for non-EU Citizens

Non-EU citizens will find it almost impossible to obtain a permanent work permit or to find a position just by looking. Nonetheless, you may inquire about procedures and requirements for temporary permits at OMI, 44, rue Bargue 75015 (tel: 01.53.69.53.70), or go to the **Centre de Réception des Etrangers** at 13, rue Miollis 75015.

If you are being transferred to France by a non-French company, you must have the *autorisation provisoire de travail* (temporary work permit), which is initially valid for six months and is renewable. Your company should be able to complete most of the bureaucratic requirements, and it should also have information and advice for settling in.

Sometimes a French corporation will hire a foreign executive or highly qualified technician. If so, it must apply to the Ministry of Labor, which then informs the Ministry of Immigration. The potential employer must prove that a French national cannot do the job. The company also informs the consular office in the potential employee's country of residence about the process. The employment contract approved, the consulate then asks the person to complete the application for a *carte de long séjour* and to have a medical exam. This should all be done well in advance of departure. Sometimes it can take four months for the details to be worked out.

Permits and Contracts

Some long-stay documents will indicate *salarié*, meaning that the holder is a salaried employee. A *carte de séjour temporaire salarié* is valid for one year. It shows the type of professional work allowed and the French *departments* in which the holder is permitted to work. The permit may be renewed two months before its expiration upon presentation of a new work contract. After the ten-year *carte de résident* has been obtained, the holder may work at any profession.

An *employé salarié* works for a monthly salary, and *Sécurité Sociale* costs are deducted. Salaries are figured either as *salaire brut* (gross salary, before deductions) or *salaire net* (net salary, after deductions). The pay is often automatically deposited into the employee's bank account, which is efficient because most checks are *chèques barrés*; a bar across the check indicates they must be deposited, not cashed. The employee receives a *fiche de paie* (pay slip) recording income and deductions.

A work contract (*contrat de travail*) is required, sometimes coming after an engagement letter (*lettre d'engagement*). The current standard work week is 39 hours. No one may be required to work on Sunday. Five weeks is the minimum vacation allowance, plus eleven national holidays, and vacation accrued is calculated as of May 1.

Contracts are of two types, as described below (although having received three paychecks is also seen as binding). Make sure all pertinent items are specified, including job description, salary, vacation, and retirement benefits. Most contracts mention the *convention collective*, a detailing of employee rights. Trial periods (*periodes d'essai*) vary from one month for lower-level jobs and up to a year for executive positions.

- **Contrat à durée indéterminée (CDI)**: a contract without a term limit, although there is generally a three-month *periode d'essai* before the contract binds either party.
- **Contrat à durée determinée (CDD)**: a contract for a fixed term, generally from three to six months.

Travailleurs indépendants are self-employed people in project-oriented professions, such as consultants, editors, or translators. An independent worker must register for *Sécurité Sociale* and make contributions, which are extremely steep, sometimes up to 40 percent of gross earnings; inquire at **URSSAF** (tel: 01.48.51. 75.75). Some companies prefer to use a *travailleur indépendant* rather than hiring a full-time employee, thus avoiding payment of high benefits. People considering working independently should therefore determine the amount they will be required to pay out from their gross earnings before setting their fees. People with a *carte de séjour* who want to engage in a business must also have the *carte de commerçant étranger*. This is not necessary for someone with a *carte de résident*.

LOOKING FOR A JOB

When applying for a position, apply only in the field of your education and experience. French employers do not often hire people with the idea of training them after employment. Make sure your resumé is translated into French, and attach a passport-size photograph. The cover letter should be no more than one page, and employers prefer that it be handwritten, not typed. Graphology is taken seriously, and French employers rely on handwriting to determine a person's character. Large corporations are sometimes flexible on this, understanding that foreigners may not have been subjected to the same stringent handwriting standards as those of French schools and that foreign handwriting may not be analyzed in the same way as French handwriting. Some companies also test for aptitude and personality as well as a foreigner's fluency in French. An advertisement may ask for an applicant's *prétentions*, meaning the salary desired. It is best to find out the salaries being paid for comparable positions before responding.

Note that open positions may not be publicly advertised. *Cooptation* (networking) is increasingly important in the more skilled positions, and even *piston* (personal influence) may play a part. Cultivating contacts, networking, and knocking on doors may be as effective as any other means of finding a job. Sometimes a favored person may be *parachuté* (dropped into) into a particular job without going through the application process.

The Job Search in Paris

EU nationals and those with a work permit may use the ANPE, the public employment service. There are more than 30 ANPE offices in Paris. Some branches specialize in particular professions, including *cadres* (see below). Inquire at the central office at 123, rue Oberkampf 75011 (tel: 01.49.23.33.00; fax: 01.43.55.99.02). See the Yellow Pages under *Administrations du Travail et de l'Emploi* and the White Pages under *ANPE*.

Each Monday *Le Figaro* publishes the most important jobs supplement. *Le Soir* carries ads as well. *Carrières et Emplois*, issued on Wednesdays, repeats already published ads, and *Les Annonces* and *Le Marché du Travail* are also ad publications. *FUSAC* lists private employment agencies advertising bilingual positions. Ads appear in *The Paris Free Voice*, and *Paris-Anglophone* lists bilingual employment agencies. Note that WICE offers courses on professional development and holds twice-monthly career network meetings.

Cadres are people with higher-education degrees or with managerial employment histories. They may use the resources of **APEC (l'Association pour l'Emploi des Cadres)** at 51, boulevard Brune 75014 (tel: 01.40.52.20.00). For *cadre* positions, look in *Le Monde*, *l'Express*, and *Les Echos*.

Americans may deposit their resumés with the **American Chamber of Commerce**, which keeps them for two months as a resource for its corporate members (see Chapter Eight).

Teaching

Teaching in an international elementary or secondary school is a possibility. Applications must arrive no later than January for the following September. You should have a college degree, teaching certificate, and proof of experience. Organizations such as **International Schools Services (ISS)** hold recruiting fairs (US tel: 609/452-0990; fax: 609/452-2690).

French public universities may hire foreigners as visiting professors or lecturers, but only French citizens may teach in French secondary schools; exceptions are teaching assistants. There are also a variety of English-speaking universities in Paris to explore (see Chapter Five).

Teaching English privately is a possibility, but non-EU citizens will have a hard time finding a position in a language school. This is a popular occupation for young expatriates from the EU, who arrive in droves with official credentials for teaching English as a Second Language (ESL). People with RSA/TEFL certificates should see *Enseignement: langues* in the Yellow Pages. WICE offers a TEFL certificate course.

Student Work Permits

Students from the EU do not need work permits. In certain cases, registered students from outside the EU may obtain an *autorisation provisoire de travail* (temporary work permit) and be allowed to work part-time during the school year and full-time between semesters. A valid student *carte de séjour* is necessary, as are student identification cards from the previous and current year, a statement from the school confirming student status, and a written promise of employment. (This does not apply to first-year students, who must prove sufficient funds for the first year.) Students at institutions that do not provide *Sécurité Sociale* medical care coverage are not eligible to work.

Students may work a maximum of 20 hours per week during the school year and up to 39 hours during the three-month summer vacation (between June and October). By law, French employers must pay all employees the legal minimum wage, but many try to bypass this with foreign students. Sometimes it is possible to work in France for a year after studies are completed. Inquire at your consulate. All earnings are taxable in the French tax system. French consulates may have copies of *Employment in France for Students*, which explains the details.

Students should apply to OMI, as above, which will then determine the appropriate course. Bring all residence and student documents, plus a letter from the prospective employer showing your name and address, the position and wages offered, plus the number of hours to be worked and the length of the employment. Students under eighteen years of age must have authorization from their parents.

American and some other full-time students from non-EU countries may work in France during vacations through a work-abroad program approved by the French government. In the United States, contact **Council on International Educational Exchange (CIEE)** at 205 East 42nd Street, New York NY 10017 (tel: 888/268-6245; fax: 212/822-2699); in Paris inquire at the **Centre Odéon Franco-Américain**: 1, place de l'Odeon 75006 (tel: 01.44.41.74.74; fax: 01.43.26.97.45).

Temporary jobs are advertised at two helpful youth organizations described in Chapter Five: **Centre Régional des Oeuvres Universitaires et Scolaires (CROUS)**, which has ANPE agents, and the **Centre d'Information et de Documentation Jeunesse (CIDJ)**.

Au Pair Work

Students (and non-students) may qualify for *au pair* work, taking care of children in a French home in exchange for room and board and a slight stipend. Other options exist, such as receiving room and board in exchange for light housework or even doing no work and paying room and board. Inquire of the agencies below. Most jobs are for young women. *Au pairs* are generally 18–30 years of age, unmarried, and plan to stay in France no longer than 18 months. Some knowledge of French is expected.

Inquire before departure about an *au pair visa*. Both the *au pair* and family must sign a work contract detailing the hours, tasks, and remuneration, and the family must declare the *au pair* a *stagiaire aide familiale*, permitting French health coverage. *Au pair* positions are monitored by the Ministry of Labor. Several agencies list *au pair* jobs, as does *FUSAC*.

- **L'Accueil Familial des Jeunes Etrangers**: 23, rue du Cherche-Midi 75006 (tel: 01.42.22.50.34)
- **L'Amicale Culturelle Internationale**: 27, rue Godot-de-Mauroy 75009 (tel: 01.47.42.94.21)

- **Arche**: 53, rue de Gergovie 75014 (tel: 01.45.45.46.39)
- **Institut Catholique**: 21, rue d'Assas 75006 (tel: 01.44.39.52.35)

Think carefully before accepting an *au pair* position. The work consists of taking care of children full-time, usually includes some housework as well, and days off are few. Such a position might not contribute to the experience of living in Paris you had in mind before coming.

CHAPTER FIVE

STUDYING IN PARIS

STUDENT VISAS

If you intend to study for a degree or certificate, you must apply for the *visa de long séjour pour études* before your departure for France. You must already have an *attestation de pré-inscription* (letter of admission) or other acceptance (*certificat d'inscription*) into an accredited institution. Occasionally the French cultural affairs officer will ask to see academic credentials, such as transcripts and diplomas. If you are coming to France to study at a language school for less than six months, you may be issued a special *visa d'étudiant pour six mois avec plusieurs entrées*, which should waive the regular student permit. While in France, you will be expected to abide by all French laws. Ignorance of a law will not be accepted as an excuse for having violated it.

Be prepared to show proof of financial means, indicating that you have enough income to maintain yourself while in France. A medical examination and proof of health insurance are mandatory.

Upon arrival in France, you should apply within thirty days for the *carte de séjour temporaire* at the Centre de Réception des Etrangers at 13, rue Miollis 75015. Bring all the same information as when you applied for the initial visa.

HEALTH INSURANCE

Students must have health insurance. Coverage required is extensive: hospitalization, outpatient treatment, dentist, medicines, and medical evacuation. EU nationals covered by their country's health plans must enclose a French translation of the insurance coverage along with the application. Remember that not all costs of treatment are covered 100 percent under the French health system. For insurance and *mutuelles* (supplemental carriers), see Chapter Seven.

RESOURCE INFORMATION

Several well-organized, state-run associations offer advice to young people on education, housing, employment, jobs, discounts on services and events, and dealing with the administration.
- **Centre d'Information et de Documentation Jeunesse (CIDJ)**: 101, quai Branly 75015 (tel: 01.44.49.12.00; fax: 01.40.65.02.61)
- **Centre Régional des Oeuvres Universitaires et Scolaires (CROUS)**: 39, avenue Georges-Bernanos 75005 (tel: 01.40. 51.37.10; lodgings tel: 01.40.51.37.21)

HOUSING

Renting an apartment, although feasible, may require a *garant* (guarantor), most often a parent, to guarantee financial responsibility and to sign the lease if you are under 18. Inquire at CROUS, and ask at the Paris Tourist Office for *Logements pour Etudiants*. If you are interested in staying with a family, ask for *Pensions de Famille*.

If you are enrolled in a school for the fall semester starting in October, start your housing search in the summer. Do not come to Paris at the end of September and expect to find decent quarters immediately, when other students are also looking. Try the resources below, as well as Allô Logement Temporaire, described in Chapter Two. The bulletin boards at the American Church and the **American Cathedral** at 23, avenue George-V 75008 often have notices of people looking for roommates or for sublets.

- **Cité Universitaire**: 19, boulevard Jourdan 75014 (tel: 01.44. 16.64.41). Housing for registered students. In summer, students with the International Student Identity Card may stay on a nightly basis (tel: 01.44.16.64.45). Americans: **Fondation des Etats-Unis** (tel: 01.53.80.68.80; fax: 01.53.80.68.99); Canadians: **Maison des Etudiants Canadiens** (tel: 01.40. 78.67.00; fax: 01.40.78.68.50). British: **Collège Franco-Britannique** (tel: 01.44.16.24.00).
- **Accueil Familial des Jeunes Etrangers**: 23, rue du Cherche-Midi 75006 (tel: 01.42.22.50.34; fax: 01.45.44.60.48). *Au pair* agency that also finds young men and women rooms in a family home.
- **Union Nationale des Etudiants Locataires**: 2, rue Pernety 75014 (tel: 01.45.41.58.18). Helps with rentals. Weekday afternoons, Wednesdays 10 am–8 pm.

Temporary Housing

Young people may stay inexpensively (and temporarily) at the *auberges de jeunesse* (youth hostels). The maximum stay is generally six nights and hostels are crowded, so book in advance. Membership cards for **Hostelling International** can be purchased before departure at travel agencies that cater to budget travel, as well as at hostels themselves. Hostels have no facilities for ensuring the safety of valuables, so if you are bringing extensive baggage or a computer, staying in an inexpensive hotel might be better than in a hostel.

Inquire at the Paris Tourist Office about youth hostels or at **Fédération Unie des Auberges de Jeunesse (FUAJ)** at 27, rue Pajol 75018 (tel: 01.44.89.87.27; fax: 01.44.89.87.10), which runs two hostels in the city center: **Jules-Ferry**: 8, boulevard Jules Ferry 75011 (tel: 01.43.57.55.60; fax: 01.40.21.79.92) and **Le d'Artagnan**: 80, rue Vitruve 75020 (tel: 01.40.32.34.56; fax: 01.40.32.34.55). Rates include breakfast. For these, you may reserve and pay in advance at any member of the International Youth Hostel Federation.

LANGUAGE SCHOOLS

Learning French should be among your first priorities upon taking up residence in Paris. Language schools for foreigners are in many convenient locations. Depending on the course and school, some qualify for the student visa. The programs of the two schools below are officially recognized, but there are many others. The Paris Tourist Office should have *Ecoles de Langues et Assimilés*, and see *FUSAC* for advertisements of language schools.

- *5e* — **Cours de Civilisation et Langue Française de la Sorbonne**: 47, rue des Ecoles (tel: 01.40.46.22.11; fax: 01.40.46.32.29). Serious language and culture courses at the Sorbonne; high school diploma required.
- *6e* — **Alliance Française**: 101, boulevard Raspail (tel: 01.45.44.38.28; fax: 01.45.44.89.42). Worldwide network of language schools. Flexible programs. Courses in French culture, literature, etc.

EU students should inquire about the EU's Socrates/Lingua program, which offers subsidies to language teaching staff for language immersion courses and assistantships for future language teachers. Contact the Language Development Department, Central Bureau for Educational Visits, 10 Spring Gardens, London SW1A 2BN (UK tel: 171/389-4840; fax: 171/389-4426).

FRENCH UNIVERSITY EDUCATION

All *lycée* graduates who have passed the stringent *baccalauréat (bac)* examinations are entitled to admission to a state-run university (*la fac*, short for *faculté*). Universities thus tend to be overcrowded, rigid in their curriculum, and impersonal. The *Institut Universitaire de Technologie (IUT)* is a two-year community college system offering certificates in professional and technical specialties.

Top *lycée* students often elect to take one or two years of additional study *(classes préparatoires* or *prépa)* to qualify for more prestigious schools, including the *Ecoles de Commerce* and the *Ecoles d'Ingénieurs*, some of which come under the heading of *Grandes Ecoles*. Graduates ultimately become the French elite: the most powerful politicians and civil servants, and the most influential business professionals in France. Among the most prestigious are *Ecole Polytechnique (X)*, *Institut d'Etudes Politiques (Sciences Po)*, and *Hautes Etudes Commerciales (HEC)*.

The **Université de Paris** (part of the **Académie de Paris**) is a conglomerate of some seventeen separate institutions offering degree programs in particular specialties. Each institution has its specialties. The most ancient and illustrious, the **Sorbonne**, founded in 1230, is also now part of the system, and it houses the University of Paris IV and I, specializing in humanities and social sciences (and parts of other faculties as well). Sorbonne information: 1, rue Victor-Cousin 75005 (tel: 01.40.46.22.11; fax: 01.40.46.25.88). See the telephone book under *Université Paris*.

Degrees

The curriculum at all universities is highly regulated. A stringent core curriculum takes up the first two years, after which the *Diplôme d'Etudes Universitaires Générales (DEUG)* is awarded, or at a technological university, the *Diplôme Universitaire de Technologie (DUT)*. After a third year the *license* is awarded. Some business or vocational programs involve a postgraduate *stage* (training internship). A *maîtrise* can be added to the *license*; it requires an added year of study and completion of a dissertation or project and is roughly the equivalent of a Master's Degree in the United States. A *Diplôme d'Etudes Supérieures Spécialisées (DESS)* is a higher degree, and a *Diplôme d'Etudes Approfondies (DEA)* is a higher degree one may take before going on to the *doctorat* (PhD).

Foreign Students

Any foreign student applying to a French university for a degree program must meet the stringent requirements of the high-quality educational system in France. British students, for example, must have passed A-levels, and American students are often required to have completed two years of college. Fluent French to the point of being able to read complicated texts is necessary, and proficiency tests are given before acceptance into a program. A few of the *Grandes Ecoles* have small quotas for foreign students, but in general foreign students are rarely admitted.

The academic year runs from September to June. Application for admission must be no later than 1 February, meaning that you must request application forms several months before. Forms and informational brochures on university study should be available at the cultural section of French embassies and consulates. In Paris, CROUS has information on higher education, as does the **Ministère de l'Education Nationale** at 61-65, rue Dutot 75015 (tel: 01.55.55.65.40).

The Socrates/Erasmus Programme offers a year of study in France to enrolled EU students who have a working knowledge of French. Inquire at your university or at **Agence Erasmus**,

10, place de la Bourse 33081 Bordeaux (tels: 05.56.79.44.10; 05.55.79.44.12). In Britain, information may be obtained from the Socrates Erasmus Council, RND Building, The University, Canterbury, Kent CT2 7PD (tel: 1227/762-712; fax: 1227/762-711).

ENGLISH-SPEAKING INSTITUTIONS

More realistic options for university study include taking a degree from one of the many fully accredited English-language schools with degree programs in Paris or taking a year abroad sponsored by a university at home. *Paris Anglophone* has an extensive listing of both, and embassies may have a current list. Some schools have better credentials than others, and some may not suit your particular needs or goals, so explore all possibilities.

- **The American University of Paris**: Admissions Office: 102, rue St-Dominique 75007 (tel: 01.40.62.06.00; fax: 01.47. 05.34.32); 60 E. 42nd St., Suite 1463, New York NY 10017 (US tel: 212/983-1414; fax: 212/983-0444). Bachelor of Arts in a variety of fields, such as art history, comparative literature, economics, and modern history; Bachelor of Science in applied economics and computers.
- **American Business School**: 12, rue Alexandre-Parodi 75010 (tel: 01.40.03.15.49; fax: 01.40.03.15.49). French school offering an American undergraduate program in business administration. Students must have the equivalent of the French *bac*, British A-levels, or an American high school diploma.
- **The British Institute in Paris**: 11, rue de Constantine 75007 (tel: 01.44.11.73.73; fax: 01.45.50.31.55). Basic and business French, culture, current events, translation. Bachelor of Arts in French studies, leading to a University of London degree.
- **Parsons School of Design**: 14, rue Letellier 75015 (tel:

01.45.77.39.66; fax: 01.45.77.10.44). Both credit and non-credit programs in illustration, fashion design, studio arts, computer graphics, etc., with flexible schedules of day, evening, and weekend courses. Bachelor of Fine Arts degree.

- **Schiller International University**: 32, boulevard de Vaugirard 75015 (tel: 01.45.38.56.01; fax: 01.45.38.54.30). Graduate, undergraduate, and business degrees. Focus is on economics and business, government, public administration. US office: 453 Edgewater Drive, Dunedin FL 34698 (tel: 813/736-5082; US toll-free 800/336-4133; fax: 813/734-0359). UK office: Royal Waterloo House, 51-55 Waterloo Road, London SE1 8TX (tel: 171/928-8484; fax: 171/620-1226).

Graduate and MBA Programs

French employers are beginning to look for advanced degrees, such as the Master's in Business Administration (MBA). Corporations are also officially required through the *CIF (congé individuel de formation)* program to sponsor continuing education (or training) of their employees. Several schools, including the two below, offer MBA programs in English; their curricula vary, so investigate several, including those mentioned above. Most require some years of work experience in addition to a college degree.

- **INSEAD**: 15, boulevard de Constance 77305 Fontainebleau (tel: 01.60.72.40.00; fax: 01.60.72.42.42). Internationally known French business school, offering a ten-month MBA and doctoral programs. Students average five years business experience.
- **American Graduate School of International Relations and Diplomacy, Paris**: 6, rue de Lubeck 75016 (tel: 01.39.73.13.40; fax: 01.39.73.62.60) MA and PhD programs. Private, accredited school, offering a joint program with the University of Paris XI, Faculté Jean-Monnet.

101

EXAM PREPARATION

Preparatory workshops for college and graduate school qualifying examinations may be taken at the **Kaplan Center**, 15, rue de Pondichéry 75015, which offers courses for the GMAT, GRE, TOEFL, SAT, ISAT, etc. (tel: 01.45.66.55.33).

NON-DEGREE EDUCATION

Some of the Anglophone universities listed above have continuing education and professional certificate programs, as does WICE, described in Chapter Two (tel: 01.45.66.75.50). The city of Paris itself offers a large range of low-fee educational courses in French for adults. Inquire at your local *mairie* or at the Hôtel de Ville.

- **ADAC (Association pour le Développement de l'Animation Culturelle de Paris)**: Hôtel de Retz, 9, rue Charlot 75003 (tel: 01.44.61.87.87; fax: 01.44.61.87.88; Minitel: 3615 PARIS ADAC). City-sponsored training organization in 175 disciplines, specializing in a wide variety of the arts, from dance to costume design, from pottery to oriental lacquer; language and other non-art courses; 400 sites throughout Paris.
- **Conservatoires municipaux**: Hôtel d'Albret, 35, rue des Francs-Bourgeois 75004 (info tel: 01.42.76.66.85). Public conservatories offering training in music, dance, and dramatic arts for people under 25.
- *5e* — **Université Inter-Ages**: 1, rue Victor-Cousin (tel: 01.40.46.26.19). Continuing education program of the Sorbonne. Non-degree courses and lectures.
- *5e* — **Collège de France**: 11, place Marcelin-Berthelot (tel: 01.44.27.12.11). Free public lectures given by illustrious scholars.
- *1er* — **Ecole du Louvre**: 34, quai du Louvre (tel: 01.40.20.56.14). Credit and auditing possibilities for a range of courses in art history and archeology.

Cooking and Wine Courses

In a country that has such a distinctive cuisine, it is rewarding to take cooking courses or classes in wine appreciation. Some of the language schools offer their own classes, and there are cooking schools that offer both serious long-term programs and short-term courses. Two of the most well-known are **Le Cordon Bleu** and **Ritz-Escoffier**. **Librairie Gourmande** at 4, rue Dante 75005 specializes in cookbooks; open Sunday (tel: 01.43.54.37.27).

- *7e* — **Ecole Princesse ERE 2001**: 18, avenue de la Motte-Picquet (tel: 01.45.51.36.34; fax: 01.43.47.38.68). School of Princess Marie-Blanche de Broglie. Easy recipes, *nouvelle cuisine*, plus special programs. Courses in French, English, and Spanish.
- *14e* — **Centre d'Information, de Documentation, et de Dégustation (CIDD):** 30, rue de la Sablière (tel: 01.45.45. 44.20). Courses in English about wine consumption, making wine, and details of the different French wine-growing regions. Wine tasting.

LIBRARIES

There are hundreds of *bibliothèques* (libraries) in Paris; there is at least one public library in each *arrondissement*. Some libraries specialize in particular fields, including some for children only. **L'Heure Joyeuse** at 6, rue des Prêtres-St-Séverin 75006 is a particularly extensive children's library. To obtain a library card, bring identification and proof of domicile. Libraries are generally open Tuesday–Friday, although some are open on Saturday. A complete list of public libraries, *Bibliothèques de la Ville de Paris*, is available at the Paris Tourist Office or at your *mairie*. And each University of Paris section has its own library for enrolled students, as does the American University of Paris.

- *4e* — **Bibliothèque Publique d'Information**: Centre Georges-Pompidou, second floor (tel: 01.44.78.12.33). Extensive multilingual research library, periodicals, a video and music listening room, software library, Internet access. Open daily; hours vary. Has moved to temporary quarters during museum renovation.

- *7e* — **American Library in Paris**: 10, rue du Général-Camou (tel: 01.53.59.12.60). Europe's largest subscription English-language library. Fiction, nonfiction, periodicals, back issues, children's books. Readings, literary programs, lectures, etc. Research facilities. Tuesday–Saturday 10 am–7 pm.
- *7e* — **Library of the British Council**: 9, rue de Constantine (tel: 01.49.55.73.00; fax: 01.47.05.77.02). Books, newspapers, research facilities, music, audio cassettes, video cassettes, CD ROMs, etc.
- *7e* — **Canadian Embassy Special Library**: 5, rue de Constantine (tel: 01.45.51.35.73). For people conducting research on Canada. Books, federal government publications, periodicals.
- *7e* — **Documentation Française**: 29, quai Voltaire (tel: 01.40.15.70.00; fax: 01.40.15.72.30). French government reference library.
- *8e* — **B. Franklin Documentation Center**: 2, rue St-Florentin (tel: 01.43.12.45.70; Minitel: 3614 Docusa). USIS Library reference materials. Open to journalists and documented researchers.
- *13e* — **Bibliothèque Nationale de France**: 11, quai François-Mauriac (tel: 01.53.79.59.59; fax: 01.53.79.43.70). Twelve million volumes (many in English), reading facilities. Exhibition center, auditorium, conference room, restaurants. Bibliothèque Nationale at 58, rue de Richelieu 75002 is the depository for manuscripts, engravings, maps, music, etc. (tel: 01.47.03.81.26).

CHAPTER SIX

BRINGING THE CHILDREN

CHILDREN IN FRANCE

Getting your children set for a long stay in Paris should not be difficult. Baby furniture is easily available and second-hand equipment is often advertised in *FUSAC*. As in most large cities, disposable diapers and pureed foods are found at supermarkets and other shops. Inoculations required are comparable to those in other countries, and there are many English-speaking pharmacists and pediatricians. Childhood diseases in Paris are the same as anywhere else, but be prepared for the usual colds and sore throats, especially when children go to school. (See Chapter Seven for health-related issues.)

French children are generally expected to be well behaved. If the French view of childhood is not as relaxed as in other countries, there seem to be countless opportunities for scheduled activities, structured events, and sports. Museums have special educational programs for children, and puppet theaters and

105

circuses schedule their entertainment for when children are not in school. After-school activities (*hors scolaires*) are encouraged and often arranged, both in the public schools and the international bilingual schools. Most public libraries have children's books, records, and videos; several are devoted entirely to children, including special toy libraries at which children may play with and borrow toys. Playgrounds and sporting facilities are in every *arrondissement*. All told, a child's experience in Paris should be rewarding and pleasant.

CONTACTS AND RESOURCES

Message is an English-speaking group for families with young children and expectant and new mothers. Message organizes meetings and events, parenthood classes, baby and toddler groups, and a working mother's group. An informative quarterly newsletter announces events, and *The ABCs of Motherhood in Paris* is an extensive guide to family living in Paris. As Message is a volunteer organization, addresses and contacts change; currently the contact is Sallie Chaballier (tel: 01.48.04.74.61).

The *mairie* has detailed information about all aspects of schooling in Paris. Ask for *L'Inscription en Maternelle* and for *Le Guide de la Rentrée*, a comprehensive guide to all phases of children's education, leisure, after-school educational activities, and children's health issues. The Paris Tourist Office may also have *Ile-de-France avec des Yeux d'Enfants*, which suggests interesting outings with children.

Inter-Service Parents at 5, impasse Bon Secours 75001 is a French advisory organization that offers free information on concerns for young children, including baby-sitting agencies, schools, and children's activities (tel: 01.44.93.44.93). CIDJ, described in the previous chapter, has information about activities for young people (tel: 01.44.49.12.00). And **Allô Sports** has information on sports programs at the municipal centers (tel: 01.42.76.54.54). For sports, also consult the *Guide du Sport à Paris*, available from the *mairie* or the Paris Tourist Office.

Pariscope and *l'Officiel des Spectacles*, the weekly events maga-zines, have listings for children's activities under the headings *Enfants/Pour les Jeunes; Figaroscope*, the weekly insert to *Le Figaro*, has a section called *Jeunes, Juniors* (summers excepted). **Kiosque Paris-Jeunes** at 25, boulevard Bourdon 75004 has information on various events and reduced-priced tickets (tel: 01.42.76. 22.60).

Paris est un Jeu d'Enfant by Isabelle Bourdial and Valérie Guidoux is a detailed guide to Paris for children, and *Paris Com-bines: Le Guide Enfants* is a compendium of good-value children's clothing stores, venues for activities, baby-sitters, etc.

DAY CARE

The French believe in early socialization for their children, so a high percentage of babies and toddlers are sent to day care. It is widely held that children who have attended day care perform better in their early school years than children who have not. Some 520 public *crèches* (day-care centers) operate within Paris. *Crèches* are subsidized, their fees based on income and need. *Crèches* are extremely over-enrolled, and many expectant moth-ers register their child even before birth. Some *crèches* are more agreeable than others, so shop around. Children are dropped off between 8 am and 10 am and picked up between 4 pm and 6 pm. A *crèche parentale* is run on the same principle, but parents volunteer in various capacities, so the fees are slightly lower. Your *mairie* should have a list of the municipal *crèches* in the *arrondissement* and advice on how to enrol a child.

An *halte garderie* is flexible in its hours. If there is a place avail-able, a parent may deposit a child for a few hours. The system is designed for mothers who need to schedule appointments or go shopping for a few hours without the child. Children are not regis-

107

tered in advance, and a place is not guaranteed on any given day. A *garderie privée* is more like a *crèche* in that the child is registered and comes on a regular basis, but the hours are flexible. Unfortunately, as with the *crèches*, there are few spaces available.

FRENCH EDUCATIONAL SYSTEM

The French public school system is demanding and rigorous. Starting at age two, children are often sent to *jardins d'enfants* (pre-nursery schools) and from 3 to 6 years to *écoles maternelles* (nursery schools). Elementary education, compulsory until age 16, begins at age six, at the *école primaire* (either coeducational or not). It progresses from preparatory to elementary to intermediate levels. By age 11, children advance to the *premier cycle* in the *collèges* (which should not be confused with the English word "college"). Here student-specific education begins according to each child's aptitude and interests. The *deuxième cycle* is the *lycée*, which starts at age 15 and lasts until the student graduates at about 18 years of age. Each student has a *carnet du liaison*, a permanent file with grades and teachers' comments entered year after year.

From age 15 to 17, the student prepares for the *baccalauréat (bac)*, which, according to the student's program and aptitudes, may also include vocational training. The *bac*, equivalent to and as stringent as the British O and A levels, is obligatory for university entrance. For university education, see Chapter Five.

Holidays and Days Off

There is a major school break (*les vacances d'été*) of more than two months each summer, and there are two shorter holidays around Christmas and Easter. There are mini-holidays at the beginning of Lent, on All Saints Day at the beginning of November, and several long weekends.

Public schools are often closed on Wednesdays. Some may be open Saturday mornings, and some may alternate their closures on every second Wednesday and every second Saturday. Many cultural attractions and entertainment, including the much-loved puppet shows and circuses, have special Wednesday programs. The **Petit Palais, musée Carnavalet,** the **Louvre, musée d'Orsay,** the **musée d'Art Moderne,** and other museums have educational programs on Wednesdays and Saturdays.

In addition, the *mairie* operates more than 500 **Centres des Loisirs,** activity centers attached to the public schools that are open on Wednesdays and during short school breaks. Inquire about brochures describing summer vacation programs.

FOREIGN CHILDREN IN SCHOOLS

Selecting a child's school, of course, will be based on many factors other than just a school's location or reputation. The age, character, and language ability of the child should be considered, as well as the expected length of stay in Paris and planned return to a school or university at home. A few parents put their children into French schools immediately. Some long-term, foreign-based parents prefer private, bilingual schools throughout the child's educational career. Others start their children in the bilingual schools, and after a period of adjustment and language learning, move them into the public or private French schools. Some people who transfer to several countries over the years prefer international schools, such as **Marymount,** where the curriculum tends to be standard and grade levels are transferable from country to country. The **Association of American Wives of Europeans** publishes a *Guide to Education*; it should be available at the American Church or at WICE.

Foreign children are accepted into French public schools if their French is adequate to progress within the instructional program. Children in primary schools may enter a conversion program to learn French (*class de CLIN*), after which they are placed · into the regular system. Schools are crowded and applications

109

should be made in the spring before the fall term. Especially in the *maternelle,* places may not be available. To enroll, bring your child's birth certificate, vaccination certificate (including small-pox, BCG, and tetanus), proof of domicile, and school records from previous schools, if appropriate. Although schools are free, there are small charges for textbooks, supplies, and meals.

Private Schools

Although some 85 percent of French schools are public, many private schools in Paris are also controlled and approved by the Ministry of Education. Some are bilingual, offering courses in both French and English. Some, even some parochial schools, are subsidized by the state (*sous contrat*), which makes the tuition reasonable. The *mairie* should have information about private schools. A directory of French private schools and other materials are available from the **Centre de documentation sur l'enseignement privé** at 20, rue Fabert 75007 (tel: 01.47.05. 32.68). See also *Enseignement privé préscolaire, Enseignement privé primaire* and *Enseignement privé secondaire* in the Yellow Pages.

International Bilingual Schools

In and around Paris there is a wide selection of international bilingual or English-language elementary and high schools. The international curriculum is stringent, for acceptance into the best European universities is highly competitive. These are all private schools and, although expensive, are generally in line with other international schools. Tuition varies greatly but may reach 82,000F for the higher grades. Transportation to schools in the suburbs can often be arranged at extra cost, although this may depend on how far into Paris the school buses go. Some important schools are in the outer suburbs, such as St-Germain-en-Laye.

Bilingual Nursery/Lower Schools and Play Groups

- *5e* — **Thomas Jefferson Bilingual Montessori School**: 13, rue de la Clef (tel: 01.43.37.93.31). Students from 3 to 9 years are taught by French and English teachers. About 50 percent of the students are French.
- *7e* — **The English Playgroup**: 3B, rue Emile-Duclaux (tel: 01.42.19.02.14). Games, music, and art provided by bilingual preschool teachers.
- *7e* — **Bilingual Montessori School**: 65, quai d'Orsay (tel: 01.45.55.13.27; fax: 01.45.51.25.12). For students 2–6 years. Other Montessori schools in other locations.
- *9e* — **Les Oursons**: 28, rue Vignon (tel: 01.49.24.05.69; fax: 01.53.70.24.00). Bilingual Montessori school for children 3–6 years. Prepares for entrance either into a French or English primary school.
- *16e* — **United Nations Nursery School**: 40, rue Pierre-Guérin (tel: 01.45.27.20.24; fax: 01.45.24.28.54). Private bilingual school with an international population. Students 2–6 years.
- *17e* — **Les Petits Dragons**: 2, rue Jacquemont (tel: 01.42.28.56.17; fax: 01.48.06.33.72). Bilingual nursery school and kindergarten. Half-day or full-day options.
- *17e* — **La Petite Ecole Bilingue**: 8, place Porte de Champerret (tel: 01.43.80.25.34; fax: 01.43.80.37.40). Ages 2–6, with full-time and part-time programs for students of all nationalities. Bilingual education.

International Elementary/High Schools

- *15e* — **Ecole Active Bilingue Jeannine-Manuel**: Upper grades and permanent secretariat at 70, rue du Théâtre (tel: 01.44.37.00.80; fax: 01.45.79.06.66). French, American, or International Baccalaureate curriculum, with most substantive courses (history, science, geography) taught in English. Preschool and primary grades: 15, rue Edgar-Faure (tel: 01.44.49.09.43); 141, avenue de Suffren (tel: 01.47.34.27.72).

- 16e — **Institut de la Tour**: 86, rue de la Tour (tel: 01.45.04.73.35; fax: 01.45.05.27.98). Catholic high school with a section for English speakers (Anglophone tel: 01.45.04.93.00). Students prepare for the *bac*.
- 16e — **International School of Paris**: 6, rue Beethoven (tel: 01.42.24.09.54; fax: 01.45.27.15.93). From preschool through high school, US and International Baccalaureate programs. French language instruction. Separate locations for lower, middle, and upper schools, all in the 16e.
- 17e — **Ecole Active Bilingue**: 117, boulevard Malesherbes (tel: 01.45.63.62.22; fax: 01.45.63.62.23). Bilingual education for ages 3–18. Helps students make the transition to the French system, leading to the *bac*, the American SAT, and British O and A levels. Locations vary depending on grade level.
- **American School of Paris**: 41, rue Pasteur 92216 Saint-Cloud (tel: 01.41.12.82.45; fax: 01.46.02.23.90). Preschool through high school. American curriculum and the International Baccalaureate. In operation since 1946, there is a good mix of nationalities; about 60 percent American. Extracurricular activities. Transportation available. Summer camp available for ages 5–12.
- **British Schools of Paris**: Senior school is at 38, quai de l'Ecluse 78290 Croissy-sur-Seine (tel: 01.34.80.45.90; fax: 01.39.76.12.69). Lower school is at Chemin du Mur-du-Parc 78380 Bougival (tel: 01.39.69.78.21; fax: 01.30.82.47.49). British curriculum, with an emphasis on French, offered from preschool through high school; about 70 percent of the students are British. Students prepare for A-levels. French classes. Boarding and day-school options. Transportation available.
- **Institut Notre-Dame**: 3, rue de Témara, BP 4259, 78104 St-Germain-en-Laye Cedex (tel: 01.30.87.17.87; fax: 01.30.61.57.67). Catholic private school, offering schooling on two campuses to children from nursery through high school.

Students prepare for the *bac*. Proficient French is required for acceptance.

- **Lycée International**: Rue du Fer-à-Cheval, BP 230, 78104 St-Germain-en-Laye Cedex (tels: British section 01.34.51. 62.64; fax: 01.34.51.39.36; American section: 01.34.51.74.85; fax: 01.30.87.00.49). Public school, with fee-paying international sections. From preschool through high school, rigorous British, American, and French curricula are offered. Foreign students take special classes, then a fully bilingual curriculum. After-school activities and cultural trips. Transport available.
- **International Sections, Collège and Lycée de Sèvres**: rue Lecoq 92310 Sèvres (tel: 01.46.23.96.35; fax: 01.45.34.22.24). French public schools, with fee-paying international sections. Bilingual education with courses in English or German; special courses for non-French speakers. Preparation for the *bac*.
- **Marymount School**: 72, boulevard de la Saussaye 92200 Neuilly-sur-Seine (tel: 01.46.24.10.51; fax: 01.46.37.07.50). Catholic co-ed school from preschool through eighth grade. American curriculum instruction with a strong French language program. About 50 percent native English speakers and the rest from other nationalities. Special education programs.

AFTER-SCHOOL ACTIVITIES

Most of the international schools arrange some after-school activities. In addition, active English-language scouting and guides troops are open to children of all ages and nationalities. Because troop leaders change, the most reliable information is usually available at the American and British embassies and the international schools.

ADAC

ADAC, Paris' public continuing education organization, offers a vast variety of courses in French for children at centers throughout Paris. (See Chapter Five.) ADAC also operates *ludothèques*, which offer play-related learning activities and games and toys to play with and to borrow. A nature-oriented *bibliothèque/ludothèque* is in the Bois de Vincennes at the Pavillon Nature in the Parc Floral (tel: 01.43.28.47.63). For information on *ludothèques*, call the **Association des Ludothèques Françaises** at 7, impasse Chartière 75005 (tel: 01.43.26.81.73; Minitel: 3615 LUDOTEK).

- 4e — 22 ter, rue des Jardins-St-Paul (tel: 01.42.77.86.09)
- 5e — 65, rue Galande (tel: 01.43.25.96.09)
- 5e — 18, rue Poliveau (tel: 01.45.35.68.95)
- 6e — 15, rue du Regard (tel: 01.45.44.67.56)
- 15e — 11, rue Linois (tel: 01.47.83.42.56)
- 17e — 65, boulevard Bessières (tel: 01.42.29.62.03)
- 17e — 2, rue de Torcy (tel: 01.40.38.67.29)

LES CENTRES D'ANIMATION

The city of Paris operates some thirty-nine **Centres d'Animation** in conjunction with its sports and exercise facilities. These offer music and dance lessons and training in hundreds of activities, including tennis, martial arts, football, swimming, and dance. Outings are organized during school holidays. Teenagers are given the highest priority, but there are programs dedicated to younger children. The centers are open on Wednesday, Saturday, and weekday evenings. To enroll your child, bring identification; there is a small fee per trimester. See the municipal sports guide for information, or the *mairie* should have the information booklet *Centres d'Animation*. *Centres d'Animation Magazine* is a bi-annual magazine that announces news of the centers and their offerings.

PARC DE LA VILLETTE

Once children have discovered the **Parc de la Villette**, they may not want to go anywhere else. On about 55 hectares at the northeastern edge of the city, this urban educational park was constructed in 1979 on the former site of the city's slaughterhouse. There are theme gardens and activity parks, a lighted promenade, playgrounds, bicycle paths, pony rides, day-care centers, restaurants, entertainment centers, and a spectacular high-tech, interactive museum. Films, concerts, a planetarium, undersea exhibits, and more are all targeted for children, from preschoolers on. The Paris Tourist Office should have brochures describing La Villette and its schedule of events.

The **Cité des Sciences et de l'Industrie** at 30, avenue Corentin-Cariou 75019 is the ultramodern, hands-on science museum. Many of the programs and exhibits require advance booking (info. tel: 08.36.68.29.30; Minitel: 3615 VILLETTE); closed Monday, May 1, and Christmas.

EDUCATIONAL ENTERTAINMENT

In addition to museum programs, educational entertainment can be found throughout the city. The American Library in Paris has a large children's section, plus readings and films for children (see Chapter Five). **The Children's English Learning Centre** at 33, rue du Fleurus 75006 has a good selection of books and audio tapes for children (tel: 01.45.44.11.66). Refer also to *Le Guide de la Rentrée*.

- 5e — **Muséum National d'Histoire Naturelle**: 57, rue Cuvier (tel: 01.40.79.30.00). In the Jardin des Plantes. Wonderful, imaginative exhibits on nature and natural history and some interactive games.
- 5e — **Le Centre de la Mer et des Eaux**: 195, rue St-Jacques (tel: 01.46.33.08.61). Interesting aquariums, films by Jacques Cousteau, book shop, and documentation center. Closed Monday.

115

- 8*e* — **Palais de la Découverte**: avenue Franklin-D.-Roosevelt (tel: 01.40.74.80.00). Planetarium, computerized and CD information, earth sciences, lessons in astronomy, films on scientific subjects.
- 12*e* — **Aquarium Tropical**: 293, avenue Daumesnil (tel: 01.44.74.84.80). At the Musée National des Arts d'Afrique et d'Océanie. Exotic fish and crocodiles. Closed Tuesday.
- 20*e* — **Géode**: La Vilette (reservations tel: 01.40.05.12.12). Enormous hemispheric screen shows Omnimax documentaries to viewers seated in the center.
- **Le Dome Imax**: 1, place du Dôme, La Défense (tel: 08.36. 67.06.06). Giant hemispheric screen, with the viewers in the middle. Interesting short documentaries and nature films.

PARKS, PLAYGROUNDS, AND ZOOS

Paris has more than 400 parks and gardens. Both the **Bois de Boulogne** to the west and **Bois de Vincennes** to the east have extensive areas of interest to children. The **Jardins du Luxembourg** and **Tuileries** are the only parks that prohibit playing on the grass, but they and most of the larger parks — the **Jardin du Ranelagh**, **Parc des Buttes-Chaumont**, and **Parc Georges-Brassens**, for example — have varied amusements for children, including pony rides. Most parks are open during daylight hours only.

Some 388 *aires de jeux* (playgrounds) can be found in the small parks throughout the city; most have large sand pits where the sand is changed frequently enough to be kept clean. Some small squares have carousels. For playgrounds with special attractions, see *La Guide de la Rentrée*.

THEATERS, MARIONNETTES, AND CIRCUSES

The weekly events guides are the best sources for current programming in theaters, marionettes, and circuses. There are many events to choose among, and they are generally held when schools are closed. Many of the smaller theaters stage programs, some educational, some with animals as the heroes, and often with magicians. The English theater **ACT** stages productions in various venues (tel: 01.40.33.64.02).

Theaters often offer reduced prices for older children, although tickets go quickly. Kiosque Paris-Jeunes at 25, boulevard Bourdon 75004 has discounted tickets for people under 26 (tel: 01.42.76.22.60) and so does **Aquaboulevard** at 4, rue Louis-Armand 75015 (tel: 01.40.60.10.00). The **Jeunesses Musicales de France (JMF)** at 20, rue Geoffroy-l'Asnier 75004 offers young subscribers reduced prices to classical music and other concerts (tel: 01.44. 61.86.86).

Guignols/marionnettes (puppet shows) are among the most popular entertainment for younger children, although for non-French speakers the shows may be difficult to understand. Some venues—at the Champ-de-Mars, Parc Montsouris, and Parc Georges-Brassens, for example—are covered and all-weather, but many famous *guignol* shows are outdoors and perform only in dry weather. The most famous (covered) *guignol* is at the Jardin du Luxembourg.

The Jardin d'Acclimatation in the Bois de Boulogne hosts puppet shows and a *cirque* (circus), **Le Cirque Diana Moreno Bormann** (tel: 01.45.00.23.01), as does the Bois de Vincennes (tel: 01.60.22.78.34). The Bois de Vincennes also has the **Théâtre Astral** for young people. Some circuses are open year-round; others hold performances during the school year.

THEME PARKS

Theme parks outside Paris are good for weekend excursions, and they are generally easy to reach by car or public transportation. There are a variety of themes to choose among, from the **Parc Astérix** (named for the beloved comic character) to **La Mer de**

Sable, an American Wild West extravaganza. **Disneyland Paris** is the most famous, but there are interesting others, such as **France Miniature**, which presents a miniature bas-relief of the historical landmarks and regions of France. The Paris Tourist Office has detailed information, and most tourist guides describe these excursions as well.

At the southern edge of Paris is the swimming complex, Aquaboulevard, mentioned above. Accessible by métro, it offers exciting indoor and outdoor swimming pool activities and is extremely popular and crowded.

EATING OUT WITH CHILDREN

Well-behaved children are welcome in most neighborhood eating establishments, although perhaps not in the most elegant restaurants, where meals are served later in the evening and where a certain decorum is desired. In addition to the varied menus at the local *bistrots* and *brasseries*, there are inexpensive Asian restaurants in every *arrondissement*, and some American-style restaurants offer hamburgers, ribs, and fries. *FUSAC*, the English-language advertising supplement, generally carries advertisements for the latter. Note that not all restaurants have *chaises hautes* (high chairs).

Some casual restaurants have children's menus, including the citywide chains of **Batifol, Chez Clément, Flunch,** and **Hippopotamus**, the sandwich chain **Pomme de Pain**, **Bistro Romain** for pasta and salads, **Léon de Bruxelles** for mussels and excellent fried potatoes, and **La Criée** for fish. Some also offer crayons or toys to keep children occupied.

Many of the pizza chains offer home delivery in neighboring areas, and delivery and takeaway are available from restaurants of all cuisines. *Paris à Domicile*, a guide to delivery services, is available at book shops.

Fast-food eateries are in every neighborhood, including **Quick**, a chain of reliable hamburger shops. **McDonald's** has some

118

100 establishments in and around Paris—so many that some areas are objecting to their coming into the neighborhood. Yet prices are reasonable, rest rooms are fairly clean, and many have play areas for children. Most important, the meat in all McDonald's hamburgers adheres to the company's standards. Although *bifteck haché et frites* (hamburger and fries) are available in many *bistrots*, unless you know the establishment and its procedures for grinding and storing meat, it is probably better to take your children to one of the chains.

BABY-SITTERS

Baby-sitting agencies can provide sitters with some English-language ability. Although it is preferable to book a sitter well in advance, most agencies can provide one given a few hours notice. Rates among companies vary somewhat. The notice board at the American Church lists people interested in baby-sitting, and CROUS, CIDJ, and Inter-Service Parents can recommend baby-sitters.

For regular child care in your home, the *mairie* should be able to direct you to resources for registered child-care providers. Ask for and check references carefully. For *au pair* and nanny agencies, see *FUSAC* and Chapter Four. See also *Garde d'Enfants* in the Yellow Pages.

- 8e — **Baby-Sitting Service**: 18, rue Tronchet (tel: 01.46.37. 51.24)
- 9e — **Home Service**: 2, rue Pierre-Sémard (tel: 01.42.82.05.04)
- 17e — **Kid Services**: 75, boulevard Péreire (tel: 01.47.66.00.52)

119

CHAPTER SEVEN

TO YOUR GOOD HEALTH!

GENERAL CONDITIONS

Medical and sanitary facilities in France are among the highest in quality in the world, and arriving in Paris requires no particular medical precautions or vaccinations. Commercially distributed milk in the cities is pasteurized, and the water in Paris has been safe to drink since the city spent 12 million francs on water purification systems more than a century ago. The water, however, has a high mineral content of *calcaire* (calcium and chalk), and Parisians tend to drink bottled water, such as Vittel, Volvic, or Evian, or slightly fizzy brands, such as Badoit, or any of the inexpensive brands found in groceries. Currently the Brita water filter is popular. To avoid *calcaire* building up in appliances, use *eau déminéralisée* (demineralized water), which is available at groceries and hardware stores.

BEFORE YOU COME

While packing, be sure to include in your carry-on case all important medications, as checked luggage occasionally goes astray. If medication includes syringes or other items that might be questioned, carry with you some proof of their medical need. To avoid needless questions, make sure that all medicines *sur ordonnances* (by prescription) are in their original, labeled containers.

Bring enough medications to tide you over until you have found a doctor and pharmacy of your own, and until you can determine which medications require prescriptions and which do not. Ask your physician to give you copies of records concerning ongoing treatments and to write new prescriptions using both the trade and generic name of the medication. Many of the pharmacies listed in this chapter can translate the prescription into the French equivalent. Bring a copy of your eyeglass prescription and an extra pair of glasses and contact lenses, as well as lens solutions, which are expensive.

CHILDREN

Obtain a copy of your children's vaccination and health records, and make sure all inoculations are current. In France, DPT and polio vaccinations are required, and a tuberculosis vaccination through the BCG combination is required before a child enters a *crèche* or the school system; *rougeole* (measles), *rubéole* (German measles), *oreillons* (mumps), and Hepatitis B vaccinations are recommended but optional, as are flu shots. For information, call the **Centre de Vaccination de la Ville de Paris** at 44, rue Charles-Moureau 75013 (tel: 01.44.97.86.80).

Check with your pediatrician to determine which medicines and other items you should have with you until you find a pediatrician in Paris. If your child has a health emergency before you are set up with a local doctor, go to a hospital (listed below by specialty) or call **Urgences Pédiatrie** for a rapid arrival at your

121

home by a pediatrician (tel: 01.43.94.35.01). Last, if you prefer to read a fever thermometer in Fahrenheit rather than Centigrade, you might think about bringing one with you.

HEALTH RESOURCES

Finding English-speaking doctors in Paris can begin before departure. The **International Association for Medical Assistance to Travelers (IAMAT)**, a non-profit association, provides a list of approved English-speaking doctors. The physicians agree to a preset fee. IAMAT information is free, but donations are encouraged. To receive a list of IAMAT centers in Paris, contact any of the following:

- **United States**: 417 Center St., Lewiston NY 14092 (tel: 716/754-4883)
- **Canada**: 40 Regal Road, Guelph, Ontario N1K1B5 (tel: 519/836-0102); 1287 St. Clair Avenue W, Toronto, Ontario M6E1B8 (tel: 416/652-0137)
- **New Zealand**: PO Box 5049, 438 Pananui Road, Christchurch 5 (tel: 03/352-9053; fax: 03/352-4630)
- **Switzerland**: 57 Voirets, 1212 Grand-Lancy-Geneva.

Credit card companies help Gold Card holders find a doctor (or a lawyer) abroad. They assist in arrangements for emergency evacuation and in relaying messages. Call your credit card company to find out about its services, and ask if it accepts collect calls. Visa participates in this referral program, and it also provides an emergency French number (toll-free tel: 08.00.90.11.79).

In Paris, you should be able to find physicians through friends and colleagues. Embassies have lists of English-speaking doctors and dentists, and *Paris Anglophone* lists physicians by specialty. **SOS Médecins** makes referrals to doctors (tel: 01.47.07.77.77). And there are two major English-speaking hospitals, the **American Hospital** and the **Hertford Franco-Britannique** (see below). *Health Care Resources in Paris* should be available at WICE.

INSURANCE

Administered by the *Caisse Primarie d'Assurance Maladie (CPAM)*, the French public health care system is part of the *Sécurité Sociale*. French health care is among the best in the world: doctors are well-trained (some make house calls), and procedures are the most modern. The entire working community—employers, employees, and the self-employed—contributes to this state-funded insurance plan. Anyone who is working is eligible for coverage.

Physicians and private clinics are either *conventionnés*, whereby they abide by the prices set by the *Sécurité Sociale*, or *non-conventionnés*, whereby they set their own prices. In the latter case, only some of the costs may be covered if it is determined that the prices for the services performed were not competitive. If a service is *nonagréé*, the particular treatment is not covered; *agréé* means the services are covered.

People choose their own *généralistes* (general practitioners) and *spécialistes* (specialists), homeopaths, and dentists. The patient pays for treatment and medicines and then is reimbursed up to about 75 percent. *Spécialistes* charge more than *généralistes*, and *honoraires libres* (doctors who set their own fees) vary their prices. To control costs, the government issues to all people in the *Sécurité*

Sociale, including children, a *carnet de santé* on which the *généraliste* is supposed to write down all particulars of treatments, including *spécialistes* recommended, medicines, etc.

Supplemental Insurance Companies
Remember that French insurance does not cover 100 percent of medical costs. Private insurance companies sell *mutuelles,* supplemental policies that pay costs otherwise not reimbursed. Shop around, for some *mutuelles* cover more costs than others. Ask about dental and eyeglass coverage. Some employers offer *mutuelles* as part of their benefit plan. See *Mutuelles d'assurances* in the Yellow Pages. Students might inquire about *mutuelles* as below:

- **MNEF**: 16, avenue Raspail, B.P. 100, 94252 Gentilly Cedex (tel: 01.30.75.08.20; fax: 01.30.32.80.48)
- **SMEREP**: 54, boulevard St-Michel 75005 (tel: 01.44.41.74.44)

Coverage for Foreigners
All EU nationals (and some others within Europe) are entitled to receive health services throughout the EU. British travelers should obtain an E111 (or E112) form before departure. It is good for three months, allowing time for registration with the French system. The E111 is available from post offices and the **Department of Health and Social Security,** as is a booklet, *Health Advice to Travelers in the European Community*. Validate the form at the post office. Health expenditures in Paris are reimbursed up to about 75 percent (with documentation and receipts), so it is important to check on supplemental insurance.

If your current company is sending you to Paris, the personnel department should be knowledgeable about health insurance coverage for employees abroad. Check to see how you will be covered and the extent of the coverage. If you will be working for a French company, you will have the documents that allow access to the French system. Once in the system, you will have a *numéro d'immatriculation*, an identification number to be used in all health care situations.

Americans on short stays should ask their insurance carriers about coverage abroad and how to file a claim. Some cover treatment for sixty days from onset of a new illness. Ask about exclusions for preexisting conditions, whether prescriptions are covered, and what the waiting time is for reimbursement. Check about coverage for long-term supplies of medications.

Older Americans should be aware that **Medicare** does not honor claims abroad (except in Mexico and Canada) and should investigate **Medigap** policies, offering coverage against catastrophes abroad. The **American Association of Retired Persons (AARP)** offers Medigap coverage and some time-specific emergency coverage abroad (US tel: 800/523-5800).

Canadians are covered by the national health plan only to the amount that similar services are covered at home, so most buy additional insurance. Provincial Ministry of Health Offices should have information, and travel agents have information about additional insurance.

For general questions and options, inquire at the *Sécurité Sociale* office dedicated to international relations at 175, rue de Bercy 75012 (tel: 01.40.19.52.01). Entering the French system may take time, so plan to have your own insurance until you are registered.

- **Advantage Insurance Associates**: 17, rue de Châteaudun 75009 (tel: 01.53.20.03.33; fax: 01.44.63.00.97). Represents various companies for health, vehicle, home, life, and business insurance. Policies in English.
- **ASA, Inc.**: PO Box 7000, Chandler AZ 85240 USA (tel: 602/857-2597; fax: 602/857-2026). Short-term and permanent plans for anybody living outside the United States.
- **Association of Americans Resident Overseas (AARO)**: BP 127, 92154 Suresnes (tel: 01.42.04.09.38; fax: 01.42.04.09.12). Health insurance for its members.

- **BUPA International**: Russell Mews, Brighton EN12NR England (tel: 1273/208-181; fax: 1273/866-583). Worldwide coverage and evacuation for expatriates.
- **Cerise Associates**: 199/207, rue des Pyrénées 75019 (tel: 01.47.97.64.80; fax: 01.47.97.95.42). Health, life, and general coverage.
- **International Medical Group**: 1328 Broadway, Suite 814, New York NY 10001 (tel: 212/268-8520; fax: 212/268-8524). Long-term medical, disability, and life insurance.
- **International Travelers Assistance Association**: 1765 Business Center Drive, Suite 100, Reston VA 20190 (tel: 800/732-5309; fax: 703/438-2279). Ten-month insurance for registered students up to 23 years of age. The **TravMed** program includes $50,000 of medical benefits and $200 of dental emergencies at a cost of $2 per day.
- **PPP International health care plan:** Phillips House, Crescent Road, Tunbridge Wells, Kent, TN12PL England (info tel: 1323/432-002; fax: 1323/432-785). Medical insurance for people living outside their home country.
- **François Sicard**: (tel: 06.06.42.15.35). Health and life insurance for foreigners in Paris; access to American Hospital and to hospitals throughout Europe.
- **Taylor-Sagassur**: 36, rue Laffitte 75009 (tel: 01.44.79.04.04; fax: 01.44.79.01.47). Health, home, and automobile insurance.
- **Wallach and Company**: 107 West Federal Street, PO Box 480, Middleburg VA 22117 (US tel: 800/237-6615). Several long-term plans, including Health Care Global and MedHelp.

PHARMACIES

Pharmacies display a green neon cross outside; the cross is lit when the shop is open. Pharmacies are not general service shops: all products have something to do with health, such as prescription and over-the-counter medications, skin preparations, suntan lotions, and tooth brushes. Most also carry homeopathic remedies. Although prescribed medicines can only be bought at pharmacies, beauty and skin products are widely available at other places, often at better prices.

To fill a prescription under French health insurance, take the *feuille de soins* (treatment statement, including fees) that your physician has given you and the *ordonnance* (prescription) to the pharmacist. The pharmacist will take a sticker indicating the medication's name and price from the medication box and affix it onto the appropriate form. The *feuille de soins* and one copy of the *ordonnance* then go to the authorities for reimbursement. Some pharmacists expect you to remove the sticker and take care of the process yourself.

Pharmacists are highly trained and extremely knowledgeable about medications, of which there are many, since French physicians tend to medicate heavily. After a discussion of symptoms, pharmacists may recommend non-prescription remedies. They also perform emergency first aid and can recommend physicians. The pharmacy in each neighborhood should display a placard indicating the nearest night and Sunday pharmacy (*pharmacie de garde*). The local *commissariat* will also indicate doctors on call and open pharmacies. For home delivery of prescriptions call a service such as **Allô Pharma,** which is open daily (tel: 01.40.54.01.02), or see *Pharmacies* in the Yellow Pages. Pharmacies marked with an asterisk are open 24 hours.

- 1er—**Anglo-American (Swann Rocher) Pharmacy**: 6, rue de Castiglione (tel: 01.42.60.72.96). English/American prescriptions and equivalent French dosages. Closed Sunday.
- 2e—**Pharmacie Opéra**: 6, boulevard des Capucines (tel: 01.42.65.88.29). Open daily until midnight; Sunday 3 pm–midnight.
- 4e—**Pharmacie des Halles**: 10, boulevard de Sébastopol (tel: 01.42.72.03.23). Open daily until midnight.

- 6e — **Pharmacie St-Germain des Pres**: 45, rue Bonaparte (tel: 01.43.26.52.92). Open daily until midnight; Sunday and holidays until 11 pm.
- 8e — **Drugstore Champs-Elysées (Publicis)**: 133, avenue des Champs-Elysées (tel: 01.47.20.39.25). Pharmacy, plus general goods, cigarettes, and food. Open until 2 am.
- 8e — **Drugstore Matignon**: 1, avenue Matignon (tel: 01.43.59. 386.70). Open daily until midnight; Sunday 3–11 pm.
- 8e — **Pharmacie Anglaise des Champs-Elysées**: 62, avenue des Champs-Elysées (tel: 01.43.59.22.52). American and British pharmaceuticals and French equivalents. Open daily until midnight.
- *8e — **Pharmacie "Les Champs"**: 84, avenue des Champs-Elysées (tel: 01. 45.62.02.41). Open 24 hours. English-speaking personnel.
- *9e — **Pharmacie Européenne**: 6, place de Clichy (tel: 01.48. 74.65.18). Open 24 hours daily.
- 9e — **British-American Pharmacy**: 1, rue Auber (tel: 01.47. 42.49.40). British and American products. Open until 8 pm; closed Sunday.
- 11e — **La Nation**: 13, place de la Nation (tel: 01.43.73.24.03). Open daily until midnight.
- 12e — **Pharmacie de la Porte de Vincennes**: 101, boulevard Soult (tel: 01.43.43.13.68). Open daily until 2 am.
- *12e — **Grande Pharmacie Daumesnil**: 6 place Félix-Eboué (tel: 01.43.43.19.03). Open daily, 24 hours.
- 13e — **Pharmacie d'Italie**: 61, avenue d'Italie (tel: 01.44.24. 19.72). Open daily until midnight.
- 14e — **Pharmacie des Arts**: 106, boulevard du Montparnasse (tel: 01.43.35.44.88). English-speaking pharmacists. Open until midnight; Sunday until 10 pm.
- 16e — **Pharmacie Mozart**: 14, avenue Mozart (tel: 01.45. 27.38.17). Weekdays until 10 pm; Saturday until 8 pm.

- 17e — **Pharmacie des Sports**: 2, place du Général-Koenig (tel : 01.45.74.31.10). Open until midnight; closed Sunday.
- 20e — **Pharmacie Bataille**: 6, rue de Belleville (tel: 01.46. 36.67.42). Open until 11:30 pm; closed Sunday.

PARAPHARMACIES

Parapharmacies, which are generally *libre-service* (self-service), carry cosmetics and non-prescription health care products, including vitamins, homeopathic remedies, and skin preparations. Not as tightly regulated as pharmacies, parapharmacies are often less expensive, and some offer a *carte de fidélité*, giving a discount for frequent purchases. Three well-stocked chains are **Euro Santé Beauté** with 11 stores in Paris, **Para+** with three, and **Conseil+** with two.

HOSPITALS

Most public hospitals have *urgences* (emergency rooms), as do the two English-speaking private hospitals listed below. See *Hôpitaux* in the Yellow Pages and *Hôpital* in the White Pages.

In a dire emergency, call **SAMU** (tel: 15) or the *pompiers* (Fire Department tel: 18) rather than go on your own to a hospital. When the emergency call is made, the caller's number is automatically registered. Response is swift and effective, and ambulances are routed to the correct hospital by trained personnel who know the procedures for the fastest treatment. A doctor, a nurse, and extensive equipment are aboard every ambulance, and in fact, SAMU ambulances are "emergency rooms on wheels." *Pompiers* have the equipment to enter an apartment in which the occupant might not be able to open the door.

For non-life threatening emergency care, go to the hospital nearest you. After treatment, you might be referred or transferred to another hospital that specializes more specifically in the treatment you require. For house calls, call **Urgences Médicales** (tel:

01.48.28.40.04) or **SOS Médecins** (24-hour tel: 01.47.07.77.77). Cardiologists from **SOS Cardiologie** also make house calls (tel: 01.47.07.50.50).

- **American Hospital of Paris**: 63, boulevard Victor-Hugo 92202 Neuilly-sur-Seine (tel: 01.46.41.25.25; emergencies: 01.47.47. 70.15). Full-service private hospital with English-speaking personnel, accredited in the United States. Dental services. Accepts Blue Cross insurance for inpatient services and provides diagnosis for outpatient reimbursement of insurance. Credit cards accepted in the emergency ward. *Agréé* but *non-conventionné*.

- **Franco-Britannique Hospital (Hertford British)**: 3, rue Barbès 92300 Levallois-Perret (tel: 01.46.39.22.22; fax: 01.46.39.22.26). Bilingual, full-service, private hospital. Priority care for British residents and tourists. No dental facilities. No emergency services for children. *Conventionné*.

The hospital system is in the process of being consolidated. In the year 2000, a major new hospital, the **Hôpital Georges-Pompidou**, will open on the quai Andre Citroën in the 15*e*, and some existing hospitals will have their services reorganized. At present, these hospitals are known for their emergency care in particular specialties:

- 4*e* — **Hôpital Hôtel Dieu**: 1, place du Parvis-Notre-Dame (tel: 01.42.34.82.34). Eye emergencies. Domestic abuse. Diabetic emergencies.
- 10*e* — **Hôpital Fernand Widal**: 200, rue du Faubourg-St-Denis (tel: 01.40.37.04.04). Poison center.
- 12*e* — **Hôpital des Quinze-Vingt**: 28, rue de Charenton (tel: 01.40.02.15.20). Eye problems.
- 12*e* — **Hôpital Trousseau**: 26, avenue du Docteur Arnold-Netter (tels: 01.44.73.74.75). Children's burn center.
- 13*e* — **Hôpital de la Pitié-Salpêtrière**: 47, boulevard de l'Hôpital, 75013 (tel: 01.42.16.00.00). Accidents. AIDS. Neurology.

- 14e — **Hôpital Cochin**: 27, rue du Faubourg-St-Jacques (tel: 01.42.34.17.58). Adult burn center; childbirth.
- 14e — **Hôpital Broussais**: 96, rue Didot (tel: 10.43.95.95.95). Major cardiac center.
- 15e — **Hôpital Boucicaut**: 78, rue de la Convention (tel: 01.53.78.80.00). Severed limbs.
- 15e — **Hôpital Necker**: 149, rue de Sèvres (tel: 01.44.49.40.00). Children's services and burn center. Ear, nose and throat services.
- 17e — **Hôpital Marmottan**: 10, rue Armaillé (tel: 01.45.74. 00.04). Drug crisis center.
- 18e — **Hôpital Bichat**: 46, rue Henri-Huchard (tel: 01.40.25. 80.80). Severed limbs.

For non-emergencies, your doctors will refer you to a hospital or clinic with which they are affiliated. It is helpful when choosing physicians to know their hospital affiliation.

Private *cliniques* (clinics) often specialize in particular fields. Although accommodations are more pleasant than in a public hospital, clinics may not be as extensively equipped.

DENTISTRY

Although Paris has excellent dental services with the most modern equipment and trained practitioners, it would be wise to have as much dental work as possible done by your regular dentist before you leave home, giving you adequate time to find a dentist in your new home. If you have particular ongoing dental problems, bring a set of x-rays with you.

Hôpital Hôtel Dieu provides 24-hour emergency *stomatologie* services (dental and mouth care), as does the American Hospital. For emergencies you can also go to **SOS Dentaire** at 87, boulevard Port-Royal 75013, preferably having called in advance (24-hour tel: 01.43.37.51.00); weekdays 8–11:30 pm, weekends

131

9:30 am–11:30 pm. **Urgences Dentaires Parisiennes** takes calls 24 hours daily (tel: 01.45.53.71.08).

PREGNANCY AND BIRTH CONTROL

Except for *préservatifs* (condoms) and *spermicides*, contraceptives require a prescription. Bring a prescription to be translated into the French equivalent, then see your doctor in Paris. Abortion is legal in France, as is the "day-after" birth-control pill.

French maternity care is excellent. In a public hospital just about all costs are covered under Sécurité Sociale, although the hospital might not provide towels, soap, lotions, or sometimes even diapers for the baby! Women in the French health care system must declare their pregnancy and undergo a minimum of four examinations and one *echographie*. A *carnet de maternité* will be provided.

As suggested above, inquire as to your obstetrician's hospital or clinic. The services at both public hospitals and private clinics can be equally good, but hospitals have more extensive equipment and facilities. Clinics can provide more comfortable surroundings, yet their services might not be *conventionnés*, and even if covered, it may take some time for reimbursement. Except for complicated deliveries, many babies in France are delivered by a *sage-femme* (midwife).

Well respected for maternity care are **Hôpital St-Vincent de Paul** at 74, avenue Denfert-Rochereau 75014 (tel: 01.40.48. 81.11) and **Hôpital Cochin,** both of which are noted for their high-risk pregnancy capabilities. Both have waiting lists, so register as soon as you know you are pregnant. Also well-known is **Hôpital des Diaconesses** at 18, rue du Sergent-Bauchat 75012 (tel: 01.44.74.10.10).

Birth and parenting classes for expectant parents are held independently by *sages-femmes* and also at many hospitals. **Hôpital Notre-Dame de Bon Secours** at 66, rue des Plantes 75014 conducts a *sophrologie* program of relaxation, including Yoga and Lamaze techniques (tel: 01.40.52.50.52). The English-speaking hospitals provide prenatal and childbirth care as well.

All births must be registered within three days at your *mairie*. The hospital provides the forms. Identification is required, and, if possible, a copy of your marriage certificate translated into French by a *traducteur assermenté*. A representative from the *mairie* comes to the hospital, so you do not have to go in person. New parents should ask for a copy of *La Naissance à Paris*. All births should also be registered immediately at your consulate.

Message, the support group for new and expectant mothers, is described in Chapter Six. *The ABCs of Motherhood in Paris* is available to members. Call Sallie Chaballier (tel: 01.48.04.74.61).

PROBLEMS WITH COPING

Both the American Church (tel: 01.40.50.26.49) and American Cathedral (tel: 01.47.23.61.13) provide space on their premises for non-sectarian, English-language support services, including counseling for individuals and families.

- **Alcoholics Anonymous** has a recorded announcement detailing the times of the daily meetings at the American Church and other venues (tel: 01.46.34.59.65).
- **SOS Help**, an English-language hotline, listens to problems and acts as a referral service to doctors and other professionals (tel: 01.47.23.80.80).

HIV/AIDS

Unfortunately, *SIDA* (AIDS) has taken hold in Paris. City-sponsored health centers do free and confidential AIDS testing, and several hospitals offer extensive care. Ask at the *mairie* for *SIDA: Solidarité et Soins*, a comprehensive resource about AIDS care in Paris. **Médecins du Monde** has a private center at 62 bis, avenue Parmentier 75011 (tel: 10.43.14.81.61).

- **FACTS**: Free AIDS telephone counseling and referrals in English (tel: 10.44.93.16.69).
- **Le Kiosque**: 36, rue Geoffroy-l'Asnier 75004 (tel: 01.44.78.00.00). Information on AIDS prevention and contraception. Also at 6, rue Dante 75005 (tel: 01.44.78.00.00).
- **SIDA Information Service** (08.00.84.08.00), hotline of **AIDES Comité Paris Ile-de-France** at 247, rue de Belleville (tel: 10.44.52.00.00).
- The **Association des Médecins Gais** provides telephone information on Wednesday evenings and Saturday afternoons (tel: 01.48.05.81.71).
- **SOS Ecoute Gay** is an evenings-only hotline for gays and lesbians (tel: 01.44.93.01.02).

DEATH

Deaths must be certified by a physician and reported to the *mairie* within 24 hours. The doctor who comes to the house to record the death will explain the procedures. Only after such official registration may a funeral or repatriation take place. Notify your embassy officially, and it will provide assistance with the paperwork.

Call **SOS Décès** for information on what to do when someone dies at home (24-hour tel: 01.42.02.99.99), or the municipal **Services Funéraires** (toll-free tel: 08.00.88.00.88). Try also:

- **Association Française d'Information Funéraire**: 9, rue Chamel 75007 (tel: 01.45.44.90.03). Information.
- **Service Municipal des Pompes Funèbres**: 104, rue d'Aubervilliers 75019 (tel: 01.44.65.34.34). Widely used public funeral service.

Chapter Eight

MINDING YOUR BUSINESS

PARIS BUSINESS SCENE

Although official policy is to decentralize French industries, the Greater Paris area remains dominant in the economic scene, its population hovering at about 13 million. Ile-de-France (the area including Paris and its surrounds) accounts for 70 percent of all company headquarters in France, 30 percent of research and development, and 25 percent of the labor force. Not only is Paris the country's political and administrative center, it is also the focus for more than 60 million tourists who visit France each year, the most visited country in the world. It is said that some 12 million visitors stay at Paris hotels each year.

About 8,000 foreign companies of all financial levels currently operate in the Paris area. La Défense, the business center on the city's western edge, is the headquarters for the major French

135

firms and multinational giants, such as IBM, Fiat, British Airways, and ELF, use the Paris area as their starting points for trade throughout Europe. A significant Anglophone expatriate community has stabilized in Paris and its suburbs: there are currently some 100,000 English-speaking residents living and working in professional occupations and consulting capacities, and many provide the expatriate community with agreeable shops and services.

UNDERSTANDING BUSINESS CUSTOMS

Before undertaking any new business endeavor, make an effort to understand how the French culture and way of life differ from your own. Read some of the literature described in the Introduction, and join some of the networking groups described in Chapter Two and below. Learn how the French do business, for it may be very different from the business customs of your home country. Hierarchical structures persist, and the French are formal and legalistic, as well as extremely courteous, in their business encounters. Traditional attitudes may mean that new ideas will be slow to take hold. But do not be discouraged by what seems to be a cold formality, or mistake it for a lack of interest. In fact, heated discussions and even negative debate about ideas and proposals may indicate a high interest in the project. Especially in initial dealings, whether by letter or telephone or in personal meetings, be formal in greetings and use the person's title as appropriate. Shake hands at the beginning of a meeting and just before leaving.

When making appointments or checking schedules, remember that France uses the 24-hour clock. Thus your business meeting (or your barber's appointment or restaurant reservation) may be set for 15:00 instead of 3 pm or at 22:00 rather than 10 pm.

Although social engagements call for a cultural understanding of how late one should be, business meetings generally start on time, but outside interruptions and distractions may be frequent and frustrating to non-French participants. Long business lunches are less popular than in the past, owing to time constraints and the tendency to eat and drink less during business hours. Younger professionals are tending to eat lunch at their desks. Nonetheless, the lunch is still seen as a pleasant method to cement a business relationship, although not to close a deal.

Using first names is not automatic; in fact, the French will let you know when — indeed if — it is time to move to first names. It will probably never be time to move from first names — still using the *vous* form of address — to the familiar *tu*. If people want you to call them by first names, they will let you know. Be cordial and respectful, but not overly familiar, and do not mistake cordiality for friendship. The French do not often mix business with pleasure and, in fact, guard their privacy. Friendly business lunches and meetings may not translate into socializing after work as friends.

Although at least 50 percent of young professional French people speak some English, French business people do not appreciate foreign business associates who make no effort to communicate with them in their country's language. First and foremost, speak French at whatever level you can. Without ability in French, you will be at a disadvantage with your EU colleagues and competitors. Write all initial letters in French, and if that is not possible, have someone translate them for you. Make sure all presentation materials are in French. If your French is not adequate to the task, bring an interpreter to initial meetings or presentations.

The watchwords for doing business in France are "do your homework." Find out in advance all particulars about the companies you wish to deal with, note the appropriate contacts, and write or call them well in advance of arrival in Paris to set up meetings; confirm a meeting the day before. Acknowledge all letters promptly. Make sure presentation materials are well organized and that they stress facts and procedures, rather than opinions. Emphasize the benefits to be gained by the endeavor. Follow up with letters, whether mailed or faxed, after all meetings.

Do not expect to have finalized orders or agreements after a first meeting, which is generally seen as an opportunity to size up the company or product. Usually the top manager or director ultimately makes the business decision, no matter with whom the initial meetings were held. Decisions may be slow, as all ramifications are considered and the French reluctance toward change is overcome, if it is. Younger people rising in the corporate structure, especially those who hold advanced degrees and have an international outlook, will soon begin to change the face of French business procedures. Some are already expressing frustration with today's "top-down," hierarchical method of decision making, although they still understand that changes will come only as generations of leaders change or if France begins to slip in international markets.

Last, take into account that in August nothing will get done, for there is no one around to do it. This also means that if you are opening a shop or other business that depends on the year-round participation of the public, you should factor into your financial forecasts the disappearance of Parisians from the city in August and somewhat in July. This also holds true, although to a lesser extent, around the New Year and Easter.

Business Cards

Business acquaintances exchange *cartes de visite* (business/visiting cards) on first meeting. Cards generally contain all the *coordonnées*, including the person's name, business affiliation and title, address, telephone and fax numbers, and Internet address if there is one. Even upon first moving to Paris and staying in temporary quarters, you should have cards to exchange with your counterparts both in business and social situations. Self-service machines offering a variety of designs and print faces can be found in train stations and some supermarkets. *Papeteries* (stationery stores) make more stylish, engraved cards.

RESOURCE MATERIALS

Fortunately, there is a wealth of information concerning the startup of businesses in Paris and about doing business within the EU; make sure you become knowledgeable about EU regulations as well as French laws. WICE regularly holds seminars on starting a business in France. French government agencies, such as **DATAR** and the semi-public **CCIP**, aid foreign investment (see below), and several Anglophone embassies maintain commercial departments to aid their citizens doing business in France. All have pertinent material, some of it for free distribution. Also inquire at **Agence Nationale pour la Valorisation de la Recherche (ANVAR)** at 43, rue Caumartin 75009 (tel: 01.40.17.83.00; fax: 01.40.17.83.19).

Private chambers of commerce and management consulting agencies also produce informative brochures as part of their services. *Setting Up a Small Business in France* and several other helpful booklets may be purchased from the **Chambre de Commerce Française de Grande-Bretagne**, Knightsbridge House, 197 Knightsbridge, London SW71RB (tel: 171/304-4040; fax: 171/304-7034). *Doing Business in France* is the same title for publications available from two different consulting companies, as well as DATAR.

- **Ernst & Young**: Tour Manhattan, 6, Place de l'Iris 92095, Paris La Défense (tel: 01.46.93.60.00; fax: 01.47.76.20.33)
- **Price Waterhouse**: 34, Place des Corolles 92908, Paris La Défense, Cedex 105 (tel: 01.41.26.16.00; fax: 01.41.26.16.16)

The *International Herald Tribune* and the Paris Stock Exchange jointly publish *French Company Handbook*, detailing profiles of all companies in the SBF 120 Index (tel: 01.41.43.93.00). Write

International Herald Tribune Offers, 37 Lambton Road, London SW20 OLW, or order by fax: 0181/944-8243. **KOMPASS**, an extensive business directory and marketing resource, can be accessed at CCIP and other chambers of commerce (Minitel: 3617 KOMPASS).

The *International Herald Tribune* sells, for US$34.95, the *International Franchise Guide*, a guide to international franchisers and opportunities. Write *IHT Guide* at PO Box 12488, Oakland CA 94604 (US tel: 510/839-5471; fax: 510/547-3245).

Assistance for British Investment

France is the United Kingdom's third largest export market after the United States and Germany. More than 1,800 UK companies have subsidiaries in France, and the prevailing opinion is that anything sold in the UK is likely to sell here. The commercial section of the British Embassy at 35, rue du Faubourg-St-Honoré 75008 provides help to British firms wanting to export to or operate in France (tel: 01.44.51.34.56; fax: 01.44.51.34.01). The embassy also maintains a commercial library with trade directories and other materials for people wishing to do business in France.

In Britain, the overseas trade services section of the **Department of Trade and Industry (DTI)** offers investors marketing information, including economic background and statistical research. It can also provide tailor-made contact lists, find agents and distributors, and participate with publicity and trade fairs. Contact your local **Business Link** (info tel: 0345/567-765) or DTI's Business in Europe desk (tel: 171/215-8885; fax: 171/215-8884).

Assistance for American Investment

The **United States and Foreign Commercial Service (US &FCS)**, located in the American Embassy at 2, avenue Gabriel 75008, assists American companies with entry into the French market in sales, licensing agreements, and joint and direct investment (tel: 01.43.12.25.32; fax: 01.43.12.21.72). The service also works with French firms that want to represent American manufacturers, use American products, or set up joint ventures. The US&FCS can brief Americans on French economic conditions and specific markets, locate and assess French agents, and set up appointments. Call for an information packet.

CCIP

Before engaging in any kind of business in France, call **CCIP (Chambre de Commerce et d'Industrie de Paris)**. Unlike private chambers of commerce, CCIP is a powerful, 4,000-employee semi-governmental agency that regulates and facilitates business and controls the ports and railroads in France, as well as the exhibition centers. CCIP represents 273,000 companies, accounting for 25 percent of all French economic activity. Although the main headquarters is at 27, avenue de Friedland 75008, it is the **Foreign Investment Department/Paris Development Agency** at 2, rue de Viarmes 75001 that aids foreign business investment (tel: 01.55.65.33.93; fax: 01.55.65.33.90). It provides information in English and assistance in setting up a business. Its **Centre de Formalités des Entreprises** is a one-stop registration process for businesses, providing liaison with other bureaucracies (tel: 01.53. 40.48.48; fax: 01.53.40.48.88).

CCIP maintains an extensive library of resource materials and sells publications concerning all aspects of French business. Ask for the English-language publication, *Documentation Pratique No. 88A, Non-French Nationals: Setting Up a Business in France.*

DATAR

DATAR (Délégation à l'Aménagement du Territoire et à l'Action Régionale) is a governmental agency that promotes foreign business investment in France (tel: 01.43.37.05.81; fax: 01.44.37.05.90), 28, rue du Docteur-Finlay 75015. DATAR provides assistance to foreigners who are considering setting up a business, and it provides liaison with the various bureaucratic agencies.

DATAR's international network, **IFA (Invest in France Agencies),** has branches worldwide. In addition to major European cities, there are IFA offices in Tokyo and Osaka, Hong Kong, Seoul, and Taipei. In the United Kingdom, IFA is at 21-24 Grosvenor Place, London SW1X7HU (tel: 171/823-1895; fax: 171/235-8453). In the United States and Canada:

- **East and Quebec**: 610 Fifth Avenue, New York NY 10020 (tel: 212/757-9340; fax: 212/245-1568)
- **Midwest and Ontario**: 401 North Michigan Avenue, Chicago IL 60611 (tel: 312/661-1640; fax: 312/661-0623)
- **South**: 5847 San Felipe Plaza, Houston TX 77057 (tel: 713/266-9772; fax: 713/266-9884)
- **West and Western Provinces**: 1801 Avenue of the Stars, Los Angeles CA 90067 (tel: 310/785-9735; fax: 310/785-9213)

THE LABOR POOL

Owing to the high unemployment rate in France, labor-intensive investments are especially encouraged. Women make up just under half the working population, this number strengthened by subsidized child care and tax breaks for home child-care workers. Since the mid-eighties, men and women are by law equal in the workplace, yet women are still paid about one-third less than their male counterparts, and few women hold top positions. Union membership has declined over the past decade and now accounts for about 12 percent of the workforce. Although strikes seem frequent, they too have declined by more than half since the early eighties.

When considering a business startup, take strongly into account the rigid labor laws and the costs of hiring employees. Social benefits, such as health and unemployment insurance and retirement benefits, are costly, both for the employer and the employee. Note also that French employees are entitled to five weeks holiday *per annum*, or two and a half days per month worked. Currently, the standard work week is 39 hours. French businesses are tending to use fewer labor-intensive procedures and to rely more on labor-saving technology, which adds to the high unemployment rate. Yet, foreign-controlled firms currently account for 22 percent of the French workforce. Some government subsidies and grants are available. Inquire at the CCIP's employment department or ask a management consultant or an *expert comptable* (certified accountant).

LEGAL FORMS OF ENTERPRISE

Business options include setting up a new, independent business, purchasing and taking over an existing business, or leasing a business in which the owner retains title but the lessee operates the business, assuming all risk. Before creating any enterprise, it is important to understand how much of your own assets will be at risk in each structure. A knowledgeable attorney will suggest the simplest structure possible and will help take care of all bureaucratic requirements. CCIP issues *Documentation Pratiques* with detailed information on each form of enterprise.

- **Entreprises Individuelles**: sole proprietorships, independent business people, and sole traders. The simplest form. One person, whose assets are at risk, receives the profit or loss. No minimum capital investment.
- **Société en Nom Collectif (SNC)**: rarely held, it is a private corporation of at least two partners, jointly and severally liable without limitation for losses.
- **Société à Responsabilité Limitée (SARL):** private limited company. Minimum capital of 50,000F. Liability limited to investment. For medium-sized business requiring little financing. Simplest type of limited-liability company. May have a minimum of two shareholders, a maximum of 50.

143

- **Unipersonnelle à Responsabilité Limitée (EURL)**: like a SARL, but with sole proprietor as a limited-liability company. Liability limited to investment in company.
- **Societé Anonyme (SA)**: corporate structure for large companies traded on the stock exchange. At least seven shareholders and a minimum capital of 250,000F. Strict auditing standards.

A *bureau de liaison* is a representative office, such as a public relations or advertising office, doing no financial business and paying no taxes. A *succursale* is a branch office of any company that is registered in France; it must keep its own accounting books (except for the balance sheet), issue its own invoices and receipts, and pay taxes. A *filiale* (subsidiary) is a separate entity of a company operating under French statutes, with new partners and new capital stock; it must be registered at the **Tribunal du Commerce.**

For alternative strategies for starting businesses and marketing ideas in France, you might consult David Applefield, the publisher of *Paris Anglophone*, at 32, rue Edouard-Vallant 93100 Montreuil (tel: 01.48.59.66.58; fax: 01.48.59.66.68).

ATTORNEYS AND EXPERT HELP

Many bilingual law firms in Paris, including those of English and American *avocats* (attorneys), specialize in *droit des affaires* (business law). All attorneys must pass the French bar exam before they may practice law under their own name. Because fees can be high, be clear as to your financial limits; on the other hand, be wary of any cut-rate offers. Some attorneys will sign with their clients a *convention d'honoraires*, which sets criteria for establishing fees.

Make sure the lawyer you are considering is expert in precisely the area you need. Many are knowledgeable about employment legislation, for instance, which is important if your business requires hiring personnel. The American and British embassies publish lists of Anglophone attorneys in the Paris district, but make no recommendations. Consulting agencies can make referrals to appropriate bilingual attorneys.

A *notaire*, as described in Chapter Two, may be helpful in rights you own concerning patents, copyrights, and royalties.

An *expert-comptable* should participate in setting up the financial reporting system to reflect the official French (and EU) method of accounting. The filling out of employee payslips, complicated in its legal intricacies, is often contracted to an *expert-comptable* rather than done in-house. A *comptable* (accountant) generally works in a company and does the financial record keeping on a daily basis. International consulting firms, although probably somewhat more expensive than local French firms, are expert in new business transactions and also serve as *experts comptables*. See *Paris Anglophone* and *Comptables* in the Yellow Pages.

- **Coopers & Lybrand**: 32, rue Guersant 75017 (tel: 01.45.72. 80.00; fax: 01.45.72.22.19)
- **KPMG, Peat Marwick Consultants**: Tour Framatome 92084 Paris La Défense, Cedex 16 (tel: 01.47.96.20.00; fax: 01.47. 96.20.58)
- **Arthur Andersen et Associés**: 41, rue Ybry 92200 Neuilly-sur-Seine (tel: 01.55.61.10.10; fax: 01.55.61.15.15)
- **BDA Deloitte et Touche**: 185, avenue Charles-de-Gaulle 92200 Neuilly-sur-Seine (tel: 01.40.88.28.00; fax: 01.40. 88.28.28)
- **HSD Ernst and Young**: Tour Manhattan, Place Iris, 92037 Paris La Défense (tel: 01.46.93.60.00; fax: 01.47.76.20.33)
- **Price Waterhouse**: 34, place des Corolles 92908 Paris La Défense, Cedex 105 (tel: 01.41.26.16.00; fax: 01.41.26.16.16)

TRADE FAIRS AND LARGE MEETINGS

Paris hosts more *salons* (trade fairs) and *congrès* (international meetings) each year than any other city in the world. The Paris Tourist Office has a calendar of the annual fairs and meetings in Paris, as does the **Fédération Française des Salons Spécialisés**: 4, place des Valois 75001 (tel: 01.42.86.82.99; fax: 01.42.86.82.97).

The **Paris Convention Bureau** at 5, avenue de l'Opéra 75001 issues *Conference and Exhibition Facilities*, provides assistance with conference sites, and offers advice on business tourism (tel: 01.47.03.16.16; fax: 01.47.03.16.18).

Most large fairs are held at **Parc des Expositions** at the Porte de Versailles. To the north of the city, near Charles-de-Gaulle Airport, is **Parc des Expositions Paris Nord** (Villepinte), a second major site. Currently, the most hi-tech site is the **Palais des Congrès** at Porte Maillot, which has television studios and satellite links. International meetings and fairs are also held at **Bercy**, at **CNIT** at La Défense, and at the **Grande Halle de la Villette**. All are accessible by public transportation.

CHAMBERS OF COMMERCE

Chambers of commerce facilitate bilateral business by publishing information of current interest, setting up meetings and seminars, etc. Some issue directories of their country's companies doing business in France, which are available to their members.

- 8*e* — **American Chamber of Commerce**: 21, avenue George-V (tel: 01.40.73.89.90; fax: 01.47.20.18.62)
- 15*e* — **Australian Centre for Commerce**: 4, rue Jean-Rey 75723 Cedex 15 (tel: 01.40.59.33.00; fax: 01.40.59.33.22)
- 8*e* — **Chambre de Commerce France-Canada**: 9, avenue Franklin-D.-Roosevelt (tel: 01.43.59.32.38; fax: 01.42.56.25.62)
- 8*e* — **Chambre de Commerce Internationale**: 38, cours Albert-1*er* (tel: 01.49.53.28.28; fax: 01.49.53.29.42)
- 8*e* — **French-American Chamber of Commerce**: 104, rue de Miromesnil (tel: 01.53.89.11.00; fax: 01.53.89.11.09)
- 8*e* — **Chambre de Commerce et d'Industrie Franco-Britannique**: 31, rue Boissy d'Anglas (tel: 01.53.30.81.30; fax: 01.53.30.81.35)

146

NETWORKING

In French business, with its rigid structures and formal approach, it is important to cultivate all opportunities for personal contact. The Anglophone community in Paris is active in networking for people of similar interests. The international **Lions Club** (tel: 01.46.34.14.10) and **Rotary Club** (tel: 01.45.04.14.44) host regular meetings. Also, inquire of your university whether there is an alumni chapter in Paris. See also *Paris Anglophone*.

- **Association of Americans Resident Overseas (AARO)**: BP 127, 92154 Suresnes Cedex (tel: 01.42.04.09.38; fax: 01.42.04.09.12). Helps Americans stay informed of current events. Tax and estate-planning seminars, meetings and social events, quarterly newsletter, and medical insurance.
- **France-Canada Association**: 5, rue de Constantine 75007 (tel: 01.45.55.83.65). Friendship association promoting contacts, conferences, and cultural events.
- **France-Amerique**: 9-11, avenue Franklin-Roosevelt 75008 (tel: 01.43.59.51.00; fax: 01.40.75.00.97). Discussions, lunches, etc. to improve cultural and economic relations between France and the Americas.
- **Business Development Network International**: Parc Croix-Marie, 4, avenue des Jonchères 78121 Crespières (tel: 01.30.54.94.66; fax: 01.30.54.94.67). A group of about 400 small businesses, consultants, and entrepreneurs meeting for business contacts and networking. French and English spoken.

OFFICE SPACE

Office space may be rented or purchased as a leasehold. If you purchase property, make sure to select an appropriate *notaire*. To rent office space, use a commercial, rather than residential, estate agent. Standard business leases are for nine years unless prior agreement is reached for another time frame. To renew a lease, the tenant should inform the landlord six months before the lease expires. EU nationals, Canadians, and Americans are afforded the same lease protections as French citizens.

The British firm, **Jones Lang Wooten**, at 49, avenue Hoche 75008 specializes in office space (tel: 01.40.55.15.15; fax: 01.46. 22.28.28). **Générale Continentale Investissements** at Immeuble Madeleine 92057 Paris La Défense Cedex 24 handles offices around avenue de Wagram (tel: 01.45.17.28.00; fax: 01.440. 90.92.91). Other agents may be found through the **Féderation Nationale des Agents Immobiliers (FNAIM)** at 129, rue du Faubourg-St-Honoré 75008 (tel: 01.53.76.03.52).

Temporary Offices

Fully equipped offices may be rented by the day, week, or month. Most offer secretarial and translation services, message taking, mail delivery, copiers, and other office services. Some have access six days a week. The *International Herald Tribune* publishes ads for temporary offices on the first Wednesday of each month. See *Location de bureaux équipés* in the Yellow Pages.

- 8e — **Multiburo**: 17, rue de la Baume (tel: 01.44.13.40.00; fax: 01.45.62.60.25); other addresses.
- 11e — **ITER International**: 33, avenue Philippe-Auguste (tel: 01.44.64.89.08; fax: 01.43.71.93.60).
- 16e — **Ibos**: 15, avenue Victor-Hugo (tel: 01.44.28.18.00; fax: 01.44.28.19.00).
- 17e — **MP Bureaux Business**: 92, rue de Lévis (tel: 01.43. 80.40.41; fax: 01.43.26.25).

CHAPTER NINE

MANAGING YOUR MONEY

THE EURO

This is a time of transition for the currency of countries within the EU. As of June 30, 2002, EU countries are planning to give up entirely their own currencies in favor of the **euro**. Although the euro itself will not be circulated until 2002, the years until then will see its gradual entry into daily life, giving people three years to accustom themselves to it. In France, many products and services will be marked with both the **franc** and the euro. Some wholesalers and corporations will begin transacting business in the euro at the beginning of January 1999, and some banks will offer accounts in euros to their customers. As of this writing, calculators designed to convert francs to euros (or vice versa) are being both given away and sold. Ask for *L'euro et moi* at the *mairie*.

CREDIT CARDS

Using a *carte de crédit* (credit card) for all major purchases is most cost efficient, especially during short- and medium-term stays and in the absence of a local bank account. Credit card companies generally get the most favorable rates of exchange—just 1 percent over the interbank rate—and although rates fluctuate, postings will be at a better rate than if you had exchanged currency in a shop or restaurant. Your bill can be paid each month from your home checking account.

Visa, MasterCard, and American Express are widely accepted for charging purchases in restaurants, shops, and hotels. Visa is the most popular because it is the country-wide, bank-issued *Carte Bleue*. MasterCard is the same as Access/Eurocard. In addition to charging purchases, you can obtain periodic cash advances from automatic teller machines (ATMs), which accept both Visa and MasterCard with a PIN (personal identification number).

The interest rates charged by the credit card companies for obtaining cash on credit cards have historically been higher than the usual interest rates, yet they may be no higher than the fees charged for currency exchange at French banks. Inquire before departure from the credit card company what the interest rate is for obtaining cash advances.

For charging purchases, Visa and MasterCard are accepted in more places than the American Express card, yet during a short sojourn in Paris, having an American Express card can be extremely helpful. With an American Express card and a PIN, members of the Amex Express Cash Service can get cash from Amex ATMs, which is then debited to their home bank account as previously arranged. More important is that card holders may also cash personal checks on their own bank accounts for up to US$1,000 in francs (in cash or traveler's checks) every three weeks, an easy way to keep supplied with cash. (Gold Card holders may cash up to US$5,000.) Credit card users may pay the monthly bill at the main office.

Other Amex services are helpful as well, such as *poste restante* and a travel agency. Amex traveler's checks are cashed free, and refunds and lost checks can be handled at the offices, as well as the replacement of lost credit cards.

The Amex office is at 11, rue Scribe 75009 (tels: 01.47.77. 77.07; 01.47.77.79.28). Hours: 9 am–6:30 pm weekdays, 10 am–5 pm Saturday; currency exchange 10 am–5 pm Sunday. The office at 38, avenue de Wagram 75008 is closed weekends (tel: 01.42.27.58.80). There is a branch at the Disneyland Hotel (tel: 01.60.45.65.20). Amex card holders may use the ATMs at rue Scribe, at Gare de Lyon and Gare de Montparnasse, and at any Crédit Lyonnais bank.

THE NEED FOR CASH

Buy a few hundred francs before your departure, at least enough to get to the city from the airport. If you cannot, exchange only enough for a day or so; the rates at airports and hotels are distinctly unfavorable. It is worth checking out several *bureaux de change* (currency exchanges). Even on the same street the rates can differ and in tourist districts can be particularly disadvantageous. Ask the rates in advance; occasionally the attractive rates posted are only for large transactions. Do not be taken in by signs that say "no commission," for no exchange may charge a commission: the profit is built into the rate. **American Express** and **Thomas Cook** are open on Sunday, as is the **Chequepoint** chain. The Paris Tourist Office also has a currency exchange. See *Change* in the Yellow Pages.

Banks offer a good rate of exchange, but they charge a commission, usually a percentage (1–2 percent) of the monies changed. Banks that do not exchange currency display a sign saying "no cash." Unfortunately, banks close earlier than currency exchanges.

Automatic Teller Machines

Cash is available 24 hours a day at the *distributeurs du billets/guichets automatiques* (ATMs). In tourist areas some ATMs have instructions in both French and English. Pictures of the cash networks accepted are displayed, making it easy to know which machines take which cards. Remember that you must have a PIN to access the machines. Generally in Europe the PIN is four numbers only; before departure, make sure that your PIN conforms to European standards.

Carte Bleue (CB) is accepted at all ATMs (see French Banking, below). Those with a debit card on the CIRRUS or Plus networks may receive cash in francs up to the daily limit of the currency of their home bank, linked to the exchange rate.

Traveler's Checks

Banks and post offices exchange foreign traveler's checks, and most, but not all, restaurants and commercial establishments will accept them as payment. Checks in francs can be harder to cash, for establishments do not make any money on the exchange. It is good to bring traveler's checks for early expenses. Traveler's checks can be canceled and are replaceable if lost or stolen, as long as the numbers of the lost checks are provided to the issuer. Keep the numbers apart from the checks themselves. Bring your passport to the bank to cash traveler's checks.

Banks may charge a service fee for cashing traveler's checks. American Express cashes its own checks at no charge, as does Thomas Cook, which has offices in the major tourist and commercial areas (info tel: 01.47.55.52.25; traveler's checks tel: 01.47.55.52.27).

Lost Articles

For lost traveler's checks, most issuers require a police report: go to the *commissariat* in the *arrondissement* in which the loss occurred. The police will issue a *récépissé de déclaration de perte ou de vol*. Bring

152

the report and your passport to the issuer of the checks. For those without offices in Paris, ask at purchase for a toll-free number to call in case of loss.

Report lost or stolen credit cards immediately. Often a replacement card with a new number can be issued within 48 hours. Be sure to inform any company that is making automatic deductions from your card (such as online services) that the number has changed.

- American Express: 11, rue Scribe 75009 (tel: 01.47.77.72.00)
- Visa and *Carte Bleue*: (tel: 01.42.77.11.90; 08.36.69.08.80)
- MasterCard and Eurocard: 16, rue Lecourbe 75015 (tel: 01.45.67.53.53)
- Diner's Club: 52, rue La Fayette 75008 (tel: 01.49.06.17.50)

Sometimes lost articles, even credit cards and traveler's checks, are turned in to the police. The **Lost and Found** department is at 36, rue des Morillons 75015 (tel: 01.55.76.20.20). Weekday hours: 8:30 am–5 pm, Tuesday and Thursday until 8 pm. For lost bank checks, call 08.36.68.32.08.

FRENCH BANKING

People with a resident card or a work permit may open a *compte bancaire* (bank account). Bring your passport and proof of domicile, which may not be as simple as it sounds. Without a bank account it is sometimes hard to obtain a lease, and without a lease it is hard to get a bank account. Proof of employment generally suffices, and using banks that have special expatriate services can be helpful. Some banks open non-resident accounts.

There are many banks to choose among. Not all banks require the same documentation. Shop around and bring to each bank a list of questions that refers to your particular banking needs. Find out the commission charged, for instance, for processing an international check, whether in francs or in your own currency. Transfers of funds can be high and vary from bank to bank. Ask how long it takes to have access to transferred funds. Find out also whether the bank has 24-hour account-information systems, and if they are free. Banks should issue a monthly statement of all transactions plus a year-end statement containing tax information.

Banks offer multi-services, such as individual and joint savings and checking accounts, money-market funds, and investment opportunities. Inquire about investment possibilities when opening an account. Checking accounts currently do not pay interest, but banks may automatically sweep funds above a certain level into interest-bearing accounts. Interest earned is taxable, so make sure you take into account in which country your taxes will be paid.

Banking in Paris is extremely impersonal. Don't expect appreciation from any bank in acquiring your account, unless you are transferring enormous funds in and out. Also, don't assume that anything is provided automatically. You must request a checkbook and a *Carte Bleue*. If you do all your banking at a smaller bank or at a local branch of one of the larger ones, you may receive some personalized services, but inquire as to the range and price of their services, which may not be competitive. The most personally helpful bank may be the **Banque Transatlantique**, listed below, which deals only with expatriates, whether in France or abroad.

Some banks require a hefty initial deposit, unless direct deposit of a salary check has been arranged. Some smaller banks may not have such stringent requirements. Opening an account takes a few days for the paperwork to be completed and longer for checks to be issued. A letter of reference from a home bank may be useful.

Checks are accepted by most establishments with proof of identity and sometimes with a minimum of 50F or 100F. The penalties for returned checks are so severe that it is extremely rare for a person to have insufficient funds when writing a check. Some banks will arrange an overdraft limit, but if the bank's procedures for covering a bounced check are not followed, the account holder may be blacklisted (*interdit bancaire*). Thus it is important to ask how your bank structures the *dates de valeur*, the amount of time it takes for deposits to be credited, including money orders and bank drafts. Withdrawals made on the same date as a deposit may result in an overdrawn account. Also note that checks are payable on the date presented, so postdating a check is not advisable.

If opening a joint account, make sure that both parties may make bank transactions and sign checks separately. Checks are not endorsable to a third party, and banks will not cash checks made out to someone else. Do not accept such checks as payment of any kind.

Determine whether the opening hours and days of a bank are convenient for you. Banks are generally open 9 am–4:30/5:00 pm, weekends and holidays excepted. Some banks are open Saturday and closed on Monday, and some close at lunchtime. If a national holiday falls on a Tuesday or Thursday, banks may *faire le pont* to bridge the long weekend, closing the previous Monday or the following Friday. Many financial institutions have two security doors: a button is pushed for access through the first door which closes behind you, then permits entry through the second door into the bank.

If your home bank is affiliated with one in France, transfers of funds from one to the other may be somewhat more efficient, although this is not always the case. **BNP** is affiliated in the United States with the Bank of the West, and **CIC** links with the Royal Bank of Scotland and with First Fidelity Bank in the United States. See *Banques* in the Yellow Pages.

Carte Bleue

Account holders may obtain the *Carte Bleue*. Unlike a credit card, it is linked to your bank account, and charges are debited to your account immediately (*débit immédiat*) or monthly (*débit différé*), according to your instructions. *Carte Bleue* cards are accepted everywhere as payment because they are seen to be safe. Monthly purchases on the card are generally limited to 10,000–15,000F, unless prior arrangements have been made.

Carte Bleue functions in *guichets automatique* with a PIN. Machines throughout Paris are electronically linked, and bank cards may be used in any of them. There is no charge for using the machines at branches of your own bank, but some banks charge for withdrawals from other banks. Card holders whose cards have been illegally used by others are generally liable for the amount withdrawn until the date they notify the bank of the problem. The PIN is a secret number; if someone else has used it, the bank considers it was negligently given out by the card holder. Some banks offer card insurance or can recommend where to obtain it.

La Poste
Post offices are the most widespread banks in France, and as they are all connected, they have more branches than any other. In terms of convenience, the local *bureau de poste* may be the most practical place to open a bank account, depending on the type of services you need. *La Poste* offers checking and savings accounts, money-market funds and investment counseling, money transfers, and access to cash machines countrywide. They are also *bureaux de change*, and many are Western Union agents. However, they are rumored to be the least flexible and personalized in service. If their convenience interests you, check out several post offices in your neighborhood. They also vary greatly in terms of efficiency, crowds, and service.

International Banks
Some foreign banks have *succursales* (branches) in Paris. While their services vary, they all adhere to French banking law. Those below provide the same services as French banks, but complicated transactions may be made in English. International banks

can provide tax information and the proper year-end forms, but they do not give tax advice. Prices for services also vary, and they may be more expensive than French banks.

- **Banque Transatlantique**: 17, boulevard Haussmann 75009 (tel: 01.40.22.80.00; fax: 01.48.24.01.75). Accounts opened at Paris office, information and preliminary paperwork at others. Representative offices in the United States: 1819 H Street NW, Suite 620, Washington DC 20006 (tel: 202/429-1909; fax: 202/296-7294); Britain: 36 St. James's Street, London SW1A 1JD (tel: 171/493-6717; fax: 495-1018); Australia: Level 11, 280 George Street, Sydney NSW (tel: 2/9231-5033; fax: 2/9223-5099). Full service bank in Jersey: 19–21 Broad Street, St. Helier, Jersey (tel: 1534/283-190; fax: 1534/283-191). Accounts available in multiple currencies. Corporate accounts available. Special services, such as ticket purchase, car rentals, hotel reservations.
- **Barclays Bank**: 6, Rond Point des Champs-Elysées 75008 (tel: 01.44.95.13.80). Full-service banking with branches throughout Paris. Checking, savings, and time deposit accounts, home and personal loans. Electronic transfers from Barclays in England. Visa debit cards available.
- **Citibank International**: Citicenter, 19, Le Parvis 92073 Paris La Défense (24-hour tel: 01.49.05.49.05; fax: 01.49.06.17.00). Full-service banking with branches throughout the city, including 24-hour phone service in English, access to account information on Minitel, Citicard debit card, access to ATMs. Residence card is not required, but you must be able to show proof of a Paris address and proof of income.
- **American Express Bank**: 11, rue Scribe (tel: 01.47.14.50.50; Minitel: 3615 FINAMEX). Full-service bank that offers interest-bearing checking accounts, time deposits, and mutual funds. Monthly statements, plus a quarterly newsletter. Accounts can be in dollars or francs. The account holder must be a resident.

157

- **Riggs Bank Europe SA**: 2, avenue Gabriel 75382 Cedex Paris 08 (tel: 01.47.42.37.22; fax: 01.47.42.38.10) Full-service bank offering accounts in francs or dollars. Inside the American Embassy complex, banking is available only by mail, except to embassy personnel. Nonetheless, mail transactions are speedy and efficient. Passport and proof of residence required.

MANAGING INVESTMENTS

Find out from your stockbroker how to track investments from Paris. There are several options, including checking market results and trading from your brokerage account on the Internet/World Wide Web. Some international companies such as **Merrill Lynch** at 96, avenue d'Iéna 75016 maintain full service offices (tel: 01.40.69.10.00; fax: 01.40.69.11.90). **Prudential Bache** has an office at 9, avenue Matignon 75008 (tel: 01.53.89.29.29; fax: 01.53.89.29.00). **Fidelity Investments** maintains a 24-hour service (toll free tel: 08.00.90.10.43).

MONEY FROM HOME

Do not expect checks or money orders sent from abroad to clear at the bank quickly enough to provide emergency funds. It is better to have money deposited into your home account and transfer it electronically. A wire transfer from home will be received within hours. Other than standard bank-to-bank transfers, there are several options. In all transactions, the sender pays the fees based on the amount sent, and these are fairly expensive, so they should be seen only as an emergency measure. **MoneyGram** (info tel: 01.47.55.52.66) transfers are available from Canada (tel: 800/933-3278), England (0800/89-7198), and the United States (tel: 800/Moneygram). In Paris, Thomas Cook is a MoneyGram agent.

Money is also available from **Western Union** (02.43.54.46.12; US tel: 800/325-6000). **Banque Rivaud** is a Western Union agent, and a convenient location is at 4, rue Cloître-Notre-

Dame 75004 (tel: 01.43.54.46.12). Some post offices are also Western Union agencies.

WHAT DO THINGS COST?

Forget the old stories that Europe is inexpensive. Currently Paris and Tokyo rank as the two cities with the highest cost of living in the world, although the current low state of the franc against many currencies favors people paid in foreign currencies or on their scale. Yet Paris is agreeably livable as its residents can attest. Most middle-class Parisians have learned how to live satisfactorily, setting their priorities and looking for good value at each turn. They frequent the discount houses and the semiannual sales for clothing purchases, shop for seasonally plentiful produce at the outdoor markets, and eat and entertain well at home, except for meals at their favorite *bistrots* or *brasseries*, at the inexpensive Asian restaurants, or on occasion in a fine restaurant.

Assume that domestic goods will be less expensive than imported ones. Fresh produce, cheeses, and breads are the least expensive, and items such as meats, gasoline, cigarettes, and canned goods may be more expensive than you are used to. Wines range from the drinkable and cheap, to the good and moderately priced, to the fabulous but astronomical. Goods in tourist areas may cost more than those in outlying neighborhoods. The cinema and theater cost about the same as in most cosmopolitan capitals, as do sporting events.

Large appliances and electronic equipment are generally more expensive in Europe than in the United States because of high import duties and taxes. Yet the price of these items is quickly becoming more competitive, especially with the advent of the *hypermarchés*. Utilities tend to be expensive, although with the privatization of France Télécom, telephone rates are decreasing. *Paris Pas Cher* and *Paris Combines* are helpful annual compendiums of shops, markets, and services recommended as good value for the money.

159

Although at first you will certainly compare prices in Paris with those at home, it is best to start early just comparing prices in francs from one shop to another. At first, though, carry a small calculator with you to understand relative prices among your own currency, the franc, and the euro. Remember that the tax is included in the price quoted in both French currencies.

FRENCH TAXES

French residents are liable for taxes on income from worldwide sources. This includes investment and real estate income as well as salaries. Non-residents are taxed only on income from French sources, and non-resident foreigners with vacation homes in France are generally not subject to income taxes. Some countries have multilateral treaties with France by which citizens working abroad are not double-taxed.

The French tax year coincides with the calendar year. Tax filing for salaried employees is due by the end of February, for independent contractors two months later. Taxes are based on *le revenu* (earned income) and *capitaux mobiliers* (unearned income). Taxes can reach up to 56 percent of the net salary, and there are also a capital gains tax, death duties, a gift tax, a wealth tax, and a land tax. There are some rebates and exemptions and a standard deduction for married people and those with children. French employers do not withhold any amount for tax. After the tax return *(déclaration des revenus)* is filed, the government calculates the tax due and sends a bill. After the first year in the tax system, the bill may be paid in three installments or debited monthly from a checking account. First-time tax payers must declare themselves and their taxable income to the appropriate **Centre des Impôts**.

If your French is up to the task, do not hesitate to consult with tax officials. Anyone may contact the **Ministère des Finances, Service de la Législation Fiscale, Bureau E-1** at 139, rue de Bercy, Télédoc 568, 75012 (tel: 01.40.24.92.00). And non-residents might also contact the **Centre fiscal des non-résidents** (tel: 01.44.76.18.00)

Family Subsidy

Residents should inquire as to the *allocations familiales*, in which families living with dependent children are entitled to a currently tax-free family allowance. Proof of enrollment in school must be provided for children over six years old. Inquire of your attorney or accountant or at **Caisse d'Allocations Familiales de Paris** at 9, rue St-Charles 75015 (tel: 01.45.71.20.00).

TAXES AT HOME

All people must determine their tax status at home and in France while living abroad. Some countries have bilateral agreements with France to avoid double taxation on earnings, but this does not exempt citizens from filing tax forms on time.

EU countries have treaties by which there is no double taxation, but since French taxation is based on the length of annual residency, all people should make sure to check with their employer or the tax bureau in their home country to determine its domicile requirements. EU nationals working in France on secondment are generally not liable for French taxes, but determinations should be reached in advance. British citizens should request a non-resident ruling by the Inspector of Taxes. Inquire at Inland Revenue: EC Unit, Room S20 West Wing, Somerset House, London WC2R 1LB (tel: 171/438-6254).

All Americans must file a federal tax return, although there is a tax exemption on income earned abroad. *A Tax Guide for U.S. Citizens and Residents Abroad* or the *Overseas Tax Package* is available from the Internal Revenue Service Forms Distribution Center, PO Box 25866, Richmond VA 23289 (US tel: 202/874-1460). Check with the tax department in your home state before departure because state requirements vary widely. Americans should

161

also note that each February, Alan Johnson, tax manager at Price Waterhouse, gives as a community service a US tax workshop at the American Church.

ACCOUNTING FIRMS

Your country's embassy should be able to provide a list of English-speaking tax consultants in Paris. International firms are current on both French and international tax laws and procedures and the treaties between countries. They offer tax preparation advice, help prepare returns, handle audits, and offer business-related services. They may, however, be more expensive than French accountants for dealing with strictly domestic matters. See also Chapter Eight.

SÉCURITÉ SOCIALE

Cotisations sociales are paid by companies and all workers, both salaried and self-employed. For salaried employees this generally covers health insurance, disability, retirement pensions, and un-employment insurance. Companies withhold from the employee's paycheck, and the amount is recorded on the pay slip. The percentage withheld can reach 20 percent of gross salary.

Some countries have bilateral agreements with France concerning Social Security to avoid double taxation of employees. This applies to both the United States and Great Britain. Both countries issue booklets that detail the rights of their citizens working abroad. (Note that non-EU nationals who do not pay French Social Security may not enter the French health insurance system, so the employer must cover health insurance, or it may be purchased privately.) Self-employed people must pay insurance to **URSSAF** and must subscribe to a basic pension plan, both of which are expensive. Payments are sent to 3, rue Franklin 93100 Montreuil (info tel: 01.48.51.75.75; tel: 01.49.20.10.10). To receive information on *Securité Sociale*, try the offices below:

- **Paris Sud**: Immeuble Le Palatino, 17, avenue de Choisy 75013. For 1–7 and 11–15 *arrondissements*.
- **Paris Nord**: 10, rue du Faubourg-Montmartre 75009. For 8–10 and 16–20 *arrondissements*.

American companies that send their employees abroad for under five years continue to pay American Social Security. People receiving Social Security or other US Government benefits may arrange in advance to have the check deposited directly into a bank account in Paris. Well before departure write the Social Security Administration, Office of International Operations, PO Box 1756, Baltimore MD 21235. It takes several months before the first payment is sent.

Bilateral agreements also apply to British salaried employees working abroad for their company under twelve months. Transferred employees will need to provide an E101 form indicating insurance coverage under the UK plan (see Chapter Seven). If employed by a French company, the worker will receive a French Social Security number and be covered by the French system.

CHAPTER TEN

STAYING IN TOUCH

THE POST OFFICE

La Poste is one of the most important institutions in France. Regular services include selling stamps, mailing letters and packages, sending telegrams, photocopy and fax facilities, and a worldwide courier service. Using **Minitel** videotext equipment in the post office, you can look up any listed address and telephone number in France. Telephone and electricity bills may be paid in cash at the post office. And, as described in the previous chapter, *La Poste* is also one of the country's major providers of financial services.

Store fronts of the *bureau de poste* are yellow with blue lettering. There are often several post offices in one neighborhood. Despite long lines, with sometimes brusque and unhelpful personnel, service is generally efficient. Post boxes, which are yellow, have two slots specifying the mail destination: *Paris et Banlieue* or *Province et Etranger*.

Post offices are open from 8 am to 7 pm weekdays and Saturday until noon. Exceptions are the two main post offices, which have extended hours. For the post office in your district, look in the Yellow Pages under *Poste.* There are two home mail deliveries daily and one on Saturday.

- **Poste Centrale**: 52, rue du Louvre 75001 (tel: 01.40.28.20.00). Open 24 hours. *Poste restante* to receive mail.
- **Poste des Champs-Elysées**: 71, avenue des Champs-Elysées 75008 (tel: 01.44.13.66.00). Open for post and telegrams until 10 pm Monday–Saturday; Sunday 10 am to noon and 2–8 pm.

Lettres recommandées (registered letters) are used routinely by the French, as they are legal proof that a person has communicated with another on a certain date, whether registering a complaint, making a request, or giving notice to terminate any kind of contract. There are two types: *avec accusé de réception*, which has a return receipt, or *recommandée simple*, which does not.

Packages mailed at the post office may weigh up to 30 kg. Books are priced according to the weight and the dimensions of the package. For heavier items, **SERNAM** sends large parcels inexpensively by land or sea (international parcels tel: 01.40. 38.56.00).

To determine the weight of a letter or package, use one of the automatic coin-operated weighing machines that then issues the correct postage. There is also a machine that dispenses the appropriate stickers for a package. To avoid flimsy packaging that may be rejected, you can buy sturdy, inexpensive mailing cartons at the post office. Some older post offices have a metal rotating window to one side of the *guichet* for accepting packages, but these are being phased out. To pick up a package or a registered letter, bring identification.

165

Rush Mail Options

Chronopost International, La Poste's express mail service, guarantees second-day delivery of packages and letters to North America and third-day service to Asia. The major international air couriers are also efficient and reliable, although expensive.

- **DHL**: 59, avenue d'Iéna 75016 (toll free: 08.00.20.25.25; tel: 01.45.01.91.00); 82, rue de Richelieu 75002 (tel: 01.42.96.14.55; fax: 01.49.27.91.62)
- **Federal Express**: 2, rue du 29 Juillet 75001 (toll-free tel: 08.00.12.38.00)
- **UPS**: 87, boulevard Aérodrome, BP 39, Orly (toll-free tel: 08.00.87.78.77)

Mailboxes, etc.

An international chain of communication service shops, **Mailboxes, etc.** offers rental post boxes, photocopiers and fax machines, packing and shipping, UPS mail, office supplies, and many other services. Addresses in Paris include:

- 5e—44, rue Monge (tel: 01.43.54.01.00; fax: 01.43.29.77.37)
- 11e—117, boulevard Voltaire (tel: 01.44.09.21.59; fax: 01.44.09.29.90)
- 13e—69, boulevard St-Marcel (tel: 01.44.08.68.68; fax: 01.47.07.47.47)
- 15e—208, rue de la Convention (tel: 01.44.19.60.20; fax: 01.44.19.60.29)
- 15e—23, rue Lecourbe (tel: 01.43.06.40.52; fax: 01.43.06.40.53)
- 17e—80, rue Legendre (tel: 01.42.63.26.10; fax: 01.42.63.26.20)

Copy Shops/Faxing

In addition to Mailboxes, etc., post offices have copiers and machines for sending (not receiving) faxes (*télécopies*). Many supermarkets and newspaper and bookshops have copiers, and shops in just about every *arrondissement* offer customized services, including color copies, binding, faxing, and sometimes computer and Internet access. At France Télécom's stores you can both send and receive faxes. **Copy Top**, with stores throughout the city, offers good services and prices.

THE TELEPHONE

France Télécom is the major telephone provider. Public telephones can be found in post offices, other public buildings, restaurants, and on the street. Some telephones still take coins, but most take the *télécarte*, a prepaid card to be inserted into the telephone. Credits are deducted according to the length of the call, and the number of units remaining on the card appears on the telephone as you speak. *Télécartes* are available in France Télécom offices, post offices, métro and train stations, in *tabacs*, and often at newsstands. Calls to emergency numbers are free from any public telephone. For operator assistance, dial 12.

Telephone numbers in France have ten digits. Those in the Paris region start with 01 and those in the rest of France with numbers from 02-05. Mobile/cellular phones have a 06 prefix. All subscribers in France can be reached with the ten-digit number, without an additional area code prefix. From abroad, do not dial the first zero. *Numéros verts* (toll-free numbers) begin with 08.00 (often depicted as 0 800); others such as *numéros indigo* and *audiotel* are toll-call numbers and often announce the rate at the beginning of the call. *Numéros azur* start with 08.01 and are nationwide numbers charged at local call rates. Many companies are changing their numbers to the more expensive 08.36 prefix (2.23F per minute); costs can mount up, especially if you are put on hold and have to wait. For international calls, dial **00,** then the country and area codes and the telephone number.

French Carriers

Until recently France Télécom controlled all telecommunications services. Its privatization, however, has allowed both domestic

167

and international competitors to enter the field. This is forcing France Télécom to reduce its own domestic and international calling prices and to offer a variety of discount plans; inquire about the *Primaliste* and *Temporalis* plans (tel: 08.00.81.98.19). Two current new competitors are **Cegetel** (tel: 08.00.77.77.77) and **First Télécom** (tel: 08.01.37.66.66), which at this writing has the overall lowest rates.

International Telephone Calls

Short-term visitors (especially people staying in hotels) often use the calling card services of their home telephone company. Calls are charged to the person's telephone bill. Below are access numbers in France for the major carriers.

- **AT&T**: 08.00.99.00.11
- **Australia Optus**: 08.00.99.20.61; **Australia Telstra**: 08.00.99.00.61
- **Canada Direct**: 08.00.99.00.16
- **MCI**: 08.00.99.00.19
- **British Telecom** 08.00.99.00.44
- **Sprint**: 08.00.99.00.87

Callback Systems

Calling cards are efficient only in temporary situations. For residents, the lower rates of the decentralized telecommunications industry are bringing new options for reasonable prices. Consider also the competitive rates of the callback systems. Some systems allow calls from predetermined numbers, while others allow calls from anywhere. Most often you dial a central number, hang up after it rings, and are called back automatically within seconds. After you hear the dial tone, you dial the call directly. Faxing is possible at the same low rates. Rates among these carriers vary. The *International Herald Tribune* and *FUSAC* often carry ads for callback systems.

AT&T International Call Plan is competitively priced. Contact AT&T at Tour Horizon, 52, quai de Dion-Bouton 92806 Puteaux Cedex (toll-free tel: 08.00.90.82.93; UK tels: 0500-626-262; 171/505-6580).

- **Phone Systems Network**: Espace Clichy, 30, rue Mozart 92110 Clichy (tel: 08.00.77.07.72; fax: 01.41.40.30.16)
- **Global Access Direct**: 36, rue des Etats-Généraux 78000 Versailles (toll-free tel: 08.00.33.39.99; tel: 01.39.07.01.01; fax: 01.39.07.00.77; US tels: 515/472-5000; toll-free: 800/338-0225; fax: 515/472-4747)
- **AXS Telecom**: 370, rue St-Honoré 75001 (tel: 08.00.90.66.50; fax: 01.53.45.22.60; UK tel: 0800/279-2223)
- **Star Telecom**: 52, rue Madeleine-Michelis 92200 Neuilly-sur-Seine (tel: 01.47.45.59.63; fax: 01.47.45.24.82); 13351 SW 131 St, Miami FL 33186 (US tel: 305/232-0900; fax: 305/232-0925)
- **New World**: 1402 Teaneck Road, Teaneck NJ (US tel: 201/287-8400; fax: 201/287-8437; UK tel: 171/360-5037; fax: 171/360-5036)

Telephone Installation

Each neighborhood has at least one commercial France Télécom office that handles telephone matters for that area, including bill payment, sales and rental of equipment, subscription to new services, sending of faxes, and access to Minitel. Telephones must be registered in the lease holder's name. To obtain service, telephones, and telephone books, bring identification and proof of domicile. Call customer service for information and installation of telephones (tel: 1014); ask for the *France Télécom Set-Up Guide* in English.

At the Télécom office, go to the *accueil* (welcome desk), where someone will direct you to the next available representative. Inquire about *signal d'appel* (call waiting), *conversation à trois* (conference calling), *transfert d'appel* (call forwarding), and *Top Message*, a voice mail service, as well as *liste rouge* (unlisted number) and *liste*

169

orange (prohibits telephone solicitation). Inquire also about the Minitel (see below).

All telephones, faxes, and answering machines must be *agréé* (approved) by France Télécom, which itself sells and rents equipment. Touch-tone telephones are provided free; *sans-fil* (cordless) phones incur a charge. *Répondeurs* (answering machines) and *télécopieurs* (fax machines) are available for purchase. Other telecommunications companies sell telephones. Equipment bought in retail stores should have two guarantee labels affixed, one from the manufacturer and the *agréé* from France Télécom. Thus, if necessary, France Télécom will repair the equipment or deal with the manufacturer.

Telephone bills are sent bimonthly and may be paid by check at France Télécom, at the post office, or deducted automatically from your French checking account. A *facture détaillée* (itemized bill) must be requested at your France Télécom office. If bills are not paid on time, it is routine for the service to be cut off and a 10 percent fine levied for reinstatement.

Mobile Phones

The **GSM** system for *mobiles/cellulaires* (mobile phones) operates throughout Europe. Each phone system has its own distance range. Determine how much distance you need to cover. Some telephone systems take messages if the phone is turned off or out of the system's range. Rates, currently high, are rapidly becoming more competitive.

France Télécom sells equipment (including varying rate options), as do its competitors **SFR** and **Bouygues Télécom** (which uses its own operating system). Advertisements for *cellulaires* can be found in free publications, such as *Boum Boum*, generally found in racks in front of stores. The telephones themselves can sometimes be obtained free with subscription to a service.

Telephone Books

Annuaires téléphonique (telephone books) are usually distributed in May. They are left in the entrance hall of apartment buildings for the tenants to take, and if they are not taken quickly, France Télécom takes them back. *Les Pages Blanches* (White Pages) are alphabetical listings, and *Les Pages Jaunes* (Yellow Pages) contain commercial listings and display advertising by category and within category by *arrondissement*. The *Pages Jaunes* come in two versions: *La Vie Pratique*, which is delivered to all homes, and *La Vie Professionnelle et Pratique*, which is designed for businesses. The center of the Yellow Pages contains an extensive information section and a street atlas.

Les Pages Minitel, the Minitel directory, can be requested from France Télécom. The *Annuaire eléctronique* is the Minitel online telephone directory, reached by dialing 3611.

L'Annuaire Soleil is divided into eight regions in the Ile de France, including Paris by region. It has helpful information in the front, such as emergency telephone numbers, food markets, and late-night services in each area. *L'Annuaire Soleil* is generally delivered with the telephone books.

The Paris Tourist Office's *Les Pages Jaunes Tourisme* provides information in five languages, maps, and listings useful to the newcomer to Paris. *Paris Anglophone* is a directory of English-speaking businesses and services in Paris, available at English-language book shops.

THE MINITEL

Minitel is a computerized, interactive, videotext service of France Télécom. Extremely popular, there are currently some 6.5 million Minitels used by 15 million people in homes and offices. Minitel accesses more than 15,000 online services: address and telephone directory, concert tickets, airline and train schedules and reservations, financial information for bank clients, health advice and

171

legal references, and the sending of faxes. Some newspapers can be read online. Minitel users can order goods from catalogues and can have groceries, pizzas, and household items delivered. There are interactive chat lines, access to the Internet, and E-mail; you can also subscribe to the Minitel with a computer modem and Minitel software.

A Minitel—a small computer screen and keyboard—may be rented or purchased through France Télécom offices. There are basic models and more extensive models. Monthly cost is determined by the time spent online. Services are required to disclose their Minitel charge in their advertisements. Access to the Minitel directory is free at post offices and France Télécom outlets. Ask at France Télécom for *Minitel User's Guide* in English.

ACCESSING THE INTERNET

Not all computer modems automatically read all telephone systems. A message saying "no dial tone," means that the modem has not found a compatible signal. If so, the software commands probably need to be changed by inserting the proper code (*X1*) to bypass the signal. For instance, if the dial prefix at home is *ATX2DT*, it may have to be changed to *ATX1DT*. Before departure, check with your communications provider to determine where in the dial prefix you should insert the *X1*, should it be necessary.

The French telephone plug is long, with an extended one-piece insert. Plugs into which the international RJ11 can be inserted can be obtained at France Télécom shops, FNAC, electronic shops, and hardware stores. France Télécom also has multiple plugs, so the modem can stay plugged in at the same time as the telephone.

The French Internet

Currently there are some 100 Internet *fournisseurs d'accès* (providers) in France, with 20 based in the Paris area. New providers are entering the field and prices vary widely, so it is worth checking out several and looking at computer magazines such as *Planète Internet* for current information. Many providers charge enrollment and monthly fees, plus an hourly charge for use; a few have flat rates. In addition to the French providers, check out the international networks, such as **AOL**, **CompuServe,** and **IBM**, which have direct Paris access and are competitively priced. With an account you can have your Internet mail from another provider forwarded. Inquire about surcharges for use abroad.

France Télécom offers **Wanadoo** software for E-mail, the Web, access to the Minitel, and online shopping (tel: 08.01.63. 34.34; from abroad: 331/47.87.88.19). Access is charged at local call rates. There is a subscription fee, as well as monthly and hourly charges. Ask about the *Primaliste* discount plan. To subscribe to Wanadoo, you must have a PC 386 minimum with Windows 3.1 or Windows 95, or Macintosh System 7.1, and a minimum modem rate of a 14.4 baud.

- **Club Internet**: (tel: 01.55.45.45.00; fax: 01.55.45.47.30; www.club-internet.fr)
- **France Net**: (tel: 01.43.92.14.49; fax: 01.43.92.14.45; infos@FranceNet.fr; www.francenet.fr)
- **Calvacom**: (tel: 01.34.63.19.19; fax: 01.34.63.19.48; scom@calva.net; www.calvanet.fr)
- **Easynet France**: (tel: 01.44.54.53.33; fax: 01.44.54.33.39; info@easynet.fr; www.easynet.fr)
- **ImagiNet**: (tel: 01.43.38.10.24; fax: 01.43.38.42.62; info@ imaginet.fr).
- **Internet Way**: (tel: 01.41.43.27.96; fax: 01.41.43.21.11; info: info@iway.fr; www.iway.fr)
- **Worldnet**: (tel: 01.40.37.90.90; fax: 01.40.37.90.89; www. worldnet.fr)

Cybercafés

For occasional Internet access, try a *cybercafé*, where you can have a cup of coffee and online access for a reasonable fee. **Espaces**

173

Internet — without the café — can be found at the Centre Georges-Pompidou, the Vidéothèque de Paris, and the Sofitel Paris Saint-Jacques, among other places. The cyber spaces at Virgin Megastore on the Champs-Elysées and inside the Gaumont-Parnasse cinema are open on Sunday. Internet access is increasingly popular as entertainment, so look for more *espaces Internet* to be opening up.

- 3e — **Web Bar**: 32, rue de Picardie (tel: 01.42.72.66.55)
- 6e — **Café Orbital**: 13, rue de Médicis (tel: 01.43.25.76.77)
- 9e — **Zowezo**: 37, rue Fontaine (tel: 01.40.23.00.71)
- 15e — **High Tech Café**: 66, boulevard du Montparnasse (tel: 01.45.38.67.61)

ENGLISH-LANGUAGE PUBLICATIONS

Many international publications are available in Paris. The *International Herald Tribune*, published in Paris, contains articles emanating from Paris, plus major articles and editorials from the *New York Times* and *The Washington Post*. It is on the newsstands and available for home delivery. *The Times, The Nikkei Financial Weekly, The Wall Street Journal Europe, USA Today, The Financial Times, The Observer, The Guardian*, and *The Independent* may all be found at newsstands, as can *Lloyds List. The European* is an English-language news tabloid. And on Sundays, *The American* is a news wrapup. International news magazines are available, sometimes in scaled-down editions.

The *Paris Free Voice*, a local tabloid, publishes ten issues a year with articles of current interest and listings for events. It is available free at English-language bookshops and pubs. Free also are *Irish Eyes* and *Canadian Content* (available at Abbey Bookstore). The *American Transatlantic* is designed for the American in Europe and is available at Shakespeare & Co bookstore.

Pariscope (a weekly events guide that is published on Wednesdays) has an English-language insert of events, restaurant and film reviews, and exhibits information. And *FUSAC*, described in Chapter Two, carries ads for restaurants and particular events, often tied to holidays.

TELEVISION

There are six non-cable *chaînes* (channels) in France. With cable, some twenty international and multi-language channels are available, including the English BBC, German ZDF, Italian RAI Uno, and the American CNN. For information and hookup, call **Lyonnaise Câble** (toll-free tel: 08.00.25.80.00; tel: 01.44.54.11.11; Minitel: 3615 LCABLE). If you have any doubts that your building is wired for cable, call the France Télécom office in your neighborhood. You can also subscribe to cable at any shop that displays the sign *TV Câble—abonnez-vous ici*. The six basic channels are as follows:

- **TF1**: Privatized channel, leaning toward light programming, plus political talk shows and a popular 8 pm news broadcast.
- **France 2** and **France 3**: State owned. Talk and game shows, soap operas, movies, news, sports, documentaries.
- **Canal Plus**: Subscriber channel (tel: 01.49.87.27.27). Television schedules indicate with a "C" which programs are *en clair* and may be viewed by non-subscribers. American network evening news in English with French *sous-titres* (subtitles) is broadcast *en clair* at 7 am the next morning, weekdays.
- **Arte**: A combined German-French effort with cultural programs, films, some in *version originale*, including English. From 6 am to 7 pm, **La Cinquième** has standard and educational programs.
- **M6**: Privately owned. International films, music videos, reruns of old series, light-hearted entertainment.

Weekly television guides are sold at newsstands, and free advertising handouts at sidewalk stands contain TV listings. Times are approximate: television programs do not always start at the

175

exact time indicated. Sports events may take precedence over regularly scheduled programming. News and weather reports are frequent throughout the day on most channels. Note that a single program is an *émission*; a schedule of *émissions* is a *programme*.

Imported televisions and *magnétoscopes* (videocassette recorders) must operate on the PAL/SECAM, the French television broadcast format. Older video players run only on SECAM, making them incompatible with American (NTSC), although they are compatible with the European PAL system. Multisystem televisions and VCRs are increasingly available. In order to tape and play the *magnétoscope*, the television set and the recorder must be compatible. There is a 700F *redevance* (yearly tax) on television sets. When a set is purchased, the store notifies the tax authority, and the bill comes from the *Service de la Redevance de l'Audiovisuel*.

RADIO

Unfortunately, there are no English-language radio stations in Paris. The **BBC** is on long wave, Radio 4 at 198 khz or medium wave at 648 khz. **RFI** at 738 khz has an afternoon program of English-language news. **BFM**, a financial station at 96.4 FM, broadcasts the daily results of Wall Street in English. *L'Annuaire Soleil* and the weekly events magazines list the many Paris FM stations, as do the television guides.

Chapter Eleven

OUT AND ABOUT

FINDING YOUR WAY

Addresses in Paris are surprisingly easy to find, given that each street has a different name assigned in no particular order. As described earlier, the twenty *arrondissements* are arranged in an outward-moving spiral, the smallest in the oldest, most central sections of town, the largest toward the edge. On streets perpendicular to the Seine, address numbers start at the river and increase as they go; *pairs* (even numbers) are on the right and *impairs* (odd numbers) on the left. Buildings on streets parallel with the river are numbered downstream from east to west. As numbers were assigned according to when particular streets were developed, do not assume that numbers on facing buildings are in the same range.

In any case, numbers increase slowly, as different buildings may bear the same number with *bis* or *ter* added to them. Of course, there are exceptions to the numbering system, especially around the *Grands Boulevards*.

Maps may be obtained at the Paris Tourist Office, bookshops, the large department stores, and many newsstands. Maps and street atlases come in varying sizes. The best for carrying around is a *Plan de Paris par arrondissement*, the generic title for the pocket-sized books with alphabetical indexes, indications of where a building number can be found, bus and métro routes, emergency numbers, and more. There are several different versions and sizes. Some atlases list a street named after a person with the first name first, others list the last name first, and some just give initials.

Walking puts you in touch with the charm of Paris at every turn. Foreigners used to driving on the left must remember to look to the left before crossing the street. Do not assume that the zebra-striped pedestrian crosswalks are havens from traffic. Paris drivers, impatient and aggressive, allow no leeway for the *piéton* (pedestrian) and are not expected to do so. On the other hand, they may look as though they are about to hit you, but they do stop promptly at red lights, which are often placed directly in front of a crosswalk rather than at the corner. Actually Parisian drivers are adept at driving in crowded conditions, maneuvering in tight situations, and going around pedestrians while hardly slowing their speed. But watch out for bicycles, mopeds, and scooters, which weave in and out of traffic and zoom around corners. The best strategy is to cross only at crosswalks and wait for traffic lights (*les feux*) to turn green in your direction.

RATP

La Régie Autonome des Transports Parisiens (RATP) is the public transit authority for *l'autobus* (buses) and *le métropolitain* (the subway, known as the *métro*). Multi-language recorded information is available 24 hours (tel: 08.36.68.41.14); a staffed telephone (with some English spoken) operates from 6 am to 9 pm (tel: 08.36.68.77.14).

Maps of the transport system (both for Paris and the sub-urbs) are available at métro stations, at the new RATP boutiques, on the backs of city maps, and in street atlases. You can also have maps mailed to you (tel: 01.44.68.21.00). Maps of the métro are easy to decipher in any of the standard sizes, but for buses, the *Petit Plan de Paris* is inadequate. Ask for the *Grand Plan de Paris*, which makes all the difference in understanding the bus system.

The public transit system is economical, efficient, well maintained, and safe. More than five million people use it daily. As in any large city, however, women alone should be careful late in the evenings; sitting in the first car behind the driver is also recommended. Petty crime is quite common on the métro, especially in tourist areas, and riders should avoid looking like tourists by not wearing expensive jewelry, intently studying maps, or carrying a thick wallet in the back pocket of trousers.

The Fares

The transit system is divided into zones; Paris is all within Zone 1. Single fare tickets are available, but a *carnet* of ten *tickets* costs about half as much per ticket. Tickets and passes are good on all RATP transport. A ticket is good for one ride of any length on the bus within the city limits and for any number of transfers within the métro, so long as you do not exit the gates. On the bus, tickets must be *oblitérés* (canceled) in the *valideur magnétique* behind the driver. (Weekly or monthly *coupons* should be shown to the driver, but not inserted into the machine.) There are no single-ticket transfers from bus to bus or to the métro. Keep your ticket, for you will have to show it if asked by an inspector. Métro tickets and coupons are inserted into a slot and then reclaimed, at which point the entry gate opens.

179

For regular use, it is best to buy the economical *carte orange* and its weekly or monthly coupon. In theory, the *carte orange* is for residents only, but just about everybody who uses public transport has one. The *coupon deux zones* for the *carte orange* allows access to the inner suburbs, which are in Zone 2. The remaining zones are the outer suburbs and the airports.

The *coupon hebdomadaire* (weekly coupon) is valid from Monday to Sunday, no matter on which day it was bought. The *coupon mensuel* (monthly coupon) is good during a calendar month. The *carte intégrale* is an annual pass, slightly discounted. You may pay for it at time of purchase or have it debited monthly from your bank account. To buy a *carte*, bring identification and a passport-size photo to any métro station.

The *Métropolitain*

Paris has one of the best underground transportation systems in the world. The métro is inexpensive, generally clean, and efficient. It has 13 lines and 370 well-maintained stations, convenient to all parts of the city. It is rare to be more than a five-minute walk from a métro.

The métro starts running at 5:30 am, and the last train leaves at 12:30 am. Rush hours are about 7:30–9:30 am and 5–8 pm. To calculate journey time, count the number of stops from the beginning to the destination and multiply by 1.5 minutes, adding five minutes for each transfer. Remember, however, that the métro runs less frequently in the evenings and on weekends.

Entrances to many métro stations are marked with a large M in a yellow circle. Some older entrances have charming grillwork. Each métro line is identified by a different number and color on the subway map; each *quai* (platform) has well-lit signs indicating the *sortie* (exit), direction of the train, and *correspondance* (interchange point) information. White signs indicate the *terminus* (last stop) in each direction. For example, the sign reading

Photo: Zeny Cieslikowski

Métro entrances in Paris are clearly marked.

M6 Nation is the Number Six line heading toward the last stop of Nation; the opposite direction is labeled *M6 Charles-de- Gaulle-Etoile*. (Most Parisians refer to the métro by the destination, not the number, so do not be surprised if they look at you blankly when you ask about the number of a particular subway line.) The *correspondance* signs are orange. *Sorties* are blue with white lettering. When there is a choice of escalator or stairs, these are also pictured in blue and white.

Large diagrams of the métro system are at the entrance to each station and along the *quais*. In each car there is a schematic of the stations and *correspondances* on that line. At the exit of many stations, either just inside or on the street, there is a map of the *quartier*.

L'Autobus

With some 2,000 city buses and 1,700 *arrêts d'autobus* (bus stops), the bus system is efficient although slower than the métro. Riding the *autobus*, however, allows a good view of the city, a not inconsiderable advantage. Fifty-eight lines run within Paris and more go to the suburbs. Some *abribus* (bus shelters) have printed information in English, especially those in tourist areas.

Bus service begins about 7 am and ends about 8:30 pm, although some buses run until about midnight. *Noctambus* (night buses), displaying a black owl in a yellow circle, run from about 1 am to 5:30 am, generally every ten or twenty minutes. Their terminus is the Place du Châtelet. Bus service is reduced on Sundays and holidays, and some buses do not run at all. There should be a schedule posted at each *arrêt*.

Buses indicate their direction by displaying the terminus. Bus routes have two digits, and those going to the suburbs have three digits. Each bus route is color coded and is displayed on the bus and at the bus stop, which makes it easy to figure out where that bus stops. A diagonal line through the number on a bus indicates partial service. People board in the front and exit from the back, except in double buses where any door may be used. Pushing a red button requests the driver to stop, and some doors must be opened by pushing a button.

RER

RER (Réseau Express Régional) underground express trains go to the suburbs. Stations and routes are specified on métro maps, drawn with thicker, different-colored lines. The RER is faster and quieter than the métro and makes fewer stops. RER trains run about every fifteen minutes, beginning around 5:30 am and ceasing about midnight. Métro tickets are valid on the RER in the two-zone Paris area; going farther requires a supplement, unless you have a pass that includes the outer zones. Lighted signs on each *quai* indicate destination and each intermediate station for the next train. There are currently four main lines (two are being added), but most fork off in different directions at some point; therefore it is important to make sure that the train you are on goes exactly to your destination. Keep your RER ticket, as inserting it into a turnstile is often necessary to exit the system.

FRENCH RAILROADS (SNCF)

Each of the six **Société Nationale des Chemins de Fer Français (SNCF)** train stations in Paris serves a different geographical region of France and farther destinations. Train reservations may be made at travel agents and train stations, by telephone, or through Minitel. Tickets may be picked up at the train station at least one and a half hours before departure (toll call info/reservations tel: 08.36.35.35.35; recorded timetables tel: 08.36.67.68.69; Eurostar info/reservations tel: 08.36.35.35.39; Minitel 3615 SNCF). See *SNCF* in the phone book.

Some trips are entitled to discounts, sometimes depending on a passenger's age or how long in advance the reservation is made. Considerably less expensive, discounted tickets are generally non-refundable or changeable. Before boarding the train, make sure to punch your ticket in one of the orange machines located at the head of the *quais*. Failure to do so brings a fine.

- 8e — **Gare Saint-Lazare**: 13, rue d'Amsterdam (tel: 01.53. 42.00.00). Northeast.
- 10e — **Gare de l'Est**: place du 11-Novembre-1918 (tel: 01.40. 18.20.00). East.
- 10e — **Gare du Nord**: 18, rue de Dunkerque (tel: 01.55.31. 10.00). North. Eurostar to London.
- 12e — **Gare de Lyon**: place Louis-Armand (tel: 01.53.33.60.00). Southeast/South.
- 13e — **Gare d'Austerlitz**: 7, boulevard de l'Hôpital (tel: 01.53.60.70.00). Southwest.
- 15e — **Gare Montparnasse**: 17, boulevard de Vaugirard (tel: 01.40.48.10.00). West/Southwest.

TAXIS

There are some 15,000 *taxis* in Paris and almost 500 taxi ranks, but this does not mean that a taxi is easy to find on a rainy day or at rush hour. The best bet is to wait at taxi stands, which are in every *arrondissement* and have blue and white signs marked *taxis*. Taxis can be engaged directly from the rank or by telephone. See *taxis* in either phone book; in the Yellow Pages, they are listed by *arrondissement*. When calling for pickup, note that the meter starts when the cab begins its trip, not when you get in. Therefore it is best to know the location of the nearest taxi stand. A cruising taxi may not pick up a customer within 50 meters of a stand unless there are no taxis or customers waiting there.

The top light on the roof of the taxi is lit when it is unoccupied. Three smaller lights indicate the type of fare (day, night, or to suburban zones). Each taxi has a *compteur* (meter), the fare determined by a combination of time and distance. Rates are strictly regulated, raised once annually, and consistent through-out the taxi system. There are supplements for each piece of bag-gage, for holidays, for pickup at the airport, and for more than three people in a cab, although often drivers refuse (legally) to accept a fourth passenger, being unwilling to have someone ride in the front seat with them (other than their dog). Do not agree to pay a driver's return trip from the airport, and be wary of cut-rate offers. The driver is usually given a 10–15 percent tip. Some taxis accept credit cards for amounts over 50F. Below are some major 24-hour radio cabs:

- **Radio Alpha**: (tel: 01.45.85.85.85)
- **Taxis 7000**: (tel: 01.42.70.00.42)
- **Taxis Bleus**: (tel: 01.49.36.10.10)
- **Taxis G7** (tel: 01.47.39.47.39; English speakers: 01.41.27.66.99)
- **Artaxi**: (tel: 01.42. 41.50.50)

Taxi drivers take several months of training and must be certified to be licensed, so they are usually knowledgeable about the city. If you have a complaint, get a receipt with the number of the cab. You can lodge complaints with the **Service des taxis, Préfecture de Police** at 36, rue des Morillons 75015 (tel: 01.55. 76.20.00).

DRIVING IN PARIS

Public transportation in Paris is so good that you should not need a car for everyday use. Rush hour traffic is extremely slow, and on rainy or snowy days it can be much worse. During rush hour, traffic on the *périphérique* slows to a crawl, and the major *portes* (exits from the *périphérique*) and large arteries are generally con-gested. *Bouchons* (traffic jams) and *embouteillages* (bottlenecks) are daily occurrences. Delivery trucks often block small, narrow streets, stopping traffic until a delivery has been made. Although drivers in Paris generally obey the traffic laws, they are aggres-sive and impatient. Take public transportation when you can.

Driver's Licenses

When driving, always carry a valid driver's license. Visitors staying under 90 days may use a license from home. The International Driving License is advisable but not required in France, but it may be required in other countries you visit. It is not available in France but may be obtained from your own automobile association. Students may use their home driver's license for the duration of their studies. Those with the *carte de séjour* may use their home driver's license, but not the International Driver's License, for one year from the date of the *carte*. The license must be valid, translated into French, and issued before the residence permit.

After residence of one year, a French *permis de conduire* (driver's license) is required of non-EU residents. Expect the process to take about two months, so apply to the *Préfecture* before the end of the year. Bring a valid, translated, driver's license, plus the *fiche d'état civil* if appropriate, proof of domicile, *carte de séjour*, two passport-sized photographs, and the current fee in the form of a *timbre fiscal*, a prepaid stamp purchased at a *tabac*. Although EU citizens theoretically do not need a French license, in practice it is often necessary for insurance and other reasons. Go to the *Préfecture*, and they will decide whether you need one, based on your nationality. (In fact, the member states of the EU are to issue a standard driving license, which will gradually replace expiring licenses.) A French driver's license is valid for life.

Some countries and some states within the United States have reciprocal agreements with France to waive the driving test, but all applicants must take the written exam concerning rules of the road. If you must take the driving exam, take a course through a certified driving school. Ask at your embassy for suggestions for *écoles de conduite* (driving schools). Some schools have sections for English speakers. **Fehrenbach Driving School** at 53, boulevard Henri-Sellier 92150 Suresnes conducts all classes in English (tel: 01.45.06.31.17; fax: 01.47.28.81.89). Both Fehrenbach's theoretical course and its coaching for the driving exam may be taken through WICE (tel: 01.45.66.75.50). *Code de la Route*, a booklet detailing the rules of the road, is available in most bookshops.

Report a lost driver's license to the police immediately. They will issue a *récépissé de déclaration de perte ou de vol de pièce d'identité*, an acknowledgment that identity documents have been lost or stolen. Carry this when you drive until you have received a replacement license.

For traffic violations, France, along with other EU countries, has a system whereby one loses points on the driver's license for each infraction: the worse the infraction, the more points lost. After twelve points are lost, so is the license. People with foreign licenses should note that, although their licenses cannot be taken away, information is computerized. If a license has become invalid in France, the information will show up on the computer. British drivers should note that French authorities contact British authorities for points to be subtracted.

For non-injury traffic offenses, the police may require an on-the-spot *consignation* (deposit) on the fine. The matter is decided by the *Tribunal de Police* (traffic court). Police occasionally stop cars to check identity papers, so make sure you are carrying a valid driver's license, along with the *carte grise* and the *certificat d'assurance* described below.

Obeying the Laws

Obey all laws, even if it looks as though other drivers are not.

- Wear a seat belt, whether in the front or back seat.
- Put your children under 10 in the back seat; babies must sit in buckled car seats or car beds.
- Give priority to cars entering your street from the right, no matter how small the street. If it does not apply at traffic-roundabouts, it will be so marked. The *priorité à droite* is one of the most important driving laws.

- Do not use the *klaxon* (horn) except in emergencies.
- Do not drive or park in the bus lanes or the AXE Rouge express lanes.
- Do not park where it says *parking interdit* or *stationnement interdit*. Although many people double park, park at corners, or edge up onto the sidewalk, this is illegal.
- Do not dash through a traffic light just as it is turning red; many traffic lights are placed not at the corner but instead just before a crosswalk, and pedestrians begin to cross immediately upon the change of the light. Do not make U-turns or cross a solid white line. Stay to the right on multi-lane roads, unless passing a car.
- Use high beam headlights only on unlit roads. Cars behind you that flash their headlights are indicating they will not slow down.
- Obey the speed limits: 130 kph on highways; 110 kph on wet highways; 90 kph on rural roads; 50 kph in the city; 80 kph on the *périphérique*.

Parking

With some 1.3-million cars in circulation each day, parking is at a premium. Fortunately, there are parking garages at the major entrances into the city, in the city center, at most shopping centers, and at numerous underground parking garages. In total there are some 65,000 spaces, and more garages are being built. Garages and parking meters are marked with a blue sign with a large white P and indicated on city maps. Most ticket machines in the garages accept credit cards. Parking spaces in these garages may be available by the month, helpful if your apartment building does not have parking facilities. See *Parkings: exploitation* in the Yellow Pages or *Parking* in the White Pages.

Many city streets have areas marked *payant*. The *horodateurs* (parking meters) operate from 9 am to 7 pm every day but Sunday;

in August some do not require payment. Purchase a ticket from the nearest meter for the length of time you intend to park and place it on the dashboard. The time of expiration should be clearly visible to any meter reader. You can also get a parking ticket that is good all day. Most meters accept coins although some only accept parking cards bought in advance at *tabacs*.

Residents may apply to the **Voierie Stationnement** at 15, boulevard Carnot 75012 for a *vignette de stationnement résidentiel*, a parking permit that allows reduced-rate parking in their *arrondissement* (tel: 01.43.46.98.30). Application forms can be picked up at the *mairie* and mailed to the *Voierie*.

Tickets are issued for overtime parking or for parking in an illegal spot. To pay the fine, purchase a *timbre fiscal* from a *tabac* and follow the instructions on the ticket for affixing the stamp. Tickets paid within 30 days are given a *remise* (discount), and they more than double in price if not paid within three months. EU citizens should note that unpaid tickets may be forwarded to your home country for payment.

If your car is not where you parked it (especially if you have parked near a sign saying *stationnement gênant*, with a picture of a car being towed away), it might have been *remorquée et mise à la fourrière* (towed and impounded). Go to the nearest *commissariat* to determine at which of the eight *préfourrières* (car depots) the car is being kept (tel: 08.36.67.22.22). After 48 hours the car goes to one of five central *fourrières* (car pounds). Fines for retrieval include the towing and storage charges, plus the original parking ticket.

Information/Road Conditions

The **Automobile Club de l'Ile-de-France** at 14, avenue de la Grande-Armée 75017 provides information and advice on driving requirements in Paris (tel: 01.40.55.43.00; fax: 01.43.80.90.51). It also gives road and weather conditions and provides an emergency road service to its members. **Automobile Club National** at 5, rue Auber 75009 also provides emergency breakdown service and 24-hour towing (tel: 01.44.51.53.99; fax: 01.49.24.93.99).

There is always some kind of road repair going on in and around Paris. Each summer, the *mairie* issues a booklet, *Travaux Eté*, that maps in detail where the roadwork will be. Reports on general road conditions around Ile-de-France may be obtained from the **Centre d'Information Routiere** (tel. for Paris: 01.48.99.33.33; tel. for all of France: 08.36.68.20.00).

Bringing a Car into France

Cars entering the country by road are not usually recorded by French Customs. For shipped cars, the shipping company will be issued a *Déclaration d'admission* at customs, given to the owner when the car is delivered. Cars that have been owned for more than six months (and on which no previous taxes are due) are considered intended for personal use and are generally exempt from customs duties. This is not true for trucks and utility vehicles. Bring all ownership and tax payment documentation pertaining to the car.

Generally, cars that are to remain in the country fewer than three months do not have to change their registration. For stays longer than three months, the car should have French *plaques d'immatriculation*. You must convert its registration to the French *carte grise* within a year at the *Préfecture* or *mairie*. Bring your *carte de séjour*, proof of residence, and car title. For questions, call the **Bureau de Paris-Douane Tourisme** at 11, rue Léon Jouhaux 75010 (tel: 01.40.40.60.35). After the status of the car has been determined, it is fairly simple to register the car at the Automobile Club de l'Ile-de-France.

Automobiles brought into France must conform to country-wide regulations, such as having a catalytic converter, and will be tested to ensure that they do. If your car is a make that is sold in France, you might call a dealer there to determine in advance what adjustments your model needs. Since not all parts for imported cars are available in France, it is advisable to bring a sufficient quantity of small spare parts to avoid frustration.

Purchasing an Automobile

When buying a car from a French dealer, you will receive a temporary ownership title; the dealer contacts the *Préfecture* for the permanent registration. You must then present the necessary *carte de séjour* and proof of residence. To determine fair prices for particular makes and models, consult the automobile purchaser's guide, *L'Argus*.

When buying a used car privately, you should get from the seller a *certificat de vente* (bill of sale). There should also be a *certificat de non-gage* (indicating that there are no liens or taxes due), the *carte grise*, and a *certificat de passage* (indicating the mechanical condition of the car). Within two weeks, you should go to the *Préfecture* to transfer the title and register for new license plates. If you have obtained French *plaques d'immatriculation* (license plates) for your car, do not use them until the car insurance reflects those plate numbers.

Automobiles bought in France to be exported within six months are issued a **TT** (temporary license plate) by French Customs. Legally, you must show proof of domicile (a utility bill in your name, for example), but you do not need to be a resident.

Automobile Insurance

All automobiles must be insured. The *carte verte/certificat d'assurance* (green insurance card) must be displayed inside the windshield, along with an annually validated *vignette* (tax sticker), which can be bought at *tabacs* in November and which must be in place by December 1. The cost of the *vignette* is based on the age, horsepower, and cubic capacity of the car.

Each car must also carry the *carte grise* (registration) and a *constat amiable d'accident*, an accident form obtained from the insurance company. In non-injury accidents, the form must be filled out, signed by both parties, and sent to the insurance company. A *contrôle technique* (safety certification) must be kept in the car, along with spare headlight bulbs.

Unlimited third-party coverage (*au tiers*) is the minimum automobile insurance required by law, and coverage must be by a French or EU company. *Au tiers limité* includes third-party fire and theft. *Tous risques* is comprehensive insurance. There are more extensive options as well.

Car theft and vandalism are common, so when considering purchase of a car, it might be helpful to consult with an insurance broker to determine which cars have the highest propensity for being stolen and thus carry the highest insurance premiums. Always lock your car and keep all valuables out of sight.

For cars driven into the country, a temporary insurance policy (*assurance-frontière*) is available at the border from French Customs. The policies can be taken for eight days to a month, either until the automobile leaves France or, in the case of a long stay, until French insurance is arranged. Generally, agents handle home and health insurance as well as automobile coverage. Policies run for one year and are generally renewed automatically. Coverage and costs vary, so shop around. Do your research carefully, for canceling an insurance policy is almost as complicated as taking one out. For other agents, see Chapter Seven.

Ask your own broker for a letter documenting your insurance record. In some cases, a discount is available after one year and is increased slightly for each year with no claims.

- **Eurofil**: 3, rue Eugène et Armand Peugeot, BP 200, 92500 Rueil-Malmaison (tel: 01.47.14.59.00)
- **MAAF**: 50, rue St-Placide 75006 (tel: 01.45.44.00.30; fax: 01.42.84.15.35)

- **Xarr Assurances**: 42, avenue Ste-Foy 92200 Neuilly (tel: 01.46.43.88.00; fax: 01.46.37.34.32)

PEOPLE WITH PHYSICAL DISABILITIES

Little of the public transit system is wheelchair accessible. Only the Number 20 bus (from Gare St-Lazare to Gare de Lyon), some RER stations, and the new automated métro line, **Météor,** are wheelchair accessible. Slow efforts are being made to upgrade the system, but public transit should not be relied on. Sidewalk curbs, however, are almost all cut for wheelchair access. Restaurants opened after 1994 are required to have wheelchair access.

The most comprehensive guide to all aspects of life in Paris for people with physical disabilities is *Personnes Handicapées*, available at the *mairie*. Minitel 3615 HANDITEL has information, and the book *Access in Paris* by Gordon Crouch and Ben Roberts may be available at book stores. See *Handicapés: matériel et services pour* in the Yellow Pages.

- **Association des Paralysés de France**: 156, rue d'Aubervilliers 75019 (tel: 01.40.34.50.36). Nationwide organization. Publishes *Où Ferons-nous Etape?*, a list of accessible hotels in France.
- **Comité National Français de Liaison pour la Rédaptation des Handicapés (CNFLRH)**: 236 bis, rue de Tolbiac 75013 (tel: 01.53.80.66.66). Publishes *Paris-Ile-de-France Pour Tous*, available also at the Paris Tourist Office.
- **Travel Information Service**: Moss Rehab Hospital, 1200 W. Tabor Road, Philadelphia PA 19141 (tel: 215/456-9600). Telephone information and referrals for disabled travelers.
- **Royal Association for Disability and Rehabilitation (RADAR)**: 12 City Forum, 250 City Road, London EC1V8AF (tel: 171/250-3222). Information for disabled travelers, including *Access in Paris*.

Although taxi drivers are obliged to take wheelchair passengers, there is no guarantee they will do so. Some companies,

193

however, offer services customized for disabled passengers. Taxis for weekends or to the airports should be reserved in advance. Try **Le Kangourou** (tel: 01.47.08.93.50), **GIHP** (tel: 01.41.83. 15.15), or **Aihrop**: (tel: 01.41.29.01.29).

THE CALL OF NATURE

Paris' sidewalk *sanisettes* (public toilets) are easy to use, sanitary, and cheap. Look for the oval structures with illuminated *Toilettes* signs throughout the city. When 2F are inserted, the door opens. Inside are a toilet, cleansing tissue, and a sink. The toilet does not flush after use—when you turn the handle to open the door and exit, the entire cabin is disinfected automatically. There are also public toilets at some métro stops, and these are generally watched by an attendant, cost a small amount, and are fairly well-maintained. Look for signs that say *Toilettes* or *WC*.

Museums, the larger hotels, restaurants, cafés, shopping centers, and department stores all have public toilet facilities. In a bar or café you will be expected to buy a cup of coffee. Some have a coin slot that takes 2F, and this usually means they are somewhat clean. In a few bars, however, you will find the old Turkish toilets with a hole in the floor and foot rests to either side. Signs on doors might read as above, or they might say *Dames* or *Femmes*, or *Hommes* or *Messieurs*. No matter where you go, always carry some tissues with you.

Chapter Twelve

EATING OUT: THE RESTAURANTS

THE WORLD CAPITAL OF FOOD

Parisians love their restaurants. They love to eat in this capital of *haute cuisine*, and they love to talk about food. Exploring different *cuisines*, each with its own approach to flavors and textures of food, will give you the unparalleled opportunity to participate in what is considered one of the world's great art forms. With some 15,000 eating establishments in Paris, ranging from casual cafés to world-renowned restaurants, dining within your budget is possible. The more refined the restaurant, of course, the higher the price. In the city center, an elegant meal will cost about 600F per person, wine not included, and even an average three-course dinner can cost about 250F. Although there is little that is truly cheap in Paris, prices are more reasonable in neighborhood *bistrots* and *brasseries* and in the interesting Asian restaurants. The food, although not

195

as beautifully presented, can be delicious. Consult the restaurant guides and experiment with restaurants until you find those that please your palate and your purse.

Ordering *à la carte*, that is, from the standard *carte* (menu), is the most expensive way to dine. Many restaurants offer a *menu conseillé* (also called the *formule* or *prix fixe*), which is a fixed-price meal of a suggested combination of courses for that day. The price is set according to the number of courses ordered. Sometimes the set menu is offered only at lunch; sometimes it includes the house wine. Often a *plat du jour* (daily special) is described on a chalk-board or printed on a paper inserted into the menu. In addition to the price, a benefit of the *plat du jour* is that the food is in season. In the fall, for instance, game dishes such as boar, hare, pheasants, and venison will appear on menus, as well as wild mushrooms—*chanterelles, cèpes,* and *girolles*. Spring and summer see the *navarin d'agneau* (spring lamb stew), *morilles*, asparagus, melons, and other seasonal produce. Some of the finer restaurants offer a *menu dégustation*, a sampling of the chef's creations.

Of course there is no such thing in France as "French cooking," for it is all French cooking, and Paris itself is not known for a particular cuisine. The finest restaurants serve *haute cuisine* or *cuisine bourgeoise*. *Nouvelle cuisine*, an adaptation of the menu to lighter foods, combinations of exotic ingredients, and small portions, did not catch on in Paris, although many people are nonetheless eating lighter foods and smaller portions. The currently popular *cuisine de terroir* offers dishes in larger portions and with more traditional recipes and regional ingredients.

Restaurants from different regions of France offer their own specialties (*cuisine de province/cuisine régionale*). These vary in quality and price, yet it is possible to sample all the *cuisines* of France without leaving Paris. Establishments may serve the sausage and sauerkraut dishes of Alsace, tomato- and olive oil-based dishes of Provence, pork dishes from Lyon, cheese dishes from Savoy, or the creamy specialties of Normandy. What counts is that the food is fresh, well prepared, and priced in line with the amenities of the restaurant. *Cuisine bonne femme* means home-cooked, and *maison* means that the particular dish is a specialty prepared in-house.

Some restaurants are beginning to cater to the desire for lighter foods by creating dishes with olive oil rather than butter and cream and experimenting with dishes to suit the tastes and budgets of a younger generation of diners that is not willing to spend 600F on one meal. The young set tends to frequent the more casual *brasseries* and *bistrots*, the wine bars and tearooms, and the inexpensive Asian restaurants. Fish restaurants and *bistrots* are increasingly attractive to people concerned about health and fitness. Fish is freshest on Friday, and some fish restaurants are closed on Monday.

Do not hesitate to discuss with the *serveur* (waiter) the ingredients in a dish, to specify politely what you can and cannot eat, and to ask advice. If a waiter says that your request "cannot be done," it may mean an intransigence on his part or it may mean that the success of the dish requires some particular method of preparation; order a different dish. Note that meat in France is cooked minimally: *bleu* is cooked well on the exterior and is warm all the way through, *saignant* is rare, *à point* is medium, and *bien cuit* is well done, although perhaps not well done enough for foreigners. Specify in advance if you insist on having your meat well done. Veal may be *rosé*, and poultry may also remain pink toward the bone. Also, if you like fish but hate the bones, ask to have it *préparé*, and your server will bone it for you.

Your server is the best source for questions concerning the meal. Being a waiter is a respected profession in France. Thus waiters take pride in what they serve and are knowledgeable about ingredients and methods of preparation. Waiters generally wear a similar uniform of black trousers, white shirt, and black bow tie. In better restaurants they wear dinner jackets, while in others they may wear a black, pocketed vest.

Start with an *entrée/hors-d'oeuvre* (appetizer), then have the *plat* (main course). *Salade* may come as an *entrée* or alone after the main course. After the *plat*, a platter of several different cheeses may be offered; select a few of different textures. Then comes *dessert* and last, *café*. It is no longer frowned upon to order two dishes instead of a three-course meal, and although "doggy bags" do not exist in France, it is acceptable to share an appetizer or dessert. Or to skip the cheese or dessert altogether. The French do not drink coffee with their meal and, except for breakfast, they do not drink *café au lait* with meals. They just drink *café*, which is small and potent.

The Wine List

The French love wine and are knowledgeable about their country's wine-growing regions and offerings. They generally understand which wines go best with each type of meal, enhancing both the appreciation of the meal and the wine. This can be easily learned. In addition to taking one of the wine appreciation courses suggested earlier and tasting wines at any of the city's many wine bars, take every opportunity to explore the *cartes des vins* (wine lists) in Paris restaurants and to discuss with a knowledgeable *sommelier* (wine steward) the wine most appropriate to the meal being ordered. It is not necessary to order an entire bottle of wine, and many people do not. Although the French have a reputation for great alcohol consumption, most people consume alcoholic beverages, primarily wine, only at mealtimes, sipping for the taste but drinking water to quench the thirst. This emphasizes the flavor of the wine and lessens the effect of the alcohol.

The finest restaurants serve the finest wines. Some of the better wines now are available in half bottles, and restaurants are beginning to serve wine by the glass. In neighborhood restaurants, the house wine generally is a decent *vin de table* and comes in several sizes: a *carafe* is a liter, a *demi* a half liter, and a *quart* a quarter of a liter. *Un picher* (a pitcher) can be had in the smaller two amounts. Regional restaurants offer a selection of wines that compliment their cuisine. Order also some water, either *une carafe d'eau*, which will be tap water and provided free, or mineral water, either sparkling (*gazeuse*) or still (*plate*).

Drinking hard liquor such as whisky before dinner is thought to deaden the taste buds. Instead, try an *apéritif*, such as vermouth, pastis, kir, which is white wine, and *crème de cassis*, or *kir royal*, made with champagne. After dinner, a *digestif* would be a subtle cognac, the fuller armagnac, calvados, *poire William*, or any fruity *eau-de-vie*.

The Agreeable Search

Reading the descriptions and reviews of restaurants can become addictive. Start with your tourist guidebook. All guides recommend restaurants, rating them according to their own standards. Some, such as *Let's Go Paris* and *The Rough Guide*, concentrate on inexpensive establishments catering to a budget traveler. Others, such as *Eyewitness Paris*, feature upscale restaurants. *Time Out Paris* has an extensive selection, describing some offbeat and interesting places, as well as some in the outer *arrondissements*.

Book stores carry an array of guides devoted to dining in Paris. The *Guide Michelin* awards up to three stars to the best restaurants, and when a three-star restaurant loses a star, the scandal makes newspapers all over the world. In English or in French, *Gault Millau* awards food ratings and *toques* (chefs' hats) for ambience, and its lively descriptions of restaurants are fun to read, except perhaps for the *restaurateur* whose establishment is being panned. *Cheap Eats in Paris* offers comparatively inexpensive dining alternatives. One of the best guides, Patricia Wells' *The Food Lover's Guide to Paris*, offers a wide range of choices, and it has a section on shopping for food. The newest addition to the scene is the famous *Zagat* guide that rates restaurants according to surveys of people who have eaten in them.

In French, the well-respected *Le Petit Lebey—des Bistrots Parisiens* lists *bistrots*, *brasseries*, and wine bars. *Paris Pas Cher* and *Paris Combines* recommend restaurants they consider good value for the money. News of restaurants also makes the daily newspapers, and Parisians keep track of new restaurants, the closing of old ones, and when a famous chef leaves one establishment for another or starts his own restaurant.

How to Decide

Categories of eating establishments overlap considerably, and what you might consider an upscale establishment with high prices, might consider itself a *bistrot*. Sometimes, too, it is hard to distinguish a bar from a café, and in reality there may be little difference. Within any category, of course, the specialties, the quality of food, the service, and the price also have their own ranges. Good establishments of any category will be crowded, as Parisians love to eat out. Except in fine restaurants, do not expect to find a quiet corner for a private conversation.

Add to the considerations of *cuisine* and price that Parisians eat outdoors whenever they can. If there is a spot of sun and a table, a Parisian will find it. Every café terrace will be crowded, and restaurants that can do so have tables outside, whether there are twenty in an elegant courtyard with white umbrellas or three small rickety tables on a too-narrow sidewalk. Some 4,000 cafés and restaurants have outdoor seating.

With so many restaurants and choices, recommendations from friends or your own exploration can be most helpful. All restaurants post their menus in their front windows, and from this you can ascertain the type of cuisine, the specialties, and the price range. When passing an inviting restaurant, stop in and ask for a *carte de visite* to make note of the location and telephone number. And look in at mealtimes to see whether a place seems filled with locals, people who already know what is good or bad, "in" or "out."

Photo: Zeny Cieslikowski

Remnants of a visit to a Paris café.

Of course it is possible to get a bad meal in Paris, as it is anywhere. Locals, for instance, rarely frequent the establishments along the *Grands Boulevards*, for they generally cater to tourists, and although the food can sometimes be good, the service tends to be impersonal and prices high. If a menu is printed in three or four languages with pictures of different countries' flags, you can be sure it caters to tourists. But in Paris, if you have heeded recommendations of friends or the suggestions of a restaurant guide, disappointments will be rare.

It is most important to decide what you want for a particular meal. Do you want a formal meal in a restaurant or something light and fast? Do you want a warm welcome and friendly, casual service? Do you want to sample an innovative dish at a particular restaurant? Do you want to be guided by a knowledgeable waiter and *sommelier* to eating and drinking *à la française*? Do you want to celebrate a great occasion and take part in a gastronomical

201

experience that you will always remember? Or on a particular day do you just want your meat cooked to a crisp and some coffee with the main course (no matter how barbaric it seems to your waiter), in which case you should stick with restaurants that cater to many nationalities. In any case, respect each restaurant for what it is. A small, local *bistrot* will not have refined, gourmet food, and a two-star restaurant may not whip up a hamburger for your kids.

Do not be hidebound. Experiment with dishes you have never heard of and foods not popular in your own country. France knows what to do with food. Even in restaurants of *haute cuisine*, expect to find beautifully prepared dishes made from inexpensive meats such as tripe, brains, or kidneys, all considered delicacies by the French. After trying them, you might see why. An inexpensive way to be adventurous is to purchase the *Entertainment Book Paris*, offering discounts (about 25 percent off the total bill) in restaurants of all categories. Go to the office at 14, rue Gaillon 75002 (tel: 01.44.51.10.00).

For moderately priced meals, try the reliable chains such as **Oh!...Poivrier, L'Amanguier, Léon de Bruxelles** for mussels, and **La Criée** for fish. Some places advertise *à volonté*, meaning that for a particular dish you may eat as much as you want for the price listed.

Business Hours

Restaurants and *bistrots* open around noon and are busiest between 1:00 and 2:30 pm. They close after lunch and reopen for dinner. Lunch is a popular meal to eat out, and restaurants are often full. When exploring a new restaurant, first try its menu at lunch, when the portions served are smaller and less expensive than at dinner but of the same quality. Dinner service starts at 7:30 pm, and restaurants begin to fill up around 8:30 pm, taking their last order about 11 pm. *Brasseries* serve food all day, as do

202

many of the *salons de thé*. Most restaurants close one day a week, and until recently it was hard to find a restaurant open on Sunday, except for kosher and Asian establishments.

Some establishments close around holidays, and some, even those of *haute cuisine*, close for a *fermeture annuelle* (annual holiday) sometime in July or August. If they stay open, they may keep an irregular schedule, closing on the weekends or for lunch on Monday. During the summer, it is best to check.

Reservations in restaurants should be made several days or a week in advance and, for the most popular, sometimes a month. *Maîtres d'hôtel* may ask for the number of *couverts* (table settings) rather than how many people. Some ask that confirmation be made on the day, and if they do not know you, may ask for your telephone number. You may request to be seated in an *espace non-fumeurs* (no smoking section), but in crowded *bistrots* this may mean little.

Cancel a reservation if you cannot make it, and do not be late to a restaurant, thinking that you will have to wait. Generally seating is prompt, the *maître d'hôtel* having gauged when the previous party will vacate the table. Many of the best restaurants have one seating only. In the best restaurants men should wear jackets and ties. Although dining out is more casual than heretofore, it is still best to dress appropriately to the establishment, and in fact, it heightens the sense of occasion. See *Restaurants* in the Yellow Pages.

Paying the Bill

An expensive three-course dinner at one of Paris' top restaurants may cost 800F per person, including an excellent wine. A moderate meal may cost around 500F with a decent wine, and an inexpensive dinner may cost around 200F, including a carafe of the *vin de la maison*. Asian restaurants, except Japanese, are generally less expensive, as are the North African. Be sure to check the bill for accuracy.

Most restaurants accept credit cards. *L'addition* (the bill) will not be brought to you automatically, for it would seem rude to presume you are finished if you are not. Signal the waiter by saying *"monsieur"* or *"s'il vous plaît,"* never *"garçon,"* even though that is what you may have been taught in elementary French class.

If using a credit card, do not write in a tip. The *pourboire* (tip) is always included in *l'addition*. The menu will indicate *service compris*. Even if the menu says *"service non compris,"* the bill will still show a service charge of 15 percent. Although the service is included one way or the other, the customer should leave a small amount on the table: in moderately priced restaurants perhaps 20F, in more elegant restaurants somewhat more.

RESTAURANTS

A *restaurant* generally indicates refined dining and refined prices. Gradations run from neighborhood restaurants to the world-famous purveyors of *haute cuisine*, but in all, the artistic presentation of the food and attentive service are part of the value of the meal. The *patron* of a small restaurant may supervise personally all dishes that come from the kitchen, make recommendations on wine, and at the end bring the bill, whereas the large establishments have several servers dedicated to each table, plus a *sommelier* to discuss the wine. Service will be efficient but not rushed, and a full meal may take two or three pleasant hours. If you are short on time, go to a *bistrot*.

BISTROTS

Some say that *bistrot* (alternatively written *bistro*) is a Russian word meaning "hurry," and introduced into France by Russian soldiers in 1815. Others claim it comes from the word *bistrouille*, which in certain northern regions is a mixture of coffee and *eau-de-vie*. *Bistrot* once conjured up the image of hearty, home-cooked food in a casual, welcoming setting, but now *bistrots* run the gamut from the proprietor-run, small, family establishment to the extremely elegant and chic. The menu is often written on a blackboard, even in the most elegant *bistrots*, and it is changed daily according to what is in season, augmenting traditional dishes such as *boeuf bourguignon* and *blanquette de veau*. Meals run from the traditional and hearty, to old favorites imaginatively presented with a modern twist. Decent house wines are often sold by the carafe, but more impressive wines can also be found. Yet with all their variety, *bistrots* still offer service somewhat faster than that in a restaurant, serve substantial dishes, have tables close together, and are reasonably priced.

Try the *bistrots* that are being opened by younger chefs who have trained under the master chefs. Offering imaginative interpretations and reasonable prices, these establishments are among the most popular. Also, some of the noted chefs themselves have opened their own *bistrots*, allowing people to savor their high-quality preparations at affordable prices. These are all generally mentioned in guidebooks, featuring the name of the chef. Be sure to book in advance.

BRASSERIES

Brasserie means "brewery." *Brasseries* began serving beer in the seventeenth century, and toward the end of the last century started offering hearty Alsatian sausages and *choucroute* (sauerkraut), plus Alsatian Riesling and Gewurtztraminer wines. Current *brasseries* tend to serve simple, light meals and fresh fish, usually nicely presented and reasonably priced. Bright, lively, and bustling, *brasseries* remain open all day and stay open late. In some of the most popular it is important to reserve in advance. Pay attention to the décor; some look like traditional beer houses and others have an inviting Belle Epoque decor or art deco wood paneling and interesting glass and mirrors. See *Cafés, bars, brasseries* in the Yellow Pages.

Master Chef Jacques Cagna

PERSONAL FAVORITES

One of the great pleasures of my stays in Paris is to collect restaurant favorites, filing away *cartes de visite*, noting down memorable meals, forming recommendations, and passing these *bonnes adresses* (good addresses) on to friends. Some restaurants are well-known, some offbeat; some offer French food, but many do not. In some I like the ambience or the *accueil* (welcome), but in all I respect the quality of the dishes prepared, no matter the level of restaurant. Although I relish the special evenings spent at **Jacques Cagna** in the heart of the Latin Quarter, at the **Pré Catalan** in the Bois de Boulogne, or at the **Jules Verne** up in the Eiffel Tower, the most elegant restaurants are too well described in guide books to include them here. All the restaurants mentioned in this chapter are my favorites.

- 1er — **Les Cartes Postales**: 7, rue Gomboust (tel: 01.42.61.02. 93). Imaginative Japanese/French cuisine, intimate ambience. Medium priced.
- 1er — **L'Escargot Montorgueil**: 38, rue Montorgueil (tel: 01.42.36.83.51). Delicious snails, fish, duck, and other dishes. Outdoor tables. Reasonably priced.
- 4e — **Chez Marianne**: 2, rue des Hospitalières St-Gervais (tel: 01.42.72.18.86). Israeli and Eastern European delicacies in a popular setting.
- 5e — **Campagne et Provence**: 25, quai de la Tournelle (tel: 01.43.54.05.17). Fish and Provençal *cuisine*, quiet and elegant, with moderate prices. Pleasant to stroll along the *quai* after dinner.
- 6e — **Cosi**: 54, rue de Seine (tel: 01.46.33.35.36). The best sandwiches! A choice of fillings to be inserted into bread steaming hot from the wood-fired oven. Friendly welcome.
- 6e — **Gustavia**: 26-28, rue des Grands-Augustins (tel: 01.40. 46.86.70). Swedish dishes and good prices in a casual setting. Gravlax, Swedish herrings, fish salads, and a *plat du jour.*
- 6e — **Le Christine**: 1, rue Christine (tel: 01.40.51.71.64). Charming ambience, excellent food, a friendly welcome, and good prices.
- 8e — **Le Cercle Ledoyen**: Carré des Champs-Elysées (tel: 01.53.05.10.02). For a summer lunch under an umbrella on a leafy terrace. Somewhat lower priced than its *haute cuisine* namesake, this is a special treat.
- 14e — **Le Bistrot du Dôme**: 1, rue Delambre (tel: 01.43.35. 32.00). Small menu changed daily, with creative fish dishes at somewhat lower cost than its flagship restaurant, **Le Dôme,** across the street.

- 14*e* — **Le Bar à Huîtres**: 112, boulevard du Montparnasse (tel: 01.43.20.71.01). This small chain serves wonderfully fresh oysters and delicious fish. The service can be indifferent, but the oysters are not.
- 19*e* — **Le Pavillon du Lac**: Place Armand-Carrel, Parc des Buttes Chaumont (tel: 01.42.02.08.97). Lovely park setting and summer terrace. Good food, a variety of *menus*.

Visitors often enjoy **Le Procope** at 13, rue de l'Ancienne-Comédie 75006, the oldest public eating establishment in Paris, which still serves good food in a delightful setting. Founded in 1686, it hosted the French revolutionaries, Napoleon Bonaparte, the American Benjamin Franklin, and such literary lights as Honoré de Balzac and Voltaire (tel: 01.40.46.79.00).

INTERNATIONAL RESTAURANTS

France having been a major colonial nation, Paris has long-established North African and Asian restaurants throughout the city. Although Asian restaurants and *traiteurs* are found in most *arrondissements*, the 13*e* is known for its inexpensive Chinese and Vietnamese restaurants, as is Belleville in the 19*e* (also popular for its North African restaurants). Couscous can also be found in kosher restaurants in the 9*e* and in the Marais.

- (African) 10*e* — **Paris-Dakar**: 95, rue du Faubourg-St-Martin (tel: 01.42.08.16.64). Senegalese cooking. Music, lively atmosphere.
- (African) 11*e* — **Mansouria**: 11, rue Faidherbe (tel: 01.43. 71.00.16). Moroccan food, couscous.
- (Asian) 13*e* — **Sala Thai**: 13, rue des Frères d'Astier-de-la-Vigerie (tel: 01.45.84.13.22). Excellent Thai and Laotian specialties with several *menus* to choose from. Tables outside.
- (Asian) 13*e* — **Tricotin**: 15, avenue de Choisy (tel: 01.45.85. 51.52). Crowded, popular, and inexpensive.

- (Chinese) 13*e* — **Miam-Miam**: 50, avenue d'Ivry (tel: 01.45. 84.55.90). Delicious Chinese noodle soup.
- (Chinese) 5*e* — **Mirama**: 17, rue St-Jacques (tel: 01.43.54.71. 77). Excellent soups, especially the noodle soup with *porc laqué*.

Italian restaurants and pizzerias are always popular. Some international restaurants are clustered in various areas; inexpensive Indian and Pakistani establishments are found in and around the Passage Brady in the 10*e* and Japanese restaurants around rue Ste-Anne in the 2*e*. Some are expensive, although the *plat du jour* is reasonable. Try these for excellent sushi and grilled, skewered, meats, and a well-priced, varied *menu*:

- 1*er* — **Foujita 2**: 27, rue du 29-Juillet (tel: 01.49.26.07.70)
- 6*e* — **Sushi House**: 50, rue Dauphine (tel: 01.43.25.54.85)
- 6*e* — **Tokyorama**: 9, rue Monsieur-le-Prince (tel: 01.43.54. 37.04)

Popular with young Parisians and North Americans are outposts of American restaurant chains and Tex-Mex establishments. Most have special events and dinners geared to the American holidays; check *FUSAC*. See also *Restaurants: Spécialités Etrangères* in the Yellow Pages.

KOSHER RESTAURANTS

Of the more than 100 kosher restaurants in Paris, many are clustered in the Jewish neighborhoods of the Marais, rue Richer, and boulevard de Belleville. Kosher is spelled variously *cacher*, *kacher*, or *kasher*. There are dairy and meat restaurants, kosher pizzerias, and even kosher Chinese restaurants. In some restaurants that are listed *cacher*, the food is all kosher, but both milk and meat dishes may be served, using only one kitchen and one set of dishes. Some do not display a Beth Din certificate, meaning that they have not paid for official certification, but are still *cacher*. Although a few establishments stay open on Friday night and Saturday, most are closed and reopen on Sunday.

    Le Guide des Bonnes Adresses Cacher en France by Guy Saint-Père is a compendium of Beth Din certified establishments in France. *Guide de la Restauration Cachere* is available from the newspaper *Actualité Juive* (tel: 01.43.71.14.14). See also Chapter Thirteen.

- 1er — **Restaurant Juliette**: 12-14 rue Duphot (tel: 01.47.60.18.10). French cooking, strictly kosher.
- 4e — **Pitchi-Poï**: 7, rue Caron (tel: 01.42.77.46.15). Polish specialties with terrace seating.
- 8e — **Cine Città Caffè**: 7, rue d'Aguesseau (tel: 01.42.68.05.03). Pastas and fish dishes in an upscale setting.
- 17e — **Fradji**: 42, rue Poncelet (tel: 01.47.54.91.40). Tunisian kosher restaurant, with fabulous couscous, welcoming service, and a lively atmosphere. Moderate prices.
- 17e — **Nini**: 24, rue Saussier-Leroy (tel: 01.46.22.28.93). North African specialties near l'Etoile.

VEGETARIAN RESTAURANTS

Given the French reliance on meats, cream sauces, and butter, at one time it was difficult to find vegetarian, much less vegan, restaurants in Paris. This is no longer true, and many restaurants will put together a platter of vegetables on request. Vegetarian fare is standard at Asian and Indian restaurants, meatless pastas are common at Italian restaurants, and some *cacher* restaurants are meatless as well.

- 2e — **Country Life**: 6, rue Daunou (tel: 01.42.97.48.51)
- 4e and 14e — **Aquarius**: 54, rue Ste-Croix-de-la-Bretonnerie (tel: 01.48.87.48.71); 40, rue de Gergovie (tel: 01.45.41.36.88)
- 5e — **Les Quatre et Une Saveurs**: 72, rue du Cardinal-Lemoine (tel: 01.43.26.88.80)
- 6e — **Guenmai**: 2 bis, rue de l'Abbaye (tel: 01.43.26.03.24)
- 13e — **Le Bol en Bois**: 35, rue Pascal (tel: 01.47.07.27.24)

Photo: Zeny Cieślikowski

All cuisines are available in Paris, from kosher pizza to felafel.

CAFÉS AND BARS

The *café* is an all-purpose eating establishment. You may linger over a breakfast *croissant* and coffee, dash in for a light lunch, stop for a cup of tea and a snack in the afternoon, or enjoy a drink in the evening. Ranging from the famous and expensive to those catering to regulars from the *quartier*, cafés generally do not bother much about decor. Many have outdoor tables and are popular late into the night. Some cafés are also *tabacs*, so you can buy items such as cigarettes, stamps, lottery tickets, and cards for the métro and telephone. What is most important is that cafés can be the community gathering places for friends. These places can be a lot of fun. Each neighborhood café has its own personality and loyal clientele (*habitués*).

211

Cafés are open all day and well into the evening. Most neighborhood cafés close around 10 pm. Those in tourist areas stay open later. If a table at a café has a placemat and table setting at mealtimes, it is reserved for those who come to eat; find a bare table if you just want to sit with a cup of coffee. For a quick coffee or a mineral water, stand at the *comptoir* (counter), where the prices are cheaper. If you order an orange juice you will most likely get something in a can. Instead, order a *citron pressé* or *orange pressée*, a freshly squeezed drink served with a carafe of water to make it the strength you like. Cafés and bars are required to post their prices (*tarifs de consommation*) and distinguish between those for service at the *comptoir* and at tables. See *Cafés, bars, brasseries* in the Yellow Pages.

- *Café:* strong black coffee. Also *expresso, un express,* or *café noir*
- *Café serré:* double strength
- *Café allongé:* coffee with hot water to dilute it
- *Café filtre:* black coffee, less strong
- *Café au lait:* coffee with milk
- *Café crème:* coffee with steamed cream or milk
- *Décaféiné or déca:* decaffeinated coffee
- *Thé nature:* plain tea
- *Thé citron:* tea with lemon
- *Thé au lait:* tea with milk
- *Tisane/Infusion:* herb tea
- *Chocolat chaud:* hot chocolate

A *bar* has more to do with atmosphere than with alcohol, and some daytime cafés are popular bars by night, serving drinks and simple meals until the wee hours. People go to their favorite bars at all times of the day: for a quick jolt of coffee in the mornings, for a simple lunch, for an *apéritif* before the theater or drink after, and just to relax in the afternoons. The "happy hour" has become popular in early evening. Some bars have pleasant terraces, others are known for their music, and some are just popular as hangouts. Probably for foreigners the most famous *bar américain* is **Harry's Bar**, founded in 1911 and for decades the hangout of American literary expatriates.

SALONS DE THÉ

Parisians drink tea but not with meals other than breakfast. If you order tea in a bar you will get something made from a tea bag or already sweetened. Instead, Paris delights in its *salons de thé* (tea rooms), which serve teas, coffees, and light meals, often in a lovely ambience. The variety of teas is excellent and the service often elegant yet relaxed. Tea rooms tend to stay open all day, many opening at breakfast and closing around 7:30–8 pm.

Tourist guides recommend the most well-known *salons* that offer a formal high tea, including hotels such as the **Ritz, Crillon**, and **Meurice**, but these can be more expensive and less friendly than the independent *salons*. Many of the local establishments sell teas to take home, including *tisanes/infusions* (herb teas). See Chapter Thirteen and *Salons de thé* in the Yellow Pages.

- 1*er* — **Angélina**: 226, rue de Rivoli (tel: 01.42.60.82.00). Teas, light meals, and unforgettable *chocolat chaud*, a wintertime favorite of Parisians.
- 4*e*, 6*e*, and 8*e* — **Mariage Frères**: 30, rue du Bourg-Tibourg (tel: 01.42.72.28.11); 13, rue des Grands-Augustins (tel: 01.40.51.82.50); 260, rue du Faubourg-St-Honoré (tel: 01.46.22.18.54). Celebrated, elegant *salon de thé*, offering hundreds of teas, light meals, and pastries.
- 5*e* — **La Mosquée**: 39, rue Geoffroy St-Hillaire (tel: 01.43.31.18.14). An interesting tea room in the Islamic mosque.
- 8*e* — **Ladurée**: 16, rue Royale (tel: 01.42.60.21.79). Fashionable, crowded, and famous for its macaroons. Salon at 75, avenue des Champs-Elysées stays open until 1 am (tel: 01.40.75.08.75).

WINE BARS

Learn about French regional wines by frequenting the city's ubiquitous *bars à vin* (wine bars). Wine has been produced from French soil since before the Romans occupied the Ile de France two thousand years ago. Currently, France produces about a quarter of the world's annual wine production, almost two billion gallons, culled from some three million planted acres. Despite the seemingly large selection in wine shops around the world, most French wines are not exported, so living in Paris affords the best opportunity to taste and learn.

The most famous wine bars are described in tourist guides; **Willi's Wine Bar** at 13, rue des Petits-Champs 75001 is British owned (tel: 01.42.61.05.09), as is **Juvenile's** at 47, rue de Richelieu 75001 (tel: 01.42.97.46.49). But Parisian *bars à vin* catering to the locals are in every *arrondissement*, each with its particular emphasis on both wines and food. Open for lunch and early evening meals, wine bars are similar to cafés, but the offerings tend to be more interesting. Wine bars can be wood-paneled and staid or modern and noisy. The food also varies, but in general includes light foods and salads. Wine bars are popular as much for their sociability as their fare, and people linger after work or late in the evening. Prices are according to wines sampled, and these range from the ordinary to the excellent. **L'Ecluse** is a well-known wine bar with five locations.

The Centre d'Information de Documentation et de Dégustation (CIDD) offers courses and programs on wine, as does the city-sponsored *ADAC* (see Chapter Five). The **Musée du Vin** at 5, square Charles-Dickens 75016 is a wine museum with the opportunity for tasting (tel: 01.45.25.63.26). *Le Guide Hachette*, an annual directory that rates current wines and lists French vineyards, can be found in bookshops.

Wine shops, such as the **Jardin des Vignes** at 91, rue de Turenne 75003, offer wine tastings (tel: 01.42.77.05.00). **La**

Dernière Goutte at 6, rue de Bourbon-le-Château 75006 has Saturday wine tastings, often with wine makers discussing their wines (tel: 01.43.29.11.62). Others that say *dégustation de vins de propriété* also offer samplings. See Chapter Thirteen for wine shops.

BEER

Parisian beer houses sell their brews in an entirely Gallic ambience. *Bière à la pression* is draft beer, and it comes in three sizes: the most common *demi* (8 oz), *sérieux* (16 oz), or *formidable* (about a liter). France produces a few bottled beers, **Kronenbourg** being the best known. If you order a *bière*, you will have asked for a bottled beer. For draft beer, order *"un demi"* or whatever size you want.

- 1er — **Le Sous-Bock**: 49, rue St-Honoré (tel: 01.40.26.48.09)
- 2e — **Le Baragouin**: 17, rue Tiquetonne (tel: 01.42.36.18.93)
- 6e — **Pub St-Germain-des-Prés**: 17, rue de l'Ancienne-Comédie (tel: 01.43.29.38.70)
- 6e — **La Taverne de Nesle**: 32, rue Dauphine (tel: 01.43.26. 38.36)

Currently it is the pub — the Irish, the Australian, the British, and the Scottish — that has hit the city hard. More pubs are opening all the time. They host special events for their country's holidays, televise sporting events, arrange dart competitions, and offer just about anything to be found in a traditional pub, including the food. Most stay open late; some stay open all night. See *Bars, pianos-bars, pubs* in the Yellow Pages.

- **The Frog & Rosbif**: 116 rue St-Denis 75002 (tel: 01.42.36. 34.73); **Frog & Princesse**: 9, rue Princesse 75006 (tel: 01.40.51. 77.38). Fresh-brewed ales from imported British ingredients and other draft beers.
- **O'Neil** at 20, rue des Canettes 75006 brews *blonde, ambrée,* and *spéciale brune* (tel: 01.46.33.36.66).

215

ICE CREAM

Glace (ice cream) has traditionally been consumed in summer, but with the international chains opening their own shops throughout Paris, it is becoming popular year round. Parisian *glaciers* (ice cream makers and parlors) often make their creations on the premises, using fresh ingredients. What makes French ice cream so delicious is that the flavors taste so true; moreover, with smaller portions and less butterfat than the imported ice creams, a dish or cone of French *glace* is not overwhelming. Despite the popularity of ice cream, Paris' most celebrated *glacier,* **Berthillon,** closes all of August, but some groceries and eating establishments carry Berthillon's ice cream, so it can still be enjoyed in August.

- 1er — **Gilles Vilfeu:** 3, rue de la Cossonnerie (tel: 01.40.26.36.40)
- 4e — **Berthillon:** 31, rue St-Louis-en-l'Ile (tel: 01.43.54.31.61)
- 7e — **Le Bac à Glaces:** 109, rue du Bac (tel: 01.45.48.87.65)
- 9e — **Baggi:** 33, rue Chaptal (tel: 01.48.74.01.39)
- 12e — **Raimo:** 59-61, boulevard de Reuilly (tel: 01.43.43.70.17)
- 14e — **Glacier Calabrese:** 15, rue d'Odessa (tel: 01.43.20.31.63)

Häagen-Dazs has more than a dozen outlets throughout Paris and is available at supermarkets, as is **Ben and Jerry's**, with its exotic flavors. Another chain, **Baskin Robbins,** has several outlets. See *Glaciers* in the Yellow Pages.

RESTAURATION RAPIDE

For quick meals it is easy to find a *casse-croûte* (snack) served at a *snack-bar* (sometimes called *le snack*). Bars offer pre-made sandwiches, bakeries make their own, and *traiteurs* (take-out groceries) are in all neighborhoods. It is also easy to stop at a café for a *croque-Monsieur* (grilled ham and cheese sandwich) or a *croque-Madame* (with a fried egg on top), or to pick up *falafel* at a North African stand or a *crêpe* at a sidewalk *crêperie*. Some restaurants offer items *sur le pouce,* for people on the run.

The Italian *panino* (sandwich), made on fresh, warm bread, has become popular. **Toastissimo** is a small chain selling good *panini*. Near St-Germain, try the freshly made sandwiches at Cosi, mentioned above. Some eateries advertise that their sandwiches are made on the bread of the famous baker Poilâne. **Lina's Sandwiches** chain makes sandwiches to order on the bread of your choice, including Poilâne. See *Restaurants: restauration rapide et libre-service* in the Yellow Pages.

Student Restaurants

Resto U (*restaurant universitaire*) is a chain of low-priced restaurants for registered students, operated by CROUS. Some are cafeterias and some are *brasseries-grill*. The food is plentiful and nourishing. People with student identification cards may buy tickets weekdays at any *resto* during lunch and dinner hours. Tickets may be bought individually or more cheaply in a *carnet* of 10. For a list of the *restos*, inquire at CROUS at 39, avenue Georges-Bernanos 75005 (tel: 01.40.51.37.10).

CHAPTER THIRTEEN

EATING IN: THE MARKETS

KNOWING HOW

Knowing how and when to shop for food is the key to eating well at home in Paris, whether you intend to cook or not. Wide-ranging options include buying fresh ingredients and starting from scratch or moving up to the artistically prepared meats from the butcher that are ready to cook, plus potatoes and vegetables already cleaned. You can also buy freshly cooked, entire meals from a *traiteur* that advertises *vente à emporter,* or even high-quality frozen meals. For times when even these easy options are not appealing, just about any type of meal can be ordered by telephone for *livraison à domicile* (home delivery), from French cuisine to Japanese sushi and Chinese dumplings, to Italian pizza or Spanish paella.

The quality of fresh ingredients in Paris is extremely high, for the food sold in groceries is regulated by law. Butter, cheese, poultry, and produce must conform to the standards set for the region from which they come, and the *appellation d'origine contrôlée* monitors the quality of both food and alcoholic beverages. Thus the highest quality of fresh foods is available, whether at an outdoor market, neighborhood *traiteur*, or the supermarkets that are conveniently located in every *quartier*. *Agents de conservation* (preservatives) are rare, so food will taste better and be fresher but may spoil quickly. Look for the *date de péremption* (expiration date) on packaged foods. Some will say *vente jusqu'à* or *consommer avant* with the expiration date. (Americans should remember that the date is written with the day, month, and year, in that order.) If you have bought a product beyond its expiration date, take your receipt and the product back to the shop, and in most cases it will be exchanged.

Groceries are open from about 8 am until 7:30 pm, although neighborhood shops may take a lunch break. Supermarkets stay open all day, many until 9 pm. *Traiteurs* and bakeries are open on Sunday mornings to supply the traditional Sunday lunch, as are outdoor markets. Most shops are closed on Monday, except supermarkets. In the summer, small shops will post signs announcing their *fermeture annuelle*, sometimes for the entire month of July or August. Supermarkets stay open, but some outdoor markets have a reduced number of stalls, and some groceries close altogether until the *rentrée* in September.

- *Alimentation générale*: grocery; *Epicerie*: small grocery
- *Boucherie*: meat market; *Boucherie chevaline*: horse-meat butcher
- *Boulangerie*: bakery; *Pâtisserie*: pastry store
- *Brûlerie/torrefaction*: coffees and teas
- *Charcuterie*: delicatessen
- *Confiserie/chocolatier*: candy, handmade chocolates
- *Fromagerie*: cheese store
- *Poissonnerie*: fish market

- *Rôtisserie*: spit-roasted meat and chicken
- *Traiteur*: prepared foods to take out
- *Triperie*: tripe and innards
- *Volailler*: poultry shop

You can find temperature conversion tables and equivalent meat cuts and food names in *Bloom Where You Are Planted*, published by the Women of the American Church. Note that *gros* indicates a wholesale market and *détail* is retail.

As Europe is on the metric system, people used to ounces and pounds will have to convert to grams and kilograms when looking at a food package. One thousand milligrams equals one gram, and one thousand grams equals a kilo, which is slightly over two pounds. With fresh produce, however, it is common to ask for *une livre* (a pound).

THE MARKETS

Shopping at the *marché* (food market) is one of the most pleasant aspects of French life. Vendors sell fish, meat, and the freshest of produce, and the quality is generally very high. Some sell candies, clothes, and gadgets. The markets listed below are *couverts* (covered) and permanent and are open daily, except Monday. Generally they close for lunch, open up again around 4 pm and close around 7 pm. Covered markets usually have only food items and flowers. Not all markets are equal in range of merchandise, quality, or price.

Remember that most often the vendor selects the produce. It is not taken kindly when a customer paws through the merchandise, although this is changing. After filling your order, the *commerçant* may ask, "*avec ceci?*" asking what else you would like. If you need nothing more, say "*ça sera tout, merci*" ("that's all, thanks") or something else polite that indicates you are finished.

- *3e*—**Rue de Bretagne**: Marché des Enfants-Rouges.
- *3e*—**Marché du Temple**: rue Perrée.

- 6e — **St-Germain:** At rue Mabillon. The old Marché Saint Germain, now incorporated into a shopping mall.
- 8e — **Rue Corvetto**: Marché Europe.
- 8e — **Rue de Castellane**: Between rue Tronchet and rue de l'Arcade.
- 10e — **Boulevard de Magenta** at Gare de l'Est: Marché St-Quentin, one of Paris' old covered markets.
- 12e — **Place d'Aligre**: The inexpensive, international Marché Beauvau. Also an extensive outdoor section
- 16e — **Rue St-Didier**: At rue Mesnil. Oriental rice, traditional produce, plus herbs and staple goods.
- 16e — **Rue Bois-le-Vent**: Marché de Passy.
- 19e — **Rue Secrétan**: A lively market near Place Stalingrad.

Open-air floating markets (*marché volant*) are in every *arrondissement* and are open on certain days in one location, moving elsewhere on others. Markets are generally open 8 am–1:00 pm; many areas have several open on different days or offering a different selection of vendors. Each market has its own personality: some have an international flavor to match that of the area. The *Annuaire Soleil* for each area lists all the nearby markets.

- 5e — **Place Monge**: Wednesday, Friday, and Sunday.
- 5e — **Maubert-Mutualité**. Tuesday, Thursday, and Saturday.
- 5e — **Boulevard Port-Royal**: Tuesday, Thursday, and Saturday.
- ◉ 6e — **Boulevard Raspail**: On Sunday: the **Marché Biologique** with organic products.
- 7e — **Avenue de Saxe**: Elegant market with a view of the Eiffel Tower. Thursday and Saturday.
- 11e — **Boulevard Richard-Lenoir**: Thursday and Sunday.
- 11e and 20e — **Boulevard de Belleville**: African specialties. Tuesday, Friday, and Sunday.
- 12e — **Daumesnil**: At boulevard de Reuilly. One of the largest markets. Tuesday and Friday.
- 13e — **Boulevard Auguste-Blanqui**: Tuesday, Friday, and Sunday.

221

- 15e — **Boulevard de Grenelle**: At rue Lourmel. Wednesday and Sunday.
- 15e — **Rue St-Charles**: Tuesday and Friday.
- 15e — **Rue de la Convention**: At rue de Vaugirard. Tuesday, Thursday, and Sunday.
- 16e — **Rue des Belles-Feuilles**. Starting at avenue Victor-Hugo.
- 16e — **Avenue du Président-Wilson**. Near Place d'Iéna. Wednesday and Saturday.
- 17e — **Batignolles**: Saturday morning organic market on boulevard des Batignolles.
- 18e — **Rue du Poteau:** At Place Jules-Joffrin, with good shops lining the street.
- 18e — **Rue Dejean**: Small pedestrian street between rue des Poissonniers and rue Poulet. Daily market.
- 18e — **Marché Barbès**: At boulevard de la Chapelle. Wednesday and Saturday. Beware of pickpockets.
- 20e — **Place de la Réunion**: Funky, interesting, international market. Thursday and Sunday; organic foods.

A *rue commerçante* is a street lined with food emporiums. Most are open Sunday morning and closed on Monday. Many are pedestrian streets, creating a *marché* atmosphere. In small shops that are not *libre-service* (self-service), you may be asked to pay at the *caisse* (cashier) after ordering your food, then to bring the receipt back to the counter to receive the packages. When paying, always count your change. Streets frequented by tourists, such as rue Mouffetard and rue de Buci, may have higher prices than streets catering to locals.

- 2e — **Rue Montorgueil**: Pedestrians only. Charming street of shops and cafés.
- 5e — **Rue Mouffetard**: Paris' most famous *rue commerçante*. Clothes, shoes, and household items.
- 6e — **Rue de Buci**: Famous *rue commerçante* with high-quality *traiteurs* and two small supermarkets.

Photo: Zeny Cieslikowski

Fruit stands offer beautifully presented, fresh, gourmet produce.

- *7e* — **Rue Cler** at **avenue de la Motte-Picquet**: High-quality, two-street-long *rue commerçante.*
- *14e* — **Rue Daguerre**: Pedestrians only, in a residential neighborhood near Denfert-Rochereau.
- *17e* — **Rue de Lévis**: Pedestrians only; old-time village atmosphere.
- *17e* — **Rue Poncelet**: Beginning at avenue des Ternes, an upscale market street.
- *18e* — **Rue Lepic**: An internationally known market street at the foot of Montmartre.

SUPERMARKETS

Supermarket chains ensure convenient one-stop shopping in just about every *quartier*; they are all *libre-service*. They range from the

223

elegant international food halls of **Marks and Spencer** and **Le Bon Marché** (see below), to the reliable, well-stocked **Monoprix** and **Franprix**, down to the unadorned **Leader Price** and **ED L'Epicier**, the original cheap supermarket chain, with its sometimes sparse stock. The department store **La Samaritaine** (Building 4) has a supermarket with a selection of international packaged goods.

People often head for the *banlieue* where gigantic *hypermarchés* offer a wide selection and low prices and also carry electronics and household items. These include **Auchan, Casino, Intermarché,** and **Carrefour**. Most supermarkets close on Sunday, and those that are open close on Monday. In the outlying areas, many are open Sunday morning. **Prisunic** at 103, rue La Boétie 75008 at the Champs-Elysées is open daily until midnight and closed Sunday (tel: 01.42.25.27.46).

Small shopping baskets are by the entrance to each supermarket. Wheeled *caddies* (carts) may be linked together by a lock, requiring the insertion of a 10F deposit, which is returned when the cart is reinserted into the rack. Plastic *sacs* (bags) are provided, but expect to bag the groceries yourself. The charge for home delivery depends on the amount spent. **Telemarket** is a telephone order supermarket; phone for a catalogue (tel: 01.53.26.55.00). See *Supermarchés et hypermarchés* in the Yellow Pages.

- 13e — **Tang Frères**: 44-48, avenue d'Ivry (tel: 01.45.70.80.00). Large Asian supermarket.
- 13e — **Supermarché Paris Store**: 21, avenue d'Ivry (tel: 01.42. 06.98.44). Asian supermarket and variety store.

FOOD HALLS

In addition to the supermarkets, food halls (usually in department stores) offer upscale and international selections, most often with high prices.

- 7e — **La Grande Epicerie de Paris**: 38, rue de Sèvres (tel: 01.44.39.80.00). Lovely food hall at the Bon Marché, with a vast international selection. Excellent baked goods, meats, fish, and *traiteur*.

- 9*e* — **Galeries Lafayette Gourmet**: 40, boulevard Haussmann (tel: 01.42.82.34.56). Beautifully presented, fresh, gourmet foods, bakery, small counters for tasting or a quick lunch.
- 9*e* and 4*e* — **Marks & Spencer**: 35, boulevard Haussmann (tel: 01.47.42.42.91). Outpost of the British department store chain. British staples, frozen foods, and international specialties. Fresh produce and breads; also at 88, rue de Rivoli (tel: 01.44.61. 08.00). Other locations in the suburbs.

GROCERIES FOR HOMESICK ANGLOPHONES

Do Americans need an Oreo once in a while, or do the English pine for Hobnobs? The shops below specialize in items from Anglophone countries. Make sure the packages have not passed the expiration date, although packaged goods can last longer than the date indicates. Supermarkets and food halls carry international packaged goods. Selection changes, so buy several of an item you particularly like.

The Pantry at 13, rue Charles-d'Orleans 78540 Vernouillet is a telephone-order service for speedily delivered, well-priced, American and British packaged foods (tel: 01.39.65.82.24). Call for a catalogue.

- 1*er* and 6*e* — **The Bagel Place**: 6, place Ste-Opportune (tel: 01.40.28.96.40). New York-style bagels, flavored cream cheeses, muffins, cheesecake, apple pie, etc; also at 24, place St-André-des-Arts (tel: 01.56.24.08.64).
- 2*e* — **Pickwick's**: 8, rue Mandar (tel: 01.40.26.06.58). British grocery off rue Montorgueil, with a reasonable selection of tinned goods, biscuits, sweets, etc.
- 3*e* — **The Bagel Store**: 31, rue de Turenne (tel: 01.44.78.06.05).

225

Small café, selling fresh bagels, cream cheese, other spreads and salads, and a few packaged American groceries.

- *4e* — **Thanksgiving**: 20, rue St-Paul (tel: 01.42.77.68.29). American grocery and restaurant, some homemade foods to take out. Closed Monday.
- *7e* and *16e* — **The General Store**: 82, rue de Grenelle (tel: 01. 45.48.63.16). American groceries, wines, and beer. American pies made to order. Also, 30, rue de Longchamp (tel: 01.47. 55.41.14).
- *7e* — **The Real McCoy**: 194, rue de Grenelle (tel: 01.45.56. 98.82). Small American grocery.
- *10e* — **Saveurs d'Irlande**: 5, cité Wauxhall (tel: 01.42.00.36.20). Irish products at reasonable prices, from smoked salmon to whiskey, bacon, and cheeses.

INTERNATIONAL GROCERIES

Many international shops are clustered around *rues commerçantes*, and the entire area of Belleville is international in flavor — Asian, African, Jewish. Many Japanese shops are found in the *2e*. The *13e* is a focal point for the Asian community. Indian groceries can be found in the Passage Brady in the *10e*, and some Indian packaged goods can be found at the Grande Epicerie. Supermarkets carry some lines of international foods, such as Old El Paso, Häagen Dazs, and Ben and Jerry's ice cream, as do the food halls mentioned above.

TRAITEURS

Traiteur means caterer. Almost every neighborhood has small *traiteurs* with *plats à emporter* (prepared dishes to take away). *Charcuteries*, particularly known for the variety of their smoked and salted pork products, also have prepared dishes, and the two categories overlap slightly (see Meat Markets below). As one would expect in Paris, the selection is mouthwatering, from stewed rabbit and guinea fowl in fricassee sauces to roasted chickens and loin of veal or beef. Potatoes, rice, vegetables, salads, and desserts round out a full meal. Dishes change according to what is in season. Monoprix has a serviceable take-out department, and the *traiteurs* at the food halls are excellent. The Asian *traiteurs* are the least expensive.

Some *traiteurs* are particularly well-known for their artistic and flavorful creations, with prices to match. The elegant **Fauchon** at 26, place de la Madeleine 75008 is by far the most famous and wide-ranging. Its series of small shops and cafés dominate two sides of the square (tel: 01.47.42.60.11). **Flo Prestige, Dalloyau**, and **Hédiard**, well-known for their high quality and extensive range of creations, all have several locations. Branches of **La Comtesse du Barry** sell *foie gras, pâté*, and exotic packaged and canned foods, soups, and other prepared dishes. Look in your nearby *rue commerçante*, and see *Traiteurs* in the Yellow Pages.

NATURAL FOODS

In addition to the organic markets, some groceries sell natural products. Look for products that say *nourriture bio* or just *bio*. In the suburbs of Neuilly, Boulogne, and Montreuil-sous-Bois are **Biocoop Les Nouveaux Robinson,** supermarkets that carry an extensive selection of organic products. **Naturalia** and **La Vie Claire** are chains for organic foods and other natural items. Look also in the restaurants mentioned in the previous chapter. *Vivre bio a Paris* by Catherine Mercadier is a French guide to natural foods in Paris.

- *4e* — **Grand Appétit**: 9, rue de la Cerisaie (tel: 01.40.27.04.95)
- *5e* — **Rendezvous de la Nature**: 96, rue Mouffetard (tel: 01.43. 36.59.34)
- *6e* — **Les Herbes du Luxembourg**: 3 rue de Médicis (tel: 01.43. 26.91.53)
- *14e* — **Alésia Biocoop**: 4 bis, rue Thibaud (tel: 01.45.53.08.00)
- *15e* — **Côté Vert**: 332, rue Lecourbe (tel: 01.40.60.60.66)
- *19e* — **Canal Bio**: 46 bis, quai de la Loire (tel: 01.42.06.44.44)

227

EATING OUT AT HOME

Just about any type of cooked meal can be delivered *à domicile*. These include restaurants of all price levels and ethnic orientation, *traiteurs*, and pizza emporiums. *Paris à Domicile* and *Home Services, Paris* are guides to businesses that deliver. Generally, a business name that starts with *Allô* offers telephone orders for home delivery of products or services. See *Restauration à domicile* in the Yellow Pages.

FROZEN FOOD

People who work late cannot always get to the stores in time to buy the appropriate ingredients for a meal. Thus, despite the abundance of markets and supermarkets, frozen food (*les surgelés*) is handy. In addition to prepared dishes ready to reheat, frozen ingredients, such as herbs, *crème fraîche*, fish filets, meats, cleaned vegetables, and desserts, are available.

The high-quality chain **Picard** has some 50 outlets in Paris. A monthly catalogue details special offers (info tel: 08.01.13.12.11; order tel: 08.03.03.90.39; Minitel 3614 PICARD). Look for shop signs that say *surgelés*. See *Surgelés: produits alimentaires* in the Yellow Pages.

BAKERIES

A *pâtisserie* specializes in desserts and often sells breads. A *boulangerie* sells bread and simple desserts as well. The distinctions overlap, and good cakes may be found in many bakeries; nonetheless, the *pâtisserie* will have refined offerings, beautifully decorated and presented. Neighborhood bakers of both types generally sell sandwiches and quiches.

Bread is *always* fresh in Paris. By law, *boulangeries* must choose their own flour and knead and bake their bread on their premises. Otherwise they may not call themselves *boulangeries*. Bakeries, *boulangeries* or not, may have a sign that says *tradition française* or *pain maison* meaning that *baguettes* (sticks), the everyday bread staple of French life, are baked on the premises. A second popular bread is the *pain de campagne*, a more substantial bread made by blending different flours. Some bakeries sell the newly popular *rétro*, which is heavier and denser and keeps longer than the more modern bread. This bread is sometimes called *tradition, passion,* or *à l'ancienne* and is generally made with unbleached flour and non-chemical leaven. A current favorite is the *boule*, a round, dark-colored country-style bread with a crunchy crust.

The weight and price of baguettes are government regulated; those of specialty breads are not. Some bakeries get around this by sprinkling the bread with flour and calling it a *baguette campagnarde*. Not all breads are equal and, of course, some *boulangeries* are better than others. With more than 1,000 in Paris, just shop around until you find what suits you best.

- *Baguette*: long bread made from flour, water, yeast, and salt. *Demi-baguette*: half a baguette. *Ficelle*: thin and crispy baguette.
- *Brioche*: sweet, buttery roll or bread made with eggs.
- *Croissant*: crescent-shaped pastry rolls, generally eaten at breakfast: without butter is *nature*, with butter, *au beurre*; *au chocolat* (not crescent-shaped) is chocolate-filled.
- *Pain*: bread loaf. *Bâtard*: loaf, similar to but thicker than a baguette. *Petit pain*: roll. *Pain de campagne*: country-style, variously shaped. *Miche*: large country bread. *Pain au levain*: sourdough.
- *Pain de mie*: sandwich bread, which can be ordered sliced.

For breakfast, baguettes are sliced lengthwise and buttered and/or spread with jam. At lunch, the bread is often used for sandwiches, and at dinner it is torn off in chunks. This is all done immediately before eating, as baguettes, made with no fat, tend to dry out quickly. Bread is baked early in the morning, late in the afternoon, and on Sunday mornings, when shops are open until lunchtime. Buy bread just before you want to eat it, but understand that everyone else is doing the same. On Sunday mornings, for example, expect to wait in line. Supermarkets carry both fresh and packaged breads. Note also that baguettes are generally not wrapped but instead are handed to the customer with a small paper square to hold while transporting home.

Pâtisseries specialize in exquisitely decorated *gâteaux* (cakes) and *tartes* (fruit pies or tarts). Some are particularly known for their elegant creations, and there is some overlap in category with chocolate shops (see below) such as the elegant multi-store **Lenôtre** and **Dalloyau**.

- *Baba au rhum:* brioche dough baked in small molds and soaked in rum
- *Charlotte russe*: ladyfingers around whipped cream
- *Dacquoise*: meringue of nuts, sugar, and shaved chocolate, layered and laced with butter or whipped cream
- *Eclair*: pastry filled with cream, topped with icing
- *Financier*: almond cake; *Madeleine*: small almond tea-cake
- *Merveille*: hot sugared doughnut
- *Mille-feuilles:* layers of pastry filled with cream, dusted with sugar
- *Palmier:* sugared, crisp cookies shaped like palm leaves
- *Sablé*: shortbread, variously flavored with chocolate or almond
- *Savarin*: large molded cake made of baba dough, sprinkled with rum and filled with cream

Each *quartier* has its *boulangeries* and *pâtisseries*, and although many close in August, at least one bakery in your neighborhood stays open. Some *traiteurs* offer desserts, and the supermarkets and food halls also sell pastries. Small bakeries generally close for lunch and then reopen until 8 pm. See *Boulangeries* or *Pâtisseries* in the Yellow Pages. Also see Kosher Foods below. Some personal favorites:

- 2e—**Stohrer**: 51, rue Montorgueil (tel: 01.42.33.38.20).

Beautiful *traiteur* founded in 1730; one of the city's best *pâtisseries* and chocolate makers. Specialty is a creamed cake *puits d'amour* (well of love).

- 6e — **Gérard Mulot**: 76, rue de Seine (tel: 01.43.26.85.77). Outstanding *boulanger, traiteur, pâtissier, chocolatier*; lovely creations, beautiful presentation.
- 6e and 15e — **Lionel Poilâne**: 8, rue du Cherche-Midi (tel: 01.45.48.42.59). One of the most celebrated bakers in Paris. Country-style breads. Also at 49, boulevard de Grenelle (tel: 01.45.79.11.49).
- 7e — **Poujauran**: 20, rue Jean-Nicot (tel: 01.47.05.80.88). *Baguettes biologiques*, nut and fruit breads, and chocolate cake.
- 15e and 1er — **Max Poilâne**: 87, rue Brancion (tel: 01.48.28.45.90). Sourdough and other specialty breads; also at 42, place du Marché-St-Honoré (tel: 01.42.61.10.53).
- 20e — **Ganachaud**: 150, rue de Ménilmontant (tel: 01.46.36.13.82). Exotic breads from wood-fired ovens.

FISH

Paris is close to the coasts of both Normandy and Brittany, so fish is generally fresh and plentiful. Fish is sold fresh at supermarkets and at the *poissonnerie* daily except Monday; it is also sold at outdoor markets. The largest true fish market in the city is an unmarked white building at the corner of rue de Castagnary and rue des Morillons, toward the southern edge of the 15e. Prices are good, and as in all *poissonneries*, there is someone to bone and slice fish. Look for the lighthouse with the sign honoring the fishermen: *"Gloire à nos marins pêcheurs."*

A large selection of *poisson* (fish) and *fruits de mer* (shellfish) is available, some of which, such as shrimp, may be precooked. The *poissonnier* will price a whole fish by weight and clean it. Fish comes in *filets* or *darnes* (steaks) and is priced by weight or the piece. Almost all *poissonneries* make fish soups. In supermarkets, soups and fish preparations are usually in refrigerators near the fish counters. Inspect the packing and expiration dates on the packages. The shops below are especially well stocked. See *Poissonneries* in the Yellow Pages.

- 12*e* — **Pêcheries Côtières**: 231, rue de Charenton (tel: 01.46. 28.41.37).
- 13*e* — **Poissonnerie Fortune des Mers**: 53, avenue d'Italie (tel: 01.45.85.76.83).
- 14*e* and 17*e* — **Daguerre Marée**: 9, rue Daguerre (tel: 01.43. 22.13.52); also at 4, rue Bayen (tel: 01.43.80.16.29).
- 14*e* — **Poissonnerie du Dôme**: 4, rue Delambre (tel: 01.43. 35.23.95).

Smoked fish is also popular, and the supermarkets have refrigerated sections for smoked fish from all over the world. **Comptoir du Saumon** sells smoked salmon and other smoked fish, caviar, and the vodka to accompany it, with snack bars for eating in. See *Epiceries fines* and *gastronomie (spécialités exotique or spécialités régionales)* in the Yellow Pages.

- 7*e* — **Pétrossian**: 18, boulevard de la Tour-Maubourg (tel: 01.44.11.32.22). World-famous purveyor of caviars, smoked fish, foie gras and truffles. Prices match its reputation.
- 8*e* — **La Maison du Caviar**: 21, rue Quentin-Bauchart (tel: 01.47.23.53.43). Eat in or take out caviar or smoked fishes in an elegant setting. Open until 2 am. Retail shop at 1, rue Vernet (tel: 01.40.70.06.39).
- 15*e* — **La Maison de l'Escargot**: 79, rue Fondary (tel: 01.45. 75.31.09). Well-prepared snails, ready to cook.
- 15*e* — **Le Comptoir du Caviar**: 130, rue Lecourbe (tel: 01.45. 30.31.60). Caviar, smoked salmon. Good prices.

KOSHER FOODS

Paris abounds with kosher groceries, *traiteurs*, butchers, and bakeries, and many restaurants are also *traiteurs*. See the comprehensive *Le Guide des Bonnes Adresses Cacher in France* by Guy Saint-Père. In general, look in rue des Rosiers (especially for the well-known bakeries **Contini** or **Korcarz**), around rues Richer and Cadet in the 9e, and by boulevard de Belleville in the 20e. As noted in the previous chapter, some shops are *cacher* but do not pay the fees to the Consistoire for the *Beth Din* certification.

- 9e, 11e, and 19e—**André**: 7, rue Geoffroy-Marie (tel: 01.47. 70.49.03). Small chain of butchers with well-cut and prepared meats and *charcuterie*. Also at 69, boulevard de Belleville (tel: 01.43.57.80.38); 135, rue Manin (tel: 01.42.38.00.43).
- 9e, 17e, and 19e—**Berbèche**: 46, rue Richer (tel: 01.47.70.50.58). Well-prepared meats, poultry, *charcuterie*; 30, rue Jouffroy-d'Abbans (tel: 01.44.40.07.59); 15, rue Henri-Ribière (tel: 01.42.08.06.06).

Some "Jewish-style" delicatessens offer kosher products. Try the famous **Jo Goldenberg** at 7, rue des Rosiers 75004 (tel: 01.48.87.20.16) and both **Finkelsztajn's** at 27, rue des Rosiers 75004 (tel: 01.42.72.78.91) and 24, rue des Ecouffes (tel: 01.48. 87.92.85). Finkelsztajn's has the best rye bread in Paris. **Goldenberg** at 69, avenue de Wagram 75017 sells kosher products and its *charcuterie* is kosher (tel: 01.42.27.34.79).

MEAT MARKETS

Meats in France are excellent. French lamb is world-famous, and beef, pork, and veal are all available at the *boucherie*. Cuts may be unfamiliar to you, but if you describe to the *boucher* what you want, he can provide it. All meats except horse meat are sold at the *boucherie*.

Note that few growth hormones are used in raising cattle. This means the meat may not be particularly tender and will require longer cooking time or thinner cuts. Meat is not aged very long, so its texture may be different from what you are used to. Chopped or minced meat is usually ground to order and should

233

be cooked and eaten the day of purchase. In fact, butchers generally cut meats to order, rather than prepackaging them, and some are known for particular specialty cuts and artistic creations. Although butchers are often closed on Mondays, the supermarkets have fresh meat every day, either packaged or freshly cut. See *Boucheries, boucheries-charcuteries* in the Yellow Pages and *Kosher Foods* above.

- *6e* — **Au Bell Viandier**: 4, rue Lobineau, at the Marché St-Germain (tel: 01. 40.46.82.82)
- *7e* — **Marc Tattevin Palais de la Viande**: 15, rue du Champs-de-Mars (tel: 01.47.05.07.02)
- *8e* — **Boucherie Marbeuf**: 35, rue Marbeuf (tel: 01.49.53.06.66)
- *16e* — **Boucherie Lamartine**: 172, avenue Victor-Hugo (tel: 01.47.27.82.29)

Other meat shops are more specialized. Flavorful, lean horse meat, less popular than heretofore, is sold in all cuts at the *boucherie chevaline*. *Marchands de volaille* or *volaillers* specialize in poultry. Some sell hot, cooked poultry and other meats, such as pork ribs or rabbit, cooked on the *tournebroche* (rotisserie). Most shops make a distinction, both in quality and price, between the *poulet fermier*, which is a free-range chicken, and the ordinary *poulet*. Many butchers also sell roasted chickens. (See *Volailles et gibiers* in the Yellow Pages.) The *triperie* sells innards, such as liver, kidneys, tripe, and sausages, such as *boudin* and *andouillette*.

Ham and fresh pork products can be bought at both the *boucherie* and *charcuterie*, although the latter is traditionally known for its pork products and has a wider range of sausages and *pâtés* and a larger selection of prepared take-out foods and salads. Both supermarkets and the *charcuteries* have a selection of thin-sliced *jambons de pays* (hams) from different regions of France, the most famous being the *jambon de Bayonne*. The kosher *charcuteries* sell the same types of products, made with beef or turkey, not pork.

234

FROMAGERIES

It was Charles de Gaulle who about fifty years ago asked rhetorically, "How can you govern, in peacetime, a people with 325 different kinds of cheese?" Currently there are some 400 cheeses, ranging from the ancient *roquefort*, said to have been a favorite of Charlemagne, to *Boursin*, a modern addition of the twentieth century. Cheese is an important part of the French *cuisine* and an interesting conversation point at any table.

Cheese is grouped into families according to their similar production, texture, flavor, and nutritive value. They are from the milk of a *vache* (cow), *brebis* (sheep), or *chèvre (*goat), each with its own flavor. They may be aged or not. They may be made from whole or skim milk, pasteurized or not (*lait cru*). They may be hard, semi-soft, or soft, and in many stages between. They may be white, creamy yellow, orange, or brown. They come in large wheels or small disks, sliced, cut, or whole. Some have edible molds and rinds, and some cheeses are seasonal. This vast variety of cheeses means, in fact, that most have not been exported. Newcomers from countries in which cheeses are pasteurized may not have tasted the most exquisite of the French cheeses, and a very pleasant education is in store.

Supermarkets and food halls carry packaged, pasteurized cheeses as well as freshly cut, unpasteurized cheeses, which are more flavorful. The best cheeses are found at the *fromageries* and *crémeries* that also sell butter, eggs, and milk. (Milk often comes in boxes marked *UHT/Ultra-Haute Température* that may be kept unrefrigerated for many months before opening.) Butter is most flavorful when cut fresh from a large slab (*beurre à la motte*); it comes *demi-sel* (lightly salted) or *doux* (sweet). In general, cheese is aged on the premises of the *fromagerie* but not at the *crémerie*. For same-day eating, soft and semi-soft cheese will be *bien fait* (perfectly ripe); for later eating, it should be *pas trop fait* (not quite ripe). Every *quartier* has its own cheese shops, each carrying a slightly different variety.

235

Cheese is served between the *plat principal* and the *dessert*, and it should be served at room temperature. Some people do not refrigerate their cheeses, keeping them instead in a special, layered, cheese container. If you choose to refrigerate, keep each cheese wrapped separately, so as not to mix flavors. Some cheeses keep longer than others, and uncut cheeses continue to age.

At dinner, serve cheeses of different textures and flavors. A *plateau de fromage* generally offers at least one mild and one strong cheese, a blue, and a variety of soft, semi-soft and hard. Begin with the mildest and move on to the strong. See *Crémeries, fromageries* in the Yellow Pages.

At **Androuet** 6, rue Arsène-Houssaye 75008 you can try a variety of cheese dishes on the premises, as well as choose from a mouthwatering selection of cut cheese (tel: 01.42.89.95.00). The same is true of the excellent **Saint Hubert**: 17-19 rue d'Antin 75002 (tel: 01.42.65.42.74) and 21, rue Vignon 75008 (tel: 01.47.42.79.20).

- *7e* — **Barthélémy**: 51, rue de Grenelle (tel: 01.45.48.56.75)
- *14e* — **Jacques Vernier**: 71, avenue du Général-Leclerc (tel: 01.43.27.93.30)
- *16e* — **Lillo**: 25, rue des Belles-Feuilles (tel: 01.47.27.69.08)
- *17e* — **Alléosse**: 13, rue Poncelet (tel: 01.46.22.50.45)
- *17e* — **Alain Dubois**: 80, rue Tocqueville (tel: 01.42.27.11.38); 79, rue de Courcelles (tel: 01.43.80.36.42)

TEA AND COFFEE

International packaged teas and coffees are in supermarkets and food halls, and some shops sell coffee beans as well. Fresh coffee beans are sold at *brûleries/torréfactions*, many of which are known for their particular selections. Some work with the customer to determine the preferred blend and then keep the recipe on file. *Torréfactions* generally offer a selection of fresh teas as well, but try the shops dedicated to tea lovers — **Mariage Frères** is the most

outstanding—which specialize in teas and the leaves for herbal *tisanes* and *infusions* (see Chapter Twelve). For English teas, try:
- 6e—**Whittard of Chelsea**: 22, rue de Buci (tel: 01.43.29.96.16). Also coffees.
- 8e—**Twining's**: 76, boulevard Haussmann (tel: 01.43.87.39.84).

CHOCOLATES

Chocolat is a year-round favorite in Paris, from the powdered hot drink found in tea rooms to the delicious creations of world-famous *chocolatiers* and down to the simple *tablettes* (bars) sold at supermarkets. Chocolates in France are so delicious because they contain a high percentage of cocoa, sometimes up to 70 percent, and the higher the percentage, the richer the confection. Even chocolate bars in supermarkets display the percentage of cocoa in each bar. Look for chocolate fish just before April Fool's Day (when people play tricks on each other, crying *"poisson d'avril"*), hearts before Valentine's Day, bunnies and chickens before Easter, and even chocolate mushrooms in the fall.

Some of the best *chocolatiers* have several locations. The most well-known is **Lenôtre**, with remarkable candies and exquisite presentation. The varied **Dalloyau** has many outlets, as do the more traditional **Maison du Chocolat** and **Jadis et Gourmande. Debauve & Gallais**, one of the city's oldest and most venerated *chocolatiers*, has three locations, and **La Maison des Bonbons** has two. Belgian *chocolatiers* **Godiva, Jeff de Bruges, Daskalidès,** and **De Neuville** all have stores throughout the city. See *Confiseries, chocolateries* in the Yellow Pages.
- 1er—**La Fontaine au Chocolat**: 201, rue St-Honoré (tel: 01.42.44.11.66).
- 6e—**Christian Constant**: 26, rue du Bac (tel: 01.47.03.30.00).
- 7e—**Richart**: 258, boulevard St-Germain (tel: 01.45.55.66.00).
- 9e—**A la Mère de Famille**: 35, rue du Faubourg-Montmartre (tel: 01.47.70.83.69).

WINE

When choosing a wine, it is often helpful to describe the meal to be served with the proprietor of the *cave*. Be clear as to the desired price range of the wine, and he will suggest the most appropriate wine, according to color and taste and the course with which it will be served. Discuss also the temperature the wine should be when served. In summer, some red wines are served slightly chilled. Note that the shape of the bottle varies according to type of wine and the region. The percentage of alcohol must be printed on the label, and this varies as well.

In addition to the local *caves* (wine shops), there are reliable chains with wines of all categories and prices. **Nicolas**, a franchise operation with more than 200 shops in Paris, has at least one shop in each *arrondissement*. The advice of the *caviste* is only as good as the owner of each franchise, but most are fairly knowledgeable. **Repaire de Bacchus**, another franchise, has more than twenty shops throughout the city. Most shops will deliver wines depending on how much is bought.

Supermarkets also have extensive selections of domestic wines; during the October *Foire aux vins*, the supermarkets offer a broader selection and knowledgeable sales personnel. Some, such as Carrefour, bottle wines under their own label. Galeries Lafayette Gourmet Food Hall and the Bon Marché have interesting selections, occasional promotional sales, and opportunities for tasting. *Traiteurs*, such as Fauchon and Hédiard, are particularly well-stocked and helpful in their advice. See *Caves* and *Vins et spiritueux* in the Yellow Pages.

La Dernière Goutte at 6, rue de Bourbon-le-Château 75006 has wine tastings on Saturdays and is open on Sunday (tel: 01.43.29.11.62). The American proprietor specializes in estate-bottled wines.

- 2e and 13e — **Cave Legrand**: 1, rue de la Banque (tel: 01.42. 60.07.12). Well-priced *vins de pays*, vintage wines, *eaux-de-vie*

Photo: Zeny Cieslikowski

Wines from the many vinyards of France.

and other brandies. Also at 119, rue du Dessous-des-Berges (tel: 01.45.83.58.88).

- *7e* — **Ryst-Dupeyron**: 79, rue du Bac (tel: 01.45.48.80.93). Known for its family-produced armagnac and aged calvados, wines from Bordeaux. Catalogue available.
- *8e* — **Les Caves Taillevent**: 199, rue du Faubourg-St-Honoré (tel: 01.45.61.14.19). A vast assortment of wines, plus regular Saturday morning wine tastings.
- *8e* — **Les Caves Augé**: 116, boulevard Haussmann (tel: 01.45.22. 16.97). Prestigious shop. Old wines and some reasonably priced younger ones.
- *14e* and *16e* — **Les Caves du Savour Club**: 120, boulevard du Montparnasse (tel: 01.43.27.12.06); 11-13 rue Gros (tel: 01.42. 30.94.18). Both shops have drive-up entries for loading wine into your car. Wines of all qualities and price ranges. Wine tasting. Catalogue for telephone orders; home delivery.

239

CHAPTER FOURTEEN

KEEPING FIT

SPECTATOR SPORTS

The French, although passionate sport spectators, are not known for being extremely *sportifs* themselves. This is changing however, as younger people are becoming fitness conscious. Gymnasiums are opening all across Paris, jogging is popular, roller blades are catching on, and some main city streets have bicycle paths. Paris offers an extensive system of public sports facilities, including tennis courts, swimming pools, gyms, and tracks, all increasingly crowded.

The main indoor public arena is the **Palais Omnisports Paris-Bercy** at 8, boulevard de Bercy 75012. It holds football matches, ice-skating competitions, horse events, tennis and volleyball matches, and rock concerts. The **Parc des Princes** is a 50,000-seat outdoor stadium at which football and rugby games are played and musical concerts held. At the southern tip of the Bois de Boulogne, it is at 24, rue Commandant-Guilbaud 75016.

The French are avid football fans (soccer to Americans). The Paris team is **Paris St-Germain Football Club (PSG)**. The football season runs from the end of July through the following April. Season tickets are available, and single tickets may be purchased at Parc des Princes or at ticket agencies. (See Chapter Seventeen.) Buy tickets well in advance, for the important matches sell out early. The 80,000-seat **Grande Stade de France**, constructed in St-Denis to hold the finals of the World Cup matches in 1998, will also hold sporting events, although at this writing they have yet to be scheduled.

Horse races are also popular. The **Hippodrome d'Auteuil** and **Hippodrome de Longchamp** are in the Bois de Boulogne, and each has its particular racing season and events. The **Hippodrome de Vincennes** in the Bois de Vincennes is known for its trotting meets. Bets may be made at the track or off-track through the *pari mutuel urbain* (*PMU*) at many *tabacs*. For information, see *Paris Turf*, a racing magazine.

Fun to watch or play is the typically French *pétanque* (also called *boules*), in which metal balls are thrown toward a small spherical target. It can be played anywhere there is a level surface, and it is played in town squares all over France, with onlookers commenting on every throw. To play, you need a set of *boules*, which are available at most sporting goods stores. In Paris there are a dozen *boulodromes*, including in the Arènes de Lutèce and the Bois de Vincennes.

RESOURCES

The Paris Tourist Office has an extensive informational booklet called *Guide du Sport à Paris*, which lists all the municipal sports centers by sport and by *arrondissement*. Each *mairie* should have detailed information about the facilities available in that *arrondissement*. The **Maison des Associations de Paris**, in the Forum des Halles, 14, Grande Galerie, has information on clubs and

241

associations. It is open Tuesday–Saturday (tel: 01.42.33.74.00). Allô Sports is the citywide sports information telephone line (tel: 01.42.76.54.54); open weekdays.

The daily sports newspaper *L'Equipe* has information on all sporting events, and the weekly events guides—*Figaroscope*, *L'Officiel des Spectacles*, and *Pariscope*—are issued on Wednesdays. They list some individual sports venues as well.

THE TWO LARGEST PARKS

The Bois de Boulogne is at the western edge of Paris, 865 hectares that run the length of the 16e down to the suburb of Boulogne-Billancourt. It is popular with all Parisians to *pique-niquer* or *se promener* (picnic or stroll). Here are the race courses and Roland Garros, the tennis stadium that is home to the French Open. Here too are running tracks, a workout course, artificial lakes, rowboat and bicycle rentals, and swimming pools. The Parc de Bagatelle has an old castle as well as lovely rose gardens. The Jardin d'Acclimatation has a children's playground and amusement park, zoo, donkey rides, and puppet shows.

The Bois de Vincennes stretches east from the 12e. Larger than the Bois de Boulogne, it is more wooded, less built up, and often more tranquil. Jogging paths, rowboat rentals on two lakes, baseball and football fields, and a large tennis facility are some of the park's attractions. In addition, at Le Parc Floral there are playgrounds, ping-pong tables, children's theater, and a working farm. The city's largest zoo is here.

RUNNING

Parisians do not often practice *le footing* (jogging) around city streets, for traffic and pollution can be unpleasant, although some people do jog along the *quais*, which have broad sidewalks and lovely views. Many runners head for the Bois de Boulogne and its 35 km of paths that wind through meadows and around lakes or to the Bois de Vincennes and its outer circuit of almost 11 km or inner circuit of 8 km. In the city center, people run in the Tuileries, the Champ-de-Mars, in Parc Monceau, Parc des Buttes-Chaumont, Parc de Montsouris, and in the Luxembourg Gardens. See *Athlétisme* and *Les Centres Sportifs d'Athlétisme* in the *Guide du Sport*.

BICYCLING

Parisians love their *vélos*, and Paris is a wonderful city for bikers. In order to cut down on pollution, the city is encouraging bicycle riding and creating bike lanes and paths throughout Paris. There are *pistes cyclables* (bicycle paths) within the Bois de Boulogne and the Bois de Vincennes, and these are connected to a set of *pistes* that run east-west across the city and join the *piste* from the north at Canal de l'Ourcq, heading south toward Porte de Vanves.

Some of the wider streets have dedicated *couloirs vélos*, bicycle lanes marked by wide white stripes. Although bicycles use them, inline skaters and delivery vehicles do too, and some car drivers think of them as parking spaces, ignoring cyclists who then have to weave around. Drivers, although aggressive and impatient, occasionally show courtesy to bikers, probably being bikers themselves. Also, if a car hits a bicycle, the car driver is usually liable. Riding bikes outside the *couloirs* during rush hour can be extremely difficult. Do not ride through a red light, as fines for automobiles also apply to bikes.

To permit easy bicycling on Sundays, the river bank express lanes are closed to car traffic from the Tuileries tunnel to the Henri-IV tunnel, along the Canal St-Martin on the Right Bank, and all along the Left Bank, as well as in a section near rue Mouffetard. Pick up the brochure *Paris à Velo* at your *mairie*. Some of the SNCF trains have bike racks and some do not charge extra for transporting bikes. Bicycles are also for rent at many SNCF train stations in the countryside. For information on cycling, call the

Fédération de Cyclisme at 5, rue de Rome 93561 Rosny-sur-Bois Cedex (tel: 01.49.35.69.00).

If you are an avid biker, think about buying a bike and then selling it upon departure. For rentals, see *Location de cycles et motocycles* in the Yellow Pages; for used bikes, see *FUSAC*.

- *4e* — **Paris à vélo, c'est sympa**: 37, boulevard Bourdon (tel: 01.48.87.60.01). Sales, rentals, tours.
- *5e* — **Paris Vélo**: 2, rue du Fer-à-Moulin (tel: 01.43.37.59.22). Rentals, sales, tours.
- *6e* — **Point Vélos**: 83, boulevard St-Michel (tel: 01.43.54.85.36). Bicycle repair and sales.
- *10e* — **La Maison du Vélo**: 11, rue Fénelon (tel: 01.42.81.24.72). Rents, buys, sells new and used bikes.
- *11e* — **Bicloune**: 7, rue Froment (tel: 01.48.05.47.75). Rentals and sales of new and used bicycles.

CLUBS

Les Grands Clubs are privately run membership organizations that offer their thousands of members multi-sport opportunities at a variety of public sporting venues. They also sponsor competitive teams, as well as training lessons for young people.

- *13e* — **Le Paris Université Club**: 17, avenue Pierre-de-Coubertin, at Charléty Stadium (tel: 01.44.16.62.62). Body building and aerobics, tennis, judo, fencing, handball, basketball, volleyball, baseball, etc.
- *11e* — **APSAP (Association des Personnes Sportives des Administrations Parisiennes)**: 12, cour Debille (tel: 01.43.79.69.87). Martial arts, exercise programs, tennis, golf, ping-pong, basketball, bicycling, horse riding, swimming, parachuting, diving, sailing, etc.
- *16e* — **Le Stade Français**: 2, rue Commandant-Guilbaud (tel: 01.40.71.33.33). Club for the entire family. Basketball, handball, tennis, golf, skiing, swimming, dance, etc.

LES CENTRES D'ANIMATION

In the municipal sports system, *Centres d'Animation* train adults and children in a wide variety of activities. Lessons in music, dance, language, and practical arts are among the cultural offerings. There are dozens of sports courses, including martial arts, tennis, fencing, golf, basketball and other ball games, water sports, and even *pétanque*. There is a small enrollment fee. Inquire at your neighborhood sports facility and look for the semi-annual publication, *Centres d'Animations Magazine,* which details the offerings.

GYMS

The more than 100 gymnasiums throughout the city vary in their facilities and programs. Refer to the *Guide du Sport* or to *Gymnases (Mairie de Paris)* in the telephone book. The facilities can be crowded, and although they meet city standards and guidelines for cleanliness, they are all pretty basic. Private clubs are opening at a rapid rate in each neighborhood. See *Clubs de forme* and *Culture physique* in the Yellow Pages.

- **Gymnase Club**: Extensive chain of gyms, pools, and tennis courts; classes, body building, steam, sauna, etc. Membership allows access to all branches. Inquire at any Gymnase Club (info tel: 01.44.37.24.24).
- **Gymnasium**: Chain of sports centers with training programs and classes for weight loss (tel: 08.36.68.14.17).
- 15e and 17e — **Vitatop**: Two well-equipped gyms and swimming pools. Hôtel Sofitel at 8, rue Louis-Armand (tel: 01.45.54. 79.00). Hôtel Concorde-Lafayette at 1, place du Général-Koenig (tel: 01.40.68.00.21).
- 3e — **Espace Vit'Halles**: 48, rue Rambuteau at place Beaubourg (tel: 01.42.77.21.71). High-tech equipment, aerobics classes, and personal trainers. Sauna and steam, swimming. Open daily. Short-term memberships.

245

- *5e* — **Club Jean de Beauvais**: 5, rue Jean-de-Beauvais (tel: 01.46.33.16.80). Well-equipped, popular facility.

TENNIS

There are some 44 public tennis centers in Paris with more than 170 courts. To belong to the public system, residents must obtain the *carte Paris-tennis*, an identification number to use when reserving a court. Applications may be obtained from tennis centers or your *mairie*. The card takes about four weeks to process (info tel: 01.42.76.54.54). Bring identification and two photos.

Courts are always crowded. Reserve them in advance. Try the Minitel 24-hour booking service (Minitel: 3615 PARIS; RTEN). Charges are by the hour and are reasonable. It costs more to play in the evening when the courts are lit.

The French Open (known in France as *Roland-Garros*) begins the last week of May at Stade Roland-Garros. The Paris Open takes place at Bercy in November. Tickets are difficult to get except for early rounds. For information (also about membership in private clubs), call the **Fédération Française de Tennis** at Stade Roland-Garros, 2, avenue Gordon-Bennet 75016 (tel: 01.47.43.48.00).

You can also join tennis clubs, which themselves have arrangements with courts around the city. See *Tennis courts et leçons* in the Yellow Pages and *Tennis* in the White Pages.

- **Gymnase Club** operates courts throughout the Paris area. Inquire at any Gymnase Club.
- *8e* — **La Ligue de Paris de Tennis**: 109, bis avenue Mozart (info tel: 01.44.14.67.89). Tennis clubs in the outer *arrondissements*. Lessons for children and adults.
- *12e* — **Centre de Tennis de La Faluère**: Bois de Vincennes, route de la Pyramide (tel: 01.43.74.40.93); 21 crowded courts.
- *15e* — **Tennis Action**: 145, rue de Vaugirard (tel: 01.44.49.37.37). Club for tennis lessons and events.

- 15*e* — **Association Tennis Sporting-Club**: 160, avenue de Suffren (tel: 01.43.06.12.14). Club using courts in the nearby *arrondissements*.
- **Tennis de Longchamp**: 19, boulevard Anatole-France, 92100 Boulogne (tel: 01.46.03.84.49). Tennis club in the Bois de Boulogne. Twenty courts, lessons, tournaments.

SWIMMING POOLS

More than 30 municipal swimming pools are sprinkled around Paris. They are well maintained, and many are quite attractive. Swimming is one of the most accessible sports, and pools are crowded year round. This means that most pools are heavily chlorinated, and to keep bathing suits from falling apart too quickly, you should rinse them out thoroughly after each use.

During the school year, students have priority except in early morning, lunchtime, and evenings. Inquire at your pool for its schedule, especially during vacations when public access is broader. Wednesday, when there is no school, is a day to avoid. In the public pools, look to see how your clothes and valuables will be kept because some facilities are more secure than others. Buying a three-month pass allows access to any public pool, and it is one of the true bargains in Paris.

The pools below are among the most interesting. See *Piscines (établissements)* in the Yellow Pages.

- 1*er* — **Piscine Suzanne-Berlioux**: Niveau 3, Forum des Halles (tel: 01.42.36.98.44). Olympic-sized pool with skylights and a tropical motif.
- 5*e* — **Piscine de Pontoise**: 19, rue de Pontoise (tel: 01.43.54. 06.23). Pool, gym, squash, jacuzzi, and sauna.
- 12*e* — **Club Roger Le Gall**: 34, boulevard Carnot (tel: 01.44. 73.81.12). Small club with a pretty pool.
- 12*e* — **Piscine Reuilly**: 13, rue Hénard (tel: 01.40.02.08.08). The newest of the city's pools. Two pools with a view of the Jardin de Reuilly.

- 13*e* — **Piscine de la Butte-aux-Cailles**: 5, place Paul-Verlaine (tel: 01.45.89.60.05). Fed from artesian wells, there are several outdoor pools and one large indoor pool.
- 15*e* — **Armand-Massard**: 66, boulevard du Montparnasse, at the Tour Montparnasse (tel: 01.42.76.78.15). Three impressive pools.
- 16*e* — **Piscine Henri de Montherlant**: 32, boulevard Lannes (tel: 01.42.76.78.21). Extensive facilities with two pools (one for children), gym, tennis, outdoor patio.
- 17*e* — **Piscine Champerret**: 36, boulevard de Reims (tel: 01.47.66.49.98). Modern pool with spiral sliding board for children.
- 18*e* — **Piscine les Amiraux**: 6, rue Hermann-Lachapelle (tel: 01.42.76.78.25). Recently redone to its former architectural splendor.
- 18*e* — **Piscine Hébert**: 2, rue des Fillettes (tel: 01.42.76.78.24). Restored in the style of the early 1900s, a lovely pool with a retractable roof.
- 19*e* — **Piscine Georges-Hermant**: 4, rue David-d'Angers (tel: 01.42.02.45.10). Large pool with a roof that slides back in clement months.
- 20*e* — **Piscine Georges-Vallerey**: 148, avenue Gambetta (tel: 01.40.31.15.20). Built for the 1924 Olympic games; roof slides open in clement weather.

GOLF

Golf is increasingly popular in France but is expensive, especially on weekends. To play golf regularly or to obtain a handicap, you must have a permit, which may be issued on a daily, trimester, or annual basis. Inquire at the **Fédération Française de Golf** at 69, avenue Victor-Hugo 75016 (tel: 01.44.17.63.00). Ask also for information about golf tournaments in the Paris area.

There are no full-sized *parcours* (golf courses) directly in Paris, but there are many throughout Ile-de-France, including Disneyland Paris (tel: 01.60.45.68.04). Some of the clubs, such as the exclusive **Golf de St-Cloud,** have waiting lists of several years, and most require recommendations. Fortunately, many are open to non-members certain days of the week. In all, you must bring the membership card to your own club and proof of your handicap. Golf shops have information on courses in the region. Ask for the booklet *Guide du Golf: Tous les Parcours Français*, which lists all the golf courses in France and gives information about membership and handicaps.

Paris itself offers driving ranges, putting greens, and golf instruction. **American Golf**, a shop at 14, rue du Regard 75006, has information about golf courses throughout France (tel: 01. 45.49.12.52). See *Golf terrains et leçons* in the Yellow Pages, and check the *Guide du Sport* for municipal facilities with golfing opportunities.

- 6e — **Squash-Golf Rennes Raspail**: 149, rue de Rennes (tel: 01.44.39.03.30). Driving and putting practice. Training. Rental of equipment.
- 15e — **Aquagolf Ecole de Golf de Paris**: 26, rue Colonel-Pierre-Avia (tel: 01.45.57.43.06). Putting green, lessons.
- 17e — **Golf Club de l'Etoile**: 10, avenue de la Grande-Armée (tel: 01.43.80.30.79). Rooftop putting green and driving range. Equipment provided, and teaching pros available.

OTHER SPORTS

Bowling/Billiards
Commercial *bowling* alleys and *billard* (billiard) parlors can be found throughout Paris and in sports complexes such as Aquaboulevard and the Jardin d'Acclimatation (tel: 01.40.67.94.00). They generally offer French (pocketless) billiards, and sometimes American

pool and British snooker. One public center, the **Centre Sportif de la Goutte-d'Or** at 10, passage de la Goutte-d'Or 75018, has *billards* and bowling (tel: 01.42.62.52.16). Contact the **Billard Club Parisien** at 1, rue Pierre-Lescot 75001 (tel: 01.40.13.95.92). See *Bowling* and *Billards* in the Yellow Pages.

Oriental Arts

Some eighteen of the municipal sports centers offer yoga, and almost all of them offer some kind of martial arts training, including *aikido, jiu-jitsu, judo, karaté* and *taekwondo*. For information, see the *Guide du Sport*. The **Fédération Française d'Hata-Yoga,** at 50, rue Vaneau, is a teaching and practice center (tel: 01.45.44.02.59). The **Fédération Karaté et Arts Martiaux Affinitaires** is at 122, rue de la Tombe-Issoire 75014 (tel: 01.43.95.42.00). See *Arts martiaux divers (salles et leçons)* in the Yellow Pages.

Skating

- 1*er*—**Tuileries Gardens**: In winter months, a small ice-skating rink toward the rue de Rivoli.
- 17*e*—**La Main Jaune**: rue Caporal-Peugeot at place de la Porte-de-Champerret (tel: 01.47.63.26.47). Roller-skating disco.

Squash

- 18*e*—**Squash Montmartre**: 14, rue Achille-Martinet (tel: 01.42.55.38.30).
- 15*e*—**Squash Front de Seine**: 21, rue Gaston de Cavaillet (tel: 01.45.75.35.37).

Rock Climbing

Of the seven walls in Paris, the highest (21 meters) is at the **Centre Sportif Poissonniers** at 2, rue Jean-Cocteau 75018 (tel: 01.42.51.24.68). For information call the **Fédération Française de Montagne et Escalade** at 8, quai de la Marne 75019 (tel:

01.40.18.75.50). Check also with the **Club Alpin Français**, 24, avenue de Laumière 75019 (tel: 01.53.38.88.61). See *Alpinisme (clubs, associations)* in the Yellow Pages.

STEAM BATHS

What could be more relaxing than a steam bath and a massage after a long day at work? The *hammams* in Paris are clean and inviting, some even luxurious. Most have different schedules for men and women; check with the *hammam*. See *Saunas, bains (établissements)* in the Yellow Pages.

* 5e — **Hammam de la Mosquée**: 39, rue Geoffroy-St-Hilaire (tel: 01.43.31.18.14). The baths of the Islamic Mosque. Closed in August.
* 14e — **Bains d'Odessa Grands**: 5, rue d'Odessa (tel: 01.43. 20.91.21). Longest-established *hammam* in Paris.

CHAPTER FIFTEEN

SHOPPING FOR CLOTHES

HAUTE COUTURE

Paris, of course, is the capital of *haute couture*, the highest fashion in clothing. If *haute couture* affects only a few men and women who can afford many thousands of francs for a handmade suit or dress and then perhaps wear it only a few times, the fashion industry nonetheless holds a prominent position in the heart of Paris and, in fact, the world. Although Paris has been known for the French *couturiers* **Dior, Chanel, Givenchy, Hermes, Lanvin,** and **Saint Laurent,** it is also now feeling the presence of international designers, such as the German **Jill Sander**, the Italian **Giorgio Armani**, the Japanese **Issey Miyake**, and the Americans **Ralph Lauren** and **Calvin Klein**.

The famous Parisian *haute couture* fashion shows take place in January and July. But unless you are a celebrity, a fashion editor at a prominent magazine or newspaper, or a particularly heavy spender, do not expect to be invited. Many of the presentations, all intricately hand stitched, many festooned with glittering ornaments, and some cut drastically up the middle or down the side, cost more than most of us spend on our annual budget for clothes. And beautiful as the creations are, they have little to do with the experience of shopping in Paris.

Many of the *couturiers*, however, also have *prét-à-porter* (ready-to-wear) salons, selling clothes and accessories under their *griffe* (designer label). Their *prêt-à-porter* are not hand-stitched but are of high quality and expensive nonetheless. Many are housed in what is known as the Golden Triangle, near the rond-point des Champs-Elysées, in streets such as avenue Montaigne or rue François-1er and rue du Faubourg-St-Honoré. Others are scattered around the city, and some have branches in fashionably strategic parts of town. The Paris Tourist Office has a list of addresses for the major designers, and they are also listed in most guidebooks. If you are really interested in exploring a *couturier*'s line of *prêt-à-porter*, do not let the sometimes frigid attitudes of the salespeople intimidate you or dissuade you from looking around.

Top designers who are not *couturiers* are called *créateurs*. Their *prêt-à-porter*, also of the highest quality, can be quite costly, but somewhat below the range of those of the *couturiers*.

Haute couture aside, clothes in general are expensive in France, although prices remain relative to other countries. A man's suit may cost over US$100 more than in the United States but hundreds of thousands of yen less than a comparable suit in Japan. Tax on clothes (included on the price tag) may be above 20 percent. Until recently there were few outlets for imported inexpensive labels; thus Parisians traditionally purchased fewer items, but of high quality, especially classic items that would not quickly go out of style. This is why style has always been more important than fashion, and why Parisian women so often seem so carefully

253

put together, with a scarf tossed over the shoulders of a classic white blouse or a pin at the collar of a tailored dress.

Today, however, the revitalization of Paris, the inclination of tourists to spend money on clothes, and the new welcome to foreign business mean increased imports at all levels of quality and price. The presence of international chains such as **Gap, Zara,** and **Esprit** is offering new options for inexpensive yet durable clothing, especially for young people. This is making shopping in Paris much like shopping in any other city, but you can still find areas of Parisian character, if you try.

WHERE TO SHOP

This chapter does not pretend to be exhaustive in terms of shopping. There are so many *boutiques* for clothes and shoes that it would take a telephone book to list them all. Tourist guides have sections on shopping, and there are several dedicated only to shopping in Paris, including *Born to Shop* by Suzy Gershman. These guides include a range of shops, both in category and price, and they often offer some offbeat ideas that are uniquely theirs, but in general they are geared toward the tourist who has discretionary funds to spend in a limited amount of time. For shops that are deemed good value for the money, including the discount shops, see *Paris Pas Cher* and *Paris Combines*.

Most of the inner *arrondissements* have their own particular shopping areas, keeping in character and economic level of the surrounding neighborhood. In addition to the fashionable streets noted above, Place des Victoires on the Right Bank is a designer nucleus, as is the area around Place des Vosges. At the top of the 16e is avenue Victor-Hugo, leading down toward aristocratic Passy, both known for an upmarket flavor.

On the Left Bank, shops on boulevard St-Germain and to its sides are increasingly fashionable. Some international top designers are opening their own boutiques to the dismay of the

254

longtime residents who would like to keep the village atmosphere of the area intact. They won't succeed. Nearby, but slightly out of the tourist scene, streets around place St-Sulpice, rue de Grenelle, and rue de Rennes are lined with boutiques of all categories and prices, from established and upcoming designers down to the most basic shops. They just take exploring to find. Inexpensive shops can be found throughout the city. For bargain shops, the streets around place de la République and the huge Paris garment district at Sentier and Place du Caire are good places to look.

DISCOUNT/SECOND-HAND CLOTHES

Paris swarms with discount clothing shops, extremely popular with Parisians. There are several types. Some shops sell new but out-of-season designer clothes, and some have the labels taken out or mutilated and are called *dégriffé*. The *dépôts-vente* (consignment shops) sell slightly used clothes of fashionable ladies who may have worn them only once. Some shops will advertise *vêtements d'occasion*, which means that the clothes are used, or have the word *troc* in their names, which occasionally means that clothes may be exchanged for others. The clothes are inspected by the shops before resale. *Fripe* means the shop specializes in "retro" (used clothes from decades past). Permanent sale shops are sometimes called *solderies*.

Some top designers maintain discount shops for their new but out-of-season designs. Some of these shops have the word *stock* in their names, meaning they sell new clothes from a particular designer or factory. Designers often contribute overstock to the always crowded semi-annual *braderies*, clothing jumble sales, at the Porte de Versailles.

Although the shops are found in all parts of the city, rue d'Alésia in the 14e is particularly noted for its discount shops, as is rue St-Placide in the 6e, off rue de Sèvres. See *Dépôts-vente: vêtements* in the Yellow Pages and *Paris Pas Cher* and *Paris Combines*.

255

Catalogue shopping is becoming popular, and companies such as **La Redoute** and **3 Suisses** sell their catalogues at newsstands. The catalogue's cost is deducted from the first order. Prices are generally fair, returns are accepted (with the appropriate paperwork), and occasionally there are special sales. La Redoute has catalogue showrooms throughout Paris.

WHEN TO SHOP

Although Parisians may be interested in the *nouveautés* (new collections), many wait for the semi-annual *soldes* (sales) to buy clothes, when all shops, including the most fashionable, offer reduced prices. During the *soldes*, the line around the block at designer boutiques can be daunting, as clever shoppers may have inspected the merchandise in the stores prior to the opening sale date. About half of all consumer purchases are made during the two annual sales. Sales are regulated by the government; they are allowed only after Christmas and in a six-week summer period, and merchandise must have been in the store for at least thirty days, so that inferior merchandise is not brought in solely for a sale. Toward the end of the sales, some stores will advertise *deuxième démarque* or *dernière démarque*, indicating further markdowns in price. Many shops also have *promotions* throughout the year, when items on the sales floor are marked for clearance or special items are brought in for a particular promotion.

Shops are generally open 10 am–7 pm. Some of the smaller shops close for a few hours at lunchtime and then may stay open until 8 pm. Department stores are open all day and generally stay open slightly later one evening a week. With only a few exceptions, shops are closed on Sundays, and some shops stay closed on Monday. August can make for difficult shopping, as many of the smaller shops close for the month. The department stores, fortunately, are open all day, six days a week, all year round.

SHOPPING ETIQUETTE

Do not shop with the idea that the "customer is always right" or even always welcome. The latter may be hard to understand but no matter, it is best just to accept the fact and be grateful if a salesperson is pleasant. In fact, shopping successfully in Paris requires some finesse. When you enter a shop, greet the *vendeuse/vendeur* (salesperson) with the polite *"bonjour, madame"* or *"bonjour, monsieur."* Sometimes salespeople ask what you want to select before you are ready. If you are still browsing, indicate that by saying *"merci, je regarde pour le moment"* or by asking if you may look around: *"puis-je jeter un coup d'oeil?"* Even if you do not make a purchase, make sure to say *"merci, madame"* or *"merci, monsieur"* as you leave.

Unless you are shopping in a store that caters to foreigners, do not ask for special treatment, such as an extra bag or special wrapping. And, although you might ask for a *remise* (discount) on merchandise that is damaged, there is no guarantee your request will be treated kindly. If, after you have left a shop it turns out the goods are damaged, bring them back with all receipts, although it is better to inspect each item before purchase. If you have any doubts before purchasing an item, inquire as to the store's return policy. If there is such a policy, it will most likely be for exchange of the merchandise rather than a refund. Depending on how long you are staying, credit at a store you might never go to again may not be attractive. Sale items are not returnable.

Size Conversions

Basically, you have to try on clothes and shoes until you see what size fits and not rely on the size shown on the label. Some companies use several factories to make their clothes, which means that different dresses or suits of a designer may not actually fit the same, despite showing the same size. And, of course, different designers have different sizing policies. In general, an American woman should add 30 to her dress size to find the comparable size. Thus a size 12 woman would look for a 42. British women should add 28. For men, a size small shirt translates into about a 37–38, and a medium is about 40.

Sizing policies may begin to change as the French woman herself is changing. With better nutrition and exercise, the French woman's waist is said to be 10 centimeters wider than just after World War II. In order to avoid their customers' having to buy larger sizes, manufacturers may well be forced to modify the cut of their creations.

DEPARTMENT STORES

As in any city, the department stores in Paris vary in their approach to their merchandising and the quality and price of the goods. The most prestigious department stores, such as **Galeries Lafayette** and **Printemps,** are called *grands magasins*, each with its own personality and approach to merchandising. Although they may cater to tourists and be staffed with English speakers, they sell what appeals to the French. Because there are so many tourists filtering through, the *grands magasins* provide services such as currency exchange, ticket and travel agencies, and tourist information. The *grands magasins* also have weekly fashion shows and offer discounts to tourists.

In some department stores, as in some food shops, it is common to select the merchandise, get the bill from the salesperson, take it to the *caisse* to pay, and only then take the validated receipt back to the salesperson to pick up your order. In some, it is possible to get one overall bill (*carnet d'achats*) and to pay for all purchases at one time.

Department stores participate in the semi-annual sales, but since there are *promotions* sales periodically on clearance merchandise, sometimes the sales prices are not much lower, although the merchandise is different. See *Centres commerciaux et grands magasins* in the Yellow Pages.

- 1er — **La Samaritaine**: 19, rue de la Monnaie (tel: 01.40.41. 20.20). Four-store complex, including one for sporting goods. "La Samar" sells everything you can imagine, including clothes, pets, toys, electronic equipment, and appliances. Grocery. Café with an excellent view. Open until 10 pm Thursday.

- 3e — **Tati**: 3, place de la République (tel: 01.48.87.72.81). Sprawling shops with merchandise at low prices. Other addresses. Lingerie is sold at 11 bis, rue Scribe (tel: 01.47.42.20.28), gold jewelry at several addresses, called Tati Or.

- 4e — **BHV (Bazar de l'Hôtel de Ville)**: 52, rue de Rivoli (01.42. 74.90.00). Known for its home-improvement items in the basement. Artists' materials, household items, a wide variety. "Do-it-yourself" annex is at 13, rue de la Verrerie (tel: 42.74. 97.23). Open until 10 pm Wednesday.

- 7e — **Le Bon Marché**: 22, rue de Sèvres (tel: 01.44.39.80.00). *Grand magasin.* Full-service department store, the city's oldest and still one of the best. Clothing, home items, carpets, antiques, watch repair, shoemaker, ticket agent, and bank. Extensive gourmet grocery, *La Grande Epicerie.*

- 9e and 4e — **Marks and Spencer**: 35, boulevard Haussmann (tel: 01.47.42.42.91). *Grand magasin.* English department store. Excellent food hall, plus clothing, all very British. Open until 8 pm Thursday. Also at 88, rue du Rivoli (tel: 01.44.61.08.00) and *centre commercial* **Les Quatre Temps** at La Défense.

- 9e and 14e — **Galeries Lafayette**: 40, boulevard Haussmann (tel: 01.42.82.34.56). *Grand magasin.* Several large buildings selling just about everything. Designer boutiques, exquisite lingerie. Hairdresser, gourmet food emporium, household items. Currency exchange, ticket agent, shoemaker. Also at *centre commercial* **Maine Montparnasse** (tel: 01.45.38.52.87). Open until 9 pm Thursday.

- 9e, 13e, and 20e — **Printemps**: 64, boulevard Haussmann (tel: 01.42.82.50.00). *Grand magasin.* Several buildings selling clothes, furniture, and other home-related items. *Brasserie* is under the Art Nouveau dome. Currency exchange, ticket agency, etc. Open until 10 pm on Thursday. Also at *centre commercial* **Italie2** (tel: 01.40.78.17.17) and 21, Cours de Vincennes (tel: 01.43.71.12.41).

- 16*e* — **Franck & Fils**: 80, rue de Passy (tel: 01.44.14.38.00). Department store for women in elegant, refurbished ambience.
- **Monoprix**: Chain of basic merchandise stores and supermarkets, with branches in most *arrondissements*. Good prices, many with the store's own label. Hours vary according to location.
- **Prisunic**: Inexpensive department stores in all districts; hours vary from store to store. Affordable housewares, cosmetics, basics, and a grocery shop with many foods under the store's own label.

SHOPPING CENTERS

Many of the *centre commerciaux* (shopping malls) have entrances into the métro, making shopping convenient in inclement weather. An easy métro ride to La Défense leads directly into **Les Quatre Temps**, the largest shopping complex in France, with hundreds of clothing and shoe shops, household stores, restaurants, services, and the *hypermarché* Auchan.

- 1*er* — **Carrousel du Louvre**: 100, rue de Rivoli. Mall attached to the Louvre. Two underground levels filled with an upscale assortment of shops. Open Sunday.
- 1*er* — **Forum des Halles**: 17, rue Pierre-Lescot. Enormous mall, with hundreds of shops of all sorts and quality levels. Large FNAC.
- 1*er* — **Les Trois Quartiers**: 23, boulevard de la Madeleine. Multi-level upscale fashion mall. Perfume store, hairdresser, plus many boutiques, some top designers.
- 6*e* — **Marché Saint-Germain**: rue Clément near métro

Mabillon. Modern mini-mall with some clothing and shoe shops, a food market, swimming pool, and parking facilities.

- 8e — **Le Drugstore Publicis Champs-Elysées**: 133, avenue des Champs-Elysées (tel: 01.44.43.79.00). Multi-level store with a bit of everything: books, records, gifts, tobacco items, plus a pharmacy, small grocery, café, etc. Open past midnight.
- 8e — **Galeries along the Champs-Elysées:** Several upscale fashion malls around 66, avenue des Champs-Elysées. Also at the intersection of the Rond Point and avenue Matignon.
- 9e — **Passage du Havre**: 69, rue de Caumartin and 107, rue St-Lazare. Modern multi-level mall anchored by FNAC, plus some small boutiques and international clothing chains. Snack bars.
- 13e — **Italie2:** Place d'Italie. Enormous complex of shops, banks, restaurants, cinema, night spots, and more.
- 14e — **Maine Montparnasse**: By Tour Maine-Montparnasse. Large mall; Galeries Lafayette and C&A.
- 15e — **Centre Beaugrenelle**: Rue Linois at place St-Charles. Multi-story mall with clothing shops, post office, dry cleaner, bookshop, etc. Cafés and a multi-screen cinema.
- 16e — **Plaza Passy**: 53, rue de Passy. A popular modern mall with international shops and a supermarket in the heart of the fashionable Passy district.
- 17e — **Boutiques du Palais des Congrès**: Porte Maillot. Upscale fashion shops, tea room, etc.

FLEA MARKETS

For inexpensive items in all categories, styles, and price, try the popular weekend *marchés aux puces* (flea markets), which stock real bargains and real junk: antiques, furniture, clothing and shoes, books, useable household items. For markets dedicated solely to clothes, try Place d'Aligre in the 12e and in the 3e at the Marché du Carreau du Temple, around rues Perrée and Dupetit-Thouars; open Tuesday-Sunday.

261

- 14e — **Les Puces de Vanves**: Porte de Vanves and Porte Didot, Avenue Georges-Lafenestre. Furniture, odds and ends, paintings, etc. sold in the mornings, used clothes in the afternoons. Weekends, 7 am–7:30 pm.
- 18e — **Les Puces Saint-Ouen/Clignancourt**: Between the Portes de Saint-Ouen and Clignancourt; Saturday, Sunday, and Monday, 7:30 am–7 pm. Huge flea market, divided into several mini-markets. The most famous of all the flea markets, selling antiques, clothes, shoes, books, records, etc.
- 20e — **Les Puces de Montreuil**: Avenue de la Porte-de-Montreuil. Appliances, old furniture, used clothing, crockery. Saturday, Sunday, and Monday, 7 am–6 pm.

CHILDREN'S CLOTHES

Surprisingly, there are some affordable shops for children's clothes. The department stores all carry a variety of children's clothes. There are also some *dépôts-ventes* that sell children's clothes, and some of the adult discount shops sell children's wear. These are usually new, end-of-the line items and designer clothes from the previous season. All clothes are inspected before display.

Tout Autre Chose, **Jacadi** and its subsidiary **Dipaki Basic**, **Du Pareil au Même**, **Prénatal**, and **Natalys** are chains of children's clothing stores, and **Magic Stock** is a discount house with several locations. **Benetton**, **Baby Gap,** and **Gap Kids** have shops throughout the city. See also *Paris Pas Cher* and *Paris Combines*.

- 13e — **Troc Lutin**: 6, rue des Cinq-Diamants (tel: 01.45.81. 44.57). *Depôt-vente* for designer clothes for kids up to 14 years, plus a sports section and games.
- 15e — **Bambin Troc**: 4, rue de l'Abbé-Groult (tel: 01.42.50. 77.93). Two-level discount shop for all children, with many designer labels. Maternity clothes.
- 15e — **Bonpoint**: 82, rue de Grenelle (tel: 01.44.39.04.95). Reasonably priced overstock shop of good-quality, fashionable clothes.

262

- 17e — **Maman Troc**: 14, rue Laugier (tel: 01.47.66.70.20). *Depôt-vente* for clothes, sports clothes, and toys, with good quality and prices. Maternity clothes.

SHOES

Shops such as **Charles Jourdan**, **Christian Louboutin**, **Walter Steiger**, or **Stéphane Kélian** offer meticulous workmanship in styles both fashionable and classic and with prices to match. The department stores, however, offer a wide selection of brands and prices, and discount shoe stores that sell end-of-line and over-stocks can make purchasing fashionable shoes much more afford-able. This holds true for children's shoes as well. Rue Meslay, near Place de la République, has several discount shoe stores, as does boulevard Magenta. For retail stores, see *Chaussures* in the Yellow Pages. For shoes at particularly good prices, including discount shops, see *Paris Pas Cher* or *Paris Combines*.

Shoe sizes are in centimeters. Width differentials are becoming more common, and some half sizes can be found. In general an American woman's size 6 to about $7^1/2$ would be sizes 37–39, and a British woman's size 6 to about $7^1/2$ would be sizes 38–40. An American man's shoe size 9 would be about a size 42, and this is approximately the same for the British man's shoe size.

Cordonneries (shoe repair shops) can be found in any *arron-dissement*, and BHV has a repair service. Some métro stations also have shoe repair and polishing booths; signs near the *WC* say *cireur*. Signs that say *talons minute* offer fast repair service.

SPORTS CLOTHES AND EQUIPMENT

Active wear can be found in department stores and at some of the discount shops. The international chains **Fila** and **Lacoste** have shops in the city, as do the sports footwear chains **Foot Locker**, **Athlete's Foot**, and **Adidas**. In these, sizes are consistent in all stores. See *Sport et loisirs: articles et vêtements (détail)* in the Yellow Pages.

- **Au Vieux Campeur**: Chain of specialized stores in the area around 48, rue des Ecoles 75005 (tel: 01.43.29.12.32). High-quality camping, climbing, and diving equipment, hammocks, sleeping bags, etc. Travel books, accessories. Knowledgeable personnel and good prices. Parking available. Several catalogues.
- **Courir**: Chain of sports shoe stores selling internationally known brands at very good prices.
- **Declathon**: Several stores selling sporting clothes and equipment, including bicyling. Good prices and service.
- **Go Sport**: Chain of sporting equipment stores. Extensive selection of clothes at reasonable prices.
- **La Clef des Marques**: Chain with discounted sporting clothes and end-of-series street wear for all the family. Hiking boots, bathing suits, goggles, etc.

CHAPTER SIXTEEN

PRODUCTS AND SERVICES

APPLIANCES AND UTILITIES

France uses 220 volt, 50 hertz electricity. Most appliances using the British 240 volts should need only an *adapteur* (adaptor plug). Otherwise, if you are thinking of bringing appliances with you, make sure they are electrically compatible, for you may need a *transformateur* (transformer) as well. Transformers change the voltage, but not the hertz, so both must be appropriate. Some appliances will not function and others such as clock-radios may run too slowly. If your appliances are brands not common in Europe and need repair, finding parts and service may be difficult. In general, it may be more economical to purchase appliances in Paris. **Appliances Overseas** sells transformers, plugs, and appliances for international use: 276 Fifth Avenue, Suite 407, New York NY 10001 (US tel: 212/545-8001; fax: 212/545-8005); ask for a catalogue. Small appliances such as hair dryers come with dual voltage and are easy to buy in Paris. Adaptors and transformers are available at electronic shops, hardware stores, and department stores.

Make sure that your large appliances are appropriate to the size of the apartment, for kitchens (and bathrooms) tend to be small. Most washing machines in France heat the water internally, using only a cold water tap, so if the washer you import depends on an external hot water source, it may wash clothes only in cold water. In addition, some apartments are not vented for dryers, but dryers with a water-gathering compartment are available.

France uses the European round, two-prong plug; the ground wire pin is above. The electrical outlets for all your large appliances, especially for desktop computers, should be grounded (*prise de terre*). Some older buildings have not yet had their outlets converted. Lamps may use one of two kinds of light bulbs: the newer screw type (*ampoule à vis*), which is compatible with standard foreign lamps, and the older but still-used bayonet with two pins (*ampoule à baïonnette*).

Major department stores sell appliances, as do the *hypermarchés*. BHV has a discount appliance outlet at 119, boulevard Paul-Vaillant-Couturier 94200 Ivry-sur-Seine (tel: 01.49.60.44. 10), and delivery to Paris is available. The FNAC chain carries an assortment of telephone and fax machines. See *Electroménager* in the Yellow Pages and ads in *FUSAC* for used appliances.

Occasionally, a shop will be slightly flexible in its prices when large, expensive items are purchased or if you are a known customer. Ask about warranties on new products and about *service après-vente/dépannage à domicile* (home repair service), for some shops require the item to be brought back to the store or charge extra for a home call. Most large appliance makers offer home service; look in the telephone book under the brand name. BHV has a repair service for cameras and watches, as well as offering a large selection of auto parts, tools, and equipment for the *bricoleur* (do-it-yourself person).

Large appliances are delivered and installed. Make sure everything works before the installer leaves. Also inspect all delivered furniture and large packages before the driver leaves to ensure that there is no damage. Some stores will claim no responsibility for repairs or exchange if damage is discovered after the delivery person has left. The driver takes back damaged goods. It is best to get warranties on products and to use licensed repairmen.

- **Darty**: Chain selling home appliances and electronics. Good prices. The warehouse in suburban Mitry-Mory has excellent prices on seconds and returned goods (tel: 01.64.27.46.04). Home delivery, repair contracts for large appliances, home servicing seven days a week.
- **France Ménager**: Chain of large appliance stores with good service and prices. Home repair service.

For electric and gas emergencies, call the *pompiers* (tel: 18). They will come quickly and will notify the Electricité de France or Gaz de France (EDF or GDF) bureau in your district of the problem. For non-emergencies, look at the top of your utilities bill where it says *"Tel: dépannage electricité* (or *gaz*)" and call the number listed. For information, call EDF (tel: 01.49.02.80.80) or GDF (tel: 01.47.54.20.20). For water problems or leaks, call SAGEP (tel: 08.02.01.20.12). For telephones, see Chapter Ten.

Paying utility bills (EDF/GDF and France Télécom) may be done several ways. You can pay them at the La Poste or ask the utility company to debit your bank account an agreed-upon amount. In a process called *TIP* (*Titre interbancaire de paiement*), you sign the bottom coupon of the bill after having provided EDF/GDF information on your bank account (*relevé de banque*); the company then processes the coupon as though it were a check. Or, having provided EDF/GDF with the *relevé d'identité bancaire*, you can call by telephone and request the amount billed to be debited from your account (tel: 01.45.42.22.22).

267

BOOKSHOPS

Paris provides many well-stocked English-language *librairies* (book-shops), and some of the larger French book stores have foreign language sections. Both FNAC on rue de Rennes and Virgin Megastore on the Champs-Elysées (open on Sunday) have foreign language titles. Expect to pay a 30 percent surcharge for a new English-language book. Several shops sell used books, and books may be borrowed from WICE or the American Library. Shops generally place special orders if the books are on the computer inventory. Some shops stay open late and a few are open on Sunday. **US to You**, a mail-order English-language book service, sells books in all categories at competitive prices; call for a catalogue (tel: 01.39.07.01.01).

Paris is also known for its *bouquinistes*, small open-air green stalls stretching along the *quais* on both sides of the Seine from the Musée d'Orsay to Pont de Sully, selling books of all conditions and prices. On weekends, the **Marché aux Livres** at Square George-Brassens 75015 sells everything from first editions of rare books down to comic books, plus some cheap books: *"tout à 10F."* The *Salon du Livre* (Paris Book Fair), held in late spring, is open to the public.

- 1er—**Galignani**: 224, rue de Rivoli (tel: 01.42.60.76.07). Books in English and French, plus its specialty of art books.
- 1er—**W.H. Smith:** 248, rue de Rivoli (tel: 01.44.77.88.99). British book chain. Open Sunday 1–6 pm.
- 2e—**Brentano's:** 37, avenue de l'Opéra (tel: 01.42.61.52.50). American titles.
- 4e—**World Data**: 10, rue Nicolas-Flamel (tel: 01.42.78.05.78). Official publications from governments and international organizations around the world in their original languages.
- 5e—**Abbey Bookshop**: 29, rue de la Parcheminerie (tel: 01.46.33.16.24). Canadian and other titles.

Photo: Zeny Ciescikowwski

English-language bookshop in the Latin Quarter.

- 5e — **Shakespeare & Company**: 37, rue de la Bûcherie (01.43.26.96.50). Famous shop packed with new and used books.
- 6e — **Australian Bookshop**: 33, quai des Grands-Augustins (tel: 01.43.29.08.65). Literature, poetry, art, and children's books.
- 6e — **Children's English Learning Centre**: 33, rue de Fleurus (tel: 01.45.44.11.66). Children's books and audio tapes.
- 6e — **San Francisco Book Co**: 17, rue Monsieur-le-Prince (tel: 01.43.29.15.70). Used books. Buys, sells, trades. Good prices.
- 6e — **Tea and Tattered Pages**: 24, rue Mayet (tel: 01.40.65.94.35). Used books and a small tea room.
- 6e — **Village Voice**: 6, rue Princesse (tel: 01.46.33.36.47). Excellent collection. Literary events and readings.

COMPUTERS

Although *ordinateurs* (computers), *imprimantes* (printers), and associated *informatique* products have traditionally been expensive, prices are becoming somewhat more competitive at least in the new megastores and in the *hypermarchés* along the *périphérique*. Nonetheless, prices vary widely from store to store, even on the same merchandise, and it pays to shop around. Check the magazines on newsstands, including *PC Direct*.

Several chains sell small electronic goods, computers, *logiciels* (software), and associated items. FNAC and Virgin Megastore carry a bit of everything hi-tech, including computers, software, and accessories. Software, of course, will be in French. If you need software in other languages, bring your own. Also note that the French keyboard does not use the Qwerty format; international computers have changeable formats, although, of course, the actual keyboard remains the same.

If you bring your own computer to France, bring your proof of purchase with serial numbers of the computer (or printer) in case customs officers ask you to prove that the equipment is yours. The computer must be used and theoretically at least six months old.

- **FNAC**: Chain with an extensive offering of CDs, cassettes, videos, computers, peripherals, software, and books; ticket agency. FNAC Micro at 71, boulevard St-Germain 75005 specializes in computer products (tel: 01.44.41.31.50). FNAC issues a catalogue that is helpful for price comparison purposes.
- **Virgin Megastore**: International chain selling CDs, records, videos, books, computer hardware, software, printers, etc. Radios, stereo equipment. Ticket agency. Open until midnight daily, until 1 am Saturday; store at 52, avenue des Champs-Elysées is open Sunday (tel: 01.49.53.50.00).
- **Extrapole**: Chain selling books, CDs, videotapes, video games, software, computer accessories, stationery.

- **Inter Discount**: Chain selling cameras, radios, televisions, computers, printers, telephones, faxes, electronic accessories, etc. at discounted prices.
- 2e — **Interpole Informatique**: 113-115, rue Réaumur (tel: 01.53.40.40.40; fax: 01.53.40.40.00). Multi-storied shop selling computers, peripherals, software.
- 8e — **Gateway 2000**: 152, boulevard Haussmann (tel: 01.53. 89.20.00; fax: 01.45.63.45.69; toll-free 08.00.90.64.88). Showroom for popular mail-order American computers. Call for a catalogue or visit showroom. Three-year warranty and tech support included in price.
- 12e — **Surcouf**: 139, avenue Daumesnil (tel: 01.53.33.20.00; fax: 01.53.33.21.01). Multi-story computer bazaar selling computer hardware, software (some in English), peripherals, etc. Tech support, repair.

Technical Support

Power outages are rare, but it is advisable to buy a UPS (uninterruptible power supply), which suppresses surges, available at computer shops and hardware stores.

Inquire of your computer manufacturer how to access its technical support in Paris. IBM's tech support is at **IBM France**: 94, rue Réaumur 75002 (software support tel: 08.01.63.10.20; hardware support tel: 08.01.63.12.13). IBM has several points of sale in Paris; look in the telephone book under IBM. For PCs in general, inquire also at shops listed above, including FNAC Micro and Surcouf. **Macintosh** has several service centers in Paris, including **Phénix** at 38, rue de Berri 75008 (tel: 01.42.56.42.56; fax: 01.42.56.02.13).

COSMETICS/PERFUMES

Department stores sell international brands of perfumes and cosmetics, and some carry their own brand names. Pharmacies carry hypo-allergenic beauty products, and parapharmacies have a wide selection. Fashion houses such as **Chanel** and **Cartier** develop their own perfumes, and a few *parfumeries* — **Annick Goutal** is well-known — create their own fragrances.

Cosmetic colors, names, and numbers differ from country to country, so a shade you have bought at home may not exist in Paris or it may have a different name: If possible, bring along your old product for comparison purposes. Inexpensive chains also carry internationally known products.

- **Rayon d'Or**: small chain of cosmetic and perfume shops with excellent prices.
- **La Parfumerie**: chain for discounted cosmetics and perfumes with shops in the city and suburbs.
- **Parfumeries Kléber**: citywide chain of perfume stores with known brand names at excellent prices.
- **Sephora**: country-wide chain; cosmetics and bath products, accessories.
- **Silver Moon**: chain of well-priced stores for beauty products and perfumes.

FLOWERS/PLANTS

Fleuristes (flower shops) are in every district, and their selection varies according to the season. Many are open on Sunday mornings. When purchasing flowers you will be asked if they are *pour offrir*, to offer as a gift. If so, the flowers will be trimmed and wrapped. Most florists deliver, and those that advertise **Interflora** can wire flowers abroad (toll-free tel: 08.00.20.32.04). **Aquarelle** and **Monceau Fleurs** are chains of well-priced shops. Food markets sell inexpensive flowers, and the markets listed below are dedicated to flowers. See *Fleuristes* in the Yellow Pages.

- *4e* — **Ile de la Cité**: Open 8 am–7:30 pm; closed Sunday. On Sunday, a bird market.

- 8e — **Place de la Madeleine**: Open 8 am–7:30 pm, Tuesday–Sunday.
- 17e — **Place des Ternes**: Open 8 am–7:30 pm; closed Monday.
  Truffaut at 85, quai de la Gare 75013 is an excellent, well-priced flower and plant supermarket (tel: 01.53.60.84.50). It can landscape your balcony or garden and has all sizes and types of plants. Open Sunday; home delivery.

HOME FURNISHINGS

Meubles (furniture) can be bought both new and used, from the elegant and expensive to the practical and cheap. The furniture in department stores is in keeping with the quality and approach of the store. See *Meubles de style et contemporains* in the Yellow Pages.

- **Habitat**: International chain with inexpensive furniture, household items, tableware. Delivery. Call for catalogue (tel: 08.00.02.70.00).
- **Ikea**: International chain selling inexpensive home furnishings. *Centre commercial* **Paris Nord 2**, rue des Buttes 95400 Gonesse (tel: 01.49.90.16.15). Call for catalogue.
- **Pier Import**: Extensive chain carrying colorful, inexpensive houseware and furniture. Tableware, casual furniture, some kitchen items (info. tel: 01.40.69.28.00).
- **Compagnie Française de l'Orient et de la Chine**: Small, upscale chain for imported Oriental furniture, table linens, fabrics, clothing, etc.
- 6e — **Roche-Bobois**: 193, boulevard St-Germain (tel: 01.42.22.11.22). Several upmarket shops with different styles of furniture. Call for catalogue (tel: 08.00.39.52.45).
- 6e and 8e — **Maison de Famille**: 29, rue St-Sulpice (tel: 01.40.46.97.47). Everything for the home in attractive, multi-storied shops; also at 10, place de la Madeleine (tel: 01.53.45.82.02).
- 7e — **The Conran Shop**: 117, rue du Bac (tel: 01.42.84.10.01). Casual furniture, kitchen accessories.

- 16e — **The Curtain Shop**: 23, rue Davioud (tel: 01.45.25.36.26). *Dépôt vente* for curtains. Occasional bargains.
- 18e — **Marché St-Pierre**: 2, rue Charles-Nodier (tel: 01.46.06. 92.25). Discount warehouse for fabrics, linens, curtains, and other items. Closed Monday morning and Sunday. Other small shops in the area.

Used furniture is available from a variety of sources including the *marchés aux puces*. See *Dépôts-vente: ameublement et divers* in the Yellow Pages, and see *FUSAC* for ads.

- 14e — **Dépôt Vente Alésia**: 123, rue d'Alésia (tel: 01.45.45. 54.54)
- 20e — **Dépôt Vente de Paris**: 81, rue Lagny (tel: 01.43.72.13.91)

Kitchen and Dining Equipment

Department stores sell kitchen and dining equipment, and some small kitchen appliances are sold in *quincailleries* (hardware stores). Shops in rue de Paradis specialize in tableware.

- 1er — **Dehillerin:** 18, rue Coquillière (tel: 01.42.36.53.13). Famous two-level, kitchen-equipment emporium.
- 1er — **Mora**: 13, rue Montmartre (tel: 01.45.08.19.24). Kitchen supplies, utensils, dishes, paperware. In business for more than 150 years.
- 2e — **A. Simon**: 36, rue Etienne-Marcel (tel: 01.42.33.71.65). Long-established supplier of kitchen equipment, dishes, gadgets. Glasses, utensils, pitchers, etc. Also at 48, rue Montmartre.
- 6e and 17e — **Culinarion**: 99, rue de Rennes (tel: 01.42.84. 02.37). Practical kitchenware shops. Also at 83 bis, rue de Courcelles (tel: 01.42.27.63.32).
- 6e and 14e — **Geneviève Lethu**: 95, rue de Rennes (tel: 01.45. 44.40.35). Chain of upscale tableware shops with a range of styles and prices. Other addresses.
- 15e — **Kitchen Bazaar**: 11, avenue du Maine (tel: 01.42.22. 91.17). Modern implements; other addresses.

HAIR AND BEAUTY SERVICES

Inexpensive chains of hairdressers offer reliable services throughout the city, charging less than the small neighborhood *coiffeurs* (hairdressers), which is causing increasing consternation among the independent operators. Yet, of course, although a *shampooing et brushing* (wash and blow-dry) or a *coupe* (cut) at the chains may cost less, the quality varies according to the stylist, as it does anywhere, and turnover of stylists tends to be higher than in neighborhood salons.

If you use hair dye, bring a few bottles with you until you find a comparable color as brands and colors are not the same as at home. Tips are not included in the price, and every person — shampoo person, hair stylist, cloakroom attendant — gets a tip based on level of service. Most shops close on Monday. Get recommendations from your friends; see *Paris Par Cher* and *Paris Combines*, and see *Coiffeurs pour dames* or *Coiffeurs pour hommes* in the Yellow Pages.

- **Jacques Dessange**: Well-known upscale chain with its own line of hair products, a dozen branches, and a training school, listed below.
- **Jean-Claude Biguine**: Extensive chain of reliable, reasonably priced hairdressers. In every *arrondissement*.
- **Maniatis**: Popular chain of hair salons, one branch in the Galeries Lafayette.
- **Saint-Algue**: Chain of reliable, inexpensive hair salons throughout Paris.

Paris is also known for *formation* (training) of hairdressers, salons that offer low-cost cuts to customers willing to take a chance on a student's ability, although students are well supervised. *Salons de perfectionnement* give established stylists the opportunity to update their techniques. Salons are open on Mondays, when regular salons are closed. See *Paris Pas Cher* and *Paris Combines* for their recommendations.

Some salons perform both hair and beauty services (*coiffure & esthétique*), but most are separate. An *institut de beauté* (beauty salon) performs manicures, pedicures, and waxing, does facials and makeup applications, and sells beauty care items. **Yves Rocher** and **Daniel Jouvance** are well-known. Some parapharmacies also offer *soins de beauté*, meaning beauty treatments.

LAUNDRY AND DRY CLEANING

Fortunately, *laveries automatiques* (self-service laundromats) are in every area, for unfurnished apartments are often not equipped with *lave-linges/machines à laver* (washers) or *séchoirs* (dryers), and apartment buildings do not have laundry rooms. Some furnished apartments come with washers but no dryers. Washers in the laundromats take one *jeton* (token) per load. Bring your own soap, bleach, and softener, rather than pay for them at laundromat rates. The *super-essorage/essoreuse* (spinner machine) removes moisture, saving money on dryers. Some laundromats also have facilities for inexpensive, self-service dry cleaning. See *Laveries pour particuliers, laveries en libre-service* in the Yellow Pages.

Many dry cleaners (*nettoyage à sec/pressing*) are also *blanchisseries* (laundries) for washing and pressing items. Cleaning and laundry are expensive because the finishing work is done by hand, rather than by machines. Less costly options are to press wrinkled clothes but not have them cleaned or to have clothes cleaned but not pressed. Some dry cleaners ask for payment in advance, and most accept checks and cash only. *Teintureries* offer high-quality cleaning at high prices but are worth it for your most elegant outfits, since the quality of cleaners can vary considerably.

Home pickup and delivery is generally available. See *Paris à Domicile* and *Nettoyage à sec* in the Yellow Pages. These cleaners are especially known for their work on fragile items:

- 8e — **Pouyanne, "Le Médecin de la Robe"**: 28, avenue Franklin-D.-Roosevelt (tel: 01.43.59.03.47).

276

- 8e — **Parfait Elève de Pouyanne**: 57, boulevard Haussmann (tel: 01.42.65.34.23).

OPTICAL SERVICES

Eye glasses and contact lenses are expensive, and most chains of *opticiens* (opticians) are no less expensive than the independent shops. **Lissac Frères** and **La Général d'Optique** are chains with reasonably priced products. See *Opticiens lunetiers* in the Yellow Pages.

Bring an extra pair of glasses with you and an up-to-date prescription. **SOS Optique** is a home repair service for eye glasses (tel: 01.48.07.22.00). If you have an eye emergency and cannot get to the Hôpital Hôtel Dieu or Hôpital des Quinze-Vingt, call **SOS Oeil** for a house call (tel: 01.40.92.93.94). The **Fondation Ophtalmologique Adolphe de Rothschild** at 25, rue Manin 75019 sees people without appointment weekday mornings (tel: 01.48. 03.65.65).

- **Alain Afflelou**: Citywide chain of well-respected opticians.
- **Fédération Mutualiste Parisienne**: Chain in Paris and suburbs. Closed Saturday afternoons.
- **Krys**: More than twenty shops throughout the city.

TOYS

Hypermarchés and inexpensive department stores sell *jouets* (toys) and *jeux* (games) at decent prices. Otherwise shop around, for similar toys can vary in price from store to store. **Au Nain** at 408, rue St-Honoré 75008 is an elegant century-old toy shop that nonetheless carries the most modern of toys (tel: 01.42.60.39.01). The toy shops below have good prices. Note that museum shops sell interesting, educational toys. See *Jouets et jeux* in the Yellow Pages, and Chapter Six for *ludothèques* where children may borrow toys.

- 5e — **EOL**: three well-stocked stores on boulevard St-Germain 75005, dedicated to model making of all sorts, including cars, airplanes, boats, and figurines (info tel: 01.43.54.01.43).

- 9e — **Comptoir des Oeuvres Ogeo**: 59 bis, rue de Rochechouart (tel: 01.48.78.01.92).
- 12e and 10e — **Pintel**: 16, rue Fabre d'Eglantine (tel: 01.43.07. 95.52); 10, rue de Paradis (tel: 01.44.83.84.00).
- La Défense — **Toys'R'Us**: *centre commercial* Les Quatre Temps, at La Défense (tel: 01.47.76.29.78). Also at Forum des Halles.

VIDEO RENTAL

When renting videos it is important to know the operating system of your television and *magnétoscope* (video cassette recorder) and the system in which the video was taped (SECAM, NTSC, or PAL), for different systems are not compatible. France uses the PAL/SECAM system.

The shops below rent films in *vo (version originale*/original language). Some have accessories, some rent video players, and some convert between operating systems. Many are open on Sunday, and some have home delivery service. See *Location de films vidéo et cinéma* in the Yellow Pages.

- 6e and 16e — **Prime Time Video**: 24, rue Mayet (tel: 01.40. 56.33.44); 12, rue Léonce-Reynaud (tel: 01.47.20.50.01)
- 7e and 16e — **Playtime**: 44, avenue Bosquet (tel: 01.45.55. 43.36); 36, avenue d'Eylau (tel: 01.42.27.56.22)
- 12e — **Reuilly Video**: 73, rue de Reuilly (tel: 01.43.45.16.62)
- 15e — **Reels on Wheels**: 12, villa Croix-Nivert (tel: 01.45. 67.64.99)
- 17e — **V.O. Only**: 25, boulevard de la Somme (tel: 01.43. 80.70.60)
- 17e — **Stéréorama**: 67, rue Legendre (tel: 01.46.27.32.22)

CHAPTER SEVENTEEN

PARIS BY NIGHT

PARIS DAY AND NIGHT

Entertainment can be found in Paris at just about any hour of any day. People who do not speak French should have few problems in this regard. Paris is a city where classical music is as important as popular music, where 300 films are shown each week in a variety of languages, where discotheques start to swing at 1 am. Two hundred and fifty theaters show dramas from the highest-quality offerings to the naughtiest revues in late-night *cabarets*. Cultural activities of all interests are extremely important to the French, and about 1 percent of the country's annual budget goes to cultural activities, more than most other nations. In Paris, the *mairie* subsidizes music and dance festivals throughout the year, and some events are free of charge.

279

RESOURCE INFORMATION

Parisians wait eagerly for the publication of the week's events guides. Available each Wednesday morning at newsstands, both *Pariscope* and *l'Officiel des Spectacles* provide detailed descriptions of the week's activities, from sporting events to museum exhibitions and art galleries, to theater, concerts, and films, to recommended restaurants, bars, and discos. *Pariscope*, which has an English-language insert by the guide publisher *Time Out*, costs only 3F, and *l'Officiel des Spectacles* costs 2F. *Figaroscope*, also published on Wednesday, is the events supplement of the daily newspaper, *Le Figaro*.

Nova, a lively monthly magazine that is increasingly popular with young people, details all the events in Paris, and occasionally it has an English-language insert. A multilingual monthly publication, *Paris Selection*, is issued by the Paris Tourist Office, which also has *What's On France* and *Programmes des Festivals*, both seasonal guides. It has 24-hour recorded information on all performances and shows in Paris (French tel: 01.49.52.53.55; English: 01.49.52.53.56).

In English, *The Paris Free Voice* keeps current on happenings, as does the magazine *Boulevard*. See *FUSAC* for English-language ads celebrating particular holidays at restaurants and bars. But refer to tourist guides, such as *Time Out Paris*, which are detailed in their descriptions.

TICKET PURCHASE

Events are crowded, especially those with big-name performers, so buy tickets as far in advance as possible. Tickets to cultural events are expensive, as they are in any major city, and season tickets are sometimes available. Consider options other than paying full price, such as ticket agencies that offer discount cards, the *kiosques* that sell half-price tickets on the day of performance, performing arts festivals, reduced-price previews, free year-round church concerts, and free rehearsals of concerts and plays. Most events have discounts for young people, senior citizens, and large groups.

Tickets are sold at the box office about two weeks before an event, for some events up to a month before. Box offices are generally open for ticket purchase from 11 am to 7 pm. Most accept telephone reservations, although lines are often busy, and they accept credit cards. Pick up tickets at least an hour before the performance. Be prepared to stand in line when purchasing tickets, when picking them up, or while waiting to enter the performance site.

Tickets to some events may be purchased half price on the day of the performance. Not all shows have such tickets, but it is worth checking the **Kiosque**, at 15, place de la Madeleine and at the Esplanade of the Tour Montparnasse. Make sure tickets do not say *sans visibilité*, meaning that at least a part of the stage will not be visible from your seats. Do not accept such tickets unless you are willing to take the chance that you will be able to move to the better seats of someone who does not show up. If an usher shows you to your seat or upgrades you to a better seat, tip 5–10F. Some theaters sell reduced-price tickets just before a performance.

Since cultural and sporting events are extremely popular, it is often best to go well in advance of an event to an agency that handles cultural, entertainment, and sporting events and that has the most current information on all dates and locations. They charge a small commission, but are worth it for the convenience. In addition to those below, the FNAC stores have ticket agencies, and they sell the *Carte FNAC*, a discount card that allows the holder a discount on tickets. Virgin Megastore, American Express, and the Paris Tourist Office all have ticket agencies with English-speaking personnel. Paying in advance for a number of productions at *théâtres subventionnés* (subsidized theaters) in some cases allows a steep discount over individual tickets.

281

Most ticket agencies take reservations over the phone with a credit card guarantee. At some, the customer is sent a voucher for the ticket, which is picked up at the event before the performance. Arrive early to do this, as there is no guarantee that a ticket will be held for very long. If you have no ticket at all, try standing at the entrance before the event is to begin and holding up a sign that says *cherche une place*; sometimes people sell their extra tickets.

- 8e — **Agence Perrossier**: 6, place de la Madeleine (tel: 01.42.60. 58.31; fax: 01.42.60.14.83). Tickets to sold-out shows.
- 8e — **Spectateurs Service**: 252, rue du Faubourg-St-Honoré (tel: 01.53.53.58.58; fax: 01.53.53.58.51). Subscription service offering reduced-price tickets to all events.
- 8e — **SOS Théâtres**: 6, place de la Madeleine (tel: 01.44. 77.88.55; fax: 01.42.60.14.83). Last-minute tickets, high fees.
- 8e — **Spectaplus**: 252, rue du Faubourg-St-Honoré (tel: 01.53. 53.58.60; fax: 01.53.53.58.61). Subscription service with reduced-price tickets to all types of events.

THEATER

Paris has more theaters than any other city in the world, but English-language productions are sparse. There are some small repertory companies, some readings at The Village Voice and Brentano's bookshops, and occasionally at Anglophone pubs such as **Finnegan's Wake** or **Sweeny's**. Check the weekly guides for performances at the **Dear Conjunction Theatre Company** or the **Company Oz,** and watch for productions in suburban theaters as well.

- 4e — **Théâtre du Tourtour**: 20, rue Quincampoix (tel: 01.48. 87.82.48)
- 6e — **Théâtre de Nesle**: 8, rue de Nesle (tel: 01.46.34.61.04)
- 11e — **Théâtre de la Main-d'Or**: 15, passage de la Main d'Or (tel: 01.48.0567.89)
- 20e — **ACT**: 84, rue de Pixérécourt (tel: 01.40.33.64.02)

Look for performances at the national theaters, especially the **Odéon** and the **Théâtre National de la Colline**, which often present plays in their original language.

CINEMA

The French regard cinema as much an art form as any other, and it receives much the same attention. Hundreds of *films* are shown each week in theaters across the city, many of them multi-screen, and they feature a wide range of international first-run films and old favorites either in French (*vf—version française*) or in the original language (*vo—version originale*) with French subtitles. The selection is outstanding: *films nouveaux* (recently released films) and *exclusivités* (films on general release) are plentiful, film *festivals* highlighting certain directors or types of films are popular, and *reprises* (older films, brought back) are often shown once a week. Check the weekly events guides for film festivals.

New films open on Wednesday. The weekly guides list the week's films by subject and by theater in each *arrondissement*. The listings state the time of the *séance*, which is when advertisements and film previews begin. They also indicate how many minutes later the film itself starts. **Allô Ciné** has recorded information on all films (tel: 01.40.30.20.10).

Arrive early for popular films and be prepared to wait outside before and after having bought a ticket. Tickets are not sold much in advance of the showing unless you have a discount card. Doors open just before the *séance* is to begin. Occasionally an *ouvreuse* (usherette) will show you to a seat. Tipping is not required, yet it is customary to give 2F. Some theaters have vending machines in the lobbies; in others, an usherette comes into the *salle* just before the show and sells snacks from a basket. Most theaters are *climatisés* (air conditioned) and smoking is prohibited.

The *Salles*

Gaumont, **UGC,** and **Mk2** are major first-run citywide cinema chains with multi-screen theaters. Generally each chain shows a particular set of films at all its theaters but at slightly different times, making it convenient to see any film. Some have a late-late show on weekends. They all show films in *vo*, as do many others. The Champs-Elysées has several cinemas on both sides of the avenue. Art films are shown across the city, with the greatest concentration of *salles* in the 5e and 6e. **Action** is a small chain that specializes in screening old films, and look for cinemas such as **L'Arlequin, Saint-André-des-Arts,** and **Quartier Latin**. See *Cinéma: salles* in the Yellow Pages.

Cinema Prices

Although prices may seem high for the cinema, discounted tickets are available on Mondays or Wednesdays in most theaters for early performances. Seniors and students are entitled to a *tarif réduit* (discount) on weekday performances. Gaumont, UGC, and Mk2 offer *cartes privilège* (discount cards). **Forum** theaters have discount programs, and some theaters offer loyal customers a *carte de fidélité*, rewarding multiple ticket purchases with a free film. In February, *18 heures 18F* is a week-long festival when showings closest to 6 pm cost 18F, and sometimes there are other cut-rate festivals. In summer, La Villette hosts the no-admission **Cinéma en Plein Air** outdoors in the park. Rent a chair and blanket and bring a picnic dinner.

MUSIC

Classical music is publicly supported at national and local levels. Paris boasts symphony orchestras, chamber groups, and church ensembles. International guest orchestras and chamber groups perform regularly, as do visiting soloists on tour. Museums and churches schedule regular concert performances. Weekly guides describe the upcoming concerts, as do the monthly *Le Monde de la Musique* and the free *Diapason*, which can be found before performances at concert halls. See *Théâtres et salles de spectacles* in the Yellow Pages.

The main concert season is October–June. Get tickets early, for concerts sell out quickly, especially those with big-name conductors or soloists. Subscriptions to series are available, and subscribers have first choice for seats. Some *salles de concerts* (concert halls) offer student discounts just before performances.

Classical festivals are held throughout the year, in the summer pleasantly out of doors. Annual festivals in Paris are listed in the calendar below. Those in the nearby suburbs, accessible by public transportation, are noted in the weekly events guides. Look also for religious-oriented music at holiday times, such as the *Festival d'art sacré*, with church music around Christmas and Easter.

Radio-France organizes the most concerts in Paris and is the sponsor of the *Orchestre National de France* and the *Orchestre Philharmonique*. The **Cité de la Musique** at 221, avenue Jean-Jaurès 75020 (info tel: 01.44.84.45.00; reservations tel: 01.44.84.44.84) puts on a varied repertoire and is home to the *Ensemble InterContemporain*. Adjacent is the **Conservatoire National Supérieur de la Musique et de Danse de Paris**.

Free Concerts

Paris has a long tradition of free concerts. In May and June, classical and jazz concerts are held at the Parc Floral in the Bois de Vincennes, and throughout the summer free concerts are held in public gardens. No admission is charged to hear programs by students at the **Ecole Normale de Musique** and the **Institut National des Jeunes Aveugles** or rehearsals at the Cité de la Musique or **Maison de Radio-France**.

Along with their paid concert season, many churches offer free concerts of sacred music throughout the year, although generally not in August. Note that many of the churches are unheated, so on winter evenings it is important to bring a warm coat and to wear shoes with soles that do not conduct the cold. Most of the older churches do not have bathrooms.

The Opera

The Paris opera is one of the strongest aspects of the Parisian musical scene, attracting international stars to its major season, which runs from September through mid-July. The **Opéra Bastille** at Place de la Bastille 75012, which opened in 1989, is one of François Mitterrand's *Grands Projets* and is the largest opera house in the world (info tel: 01.43.43.96.96; reservations tel: 08.36.69.78.68). The Bastille offers grand opera in the *Grande Salle,* and other concerts and performing art festivals in the smaller *Amphithéâtre* and *Studio*. It generally stages sixteen operas per season in a varied repertoire. Although the opera is always an elegant occasion, formal dress is not required, except perhaps for opening nights.

When the Opéra Bastille was built, it was originally intended that the beautiful **Opéra Garnier** at Place de la Opéra 75009 be used only for ballet and other dance concerts. Now, however, it also hosts opera, putting on smaller works and special programs (tel: 01.40.01.17.89).

The best seats, of course, are expensive. Relatively inexpensive tickets are available with effort, and occasionally reduced-price tickets are sold to students and seniors just before show time. The box office sells tickets two weeks prior to a performance, and it is best to go on the first day that tickets are available and to wait in line. Although the box office opens at 11 am, some people arrive by 7 am for tickets to the most popular performances.

DANCE

The *Ballet de l'Opéra National de Paris* performs primarily at the Opéra Garnier, mixing some contemporary works into its classical repertoire. The Bastille also hosts international productions. Contemporary dance can be found at the city-subsidized **Théâtre de la Ville** at 2, place du Châtelet 75001 (tel: 01.42.74.22.77), which was founded by Sarah Bernhardt. There are also regularly scheduled ballet performances at the **Palais des Congrès** and the **Théâtre des Champs-Elysées**.

Currently, however, it is the offbeat theaters that are staging the most interesting performances. Look for Asian and Middle Eastern dance troupes at the **Centre Mandapa** at 6, rue Wurtz 75013 (tel: 01.45.89.01.60) and at **Danse, Théâtre et Musique** at 6, rue de la Folie-Méricourt 75011. You will find dance, musical performances, children's programs, and classes (tel: 01.47.00.19.60). Also in the 11e is the **Café de la Danse** at 5, passage Louis-Philippe, which hosts dance performances and other events from rock concerts to poetry readings (tel: 01.47.00.57.59).

NIGHTLIFE

From blues and jazz to the most mellow of *chansons*, from music bars and discotheques to enormous stadiums, there is not an evening in Paris when something is not going on. Radio Nova at 101.5 FM gives details each evening of what is happening. At newsstands, get *Les Inrockuptibles*, which details the current music scene. *LYLO*, a free publication, can be picked up at clubs around the city. Otherwise the best bet is to check the weekly events guides, the *Paris Free Voice*, or to ask at FNAC, Virgin Megastore, or other shops. Nightspots come and go, and some are closed occasionally for drug problems or other undesirable elements, so it is best to keep informed.

Many clubs impose a cover charge, often including the first drink (*consommation*). If not, the first drink can be expensive.

Occasionally entrance fees are waived, and some clubs distribute entry-free coupons around town.

If you have patience, your favorite group will eventually come to Paris, for they all do at one time or another. The major stadium for big musical events is the **Palais Omnisports de Paris-Bercy**; another large site is **Zénith** at 211, avenue Jean-Jaurès 75019 at La Villette. Throughout Paris, though, different styles overlap, especially Latin and African music, which can now be found just about everywhere. The ever-popular **New Morning**, for instance, at 7–9, rue des Petites-Ecuries 75010, hosts jazz, salsa, world music, blues, and just about anything else interesting that is passing through Paris (tel: 01.45.23.51.41).

Rock stars come through regularly to play at the clubs, and most of the best perform at **Arapaho**, at the *centre commercial* Italie2 75013 (tel: 01.45.89.65.05). The beautiful **Bataclan** at 50, boulevard Voltaire 75011 is perennially popular (tel: 01.47. 00.55.22).

The *Banlieues Bleues* jazz festival held in the spring draws internationally known jazz performers. **Le Caveau de la Huchette** at 5, rue de la Huchette 75005 is most famous for traditional jazz (tel: 01.43.26.65.05), and **Au Duc des Lombards** at 42, rue des Lombards 75001 is one of the coolest jazz spots in the city (tel: 01.42.33.22.88)

- 6e — **La Villa**: 29, rue Jacob (tel: 01.43.26.60.00)
- 14e — **Le Petit Journal Montparnasse**: 13, rue du Com-mandant-Mouchotte (tel: 01.43.21.56.70)

The truly *branché* (plugged in) crowd changes its preferences seemingly with the wind, but whatever the wind, it does not start blowing until late. *Boîtes* (discotheques) are popular, but not before midnight, and dancing can last until dawn. One stalwart favorite, despite its selection process at the door, is **Les Bains** at 7, rue du Bourg-l'Abbé 75002 (tel: 01.48.87.01.80). And one of the most varied is the comparatively inexpensive **La Locomotive** at 90, boulevard de Clichy 75018 (tel: 08.36.69.69.28). **Slow Club** at 130, rue de Rivoli offers a variety of styles, including boogie-woogie (tel: 01.42.33.84.30).

PHILOSOPHY CAFÉS

Trendy now are the *cafés des philosophes* at which people get to-gether to discuss philosophy. Topics are chosen in advance, and a leader guides the discussion. Most discussions are in the evening, but the **Café des Phares** at 7, Place de la Bastille 75004 is known for its discussion at 11 am on Sunday mornings. There are about a dozen philosophy cafés in Paris and the suburbs. For Anglo-phones, the **Café de Flore** at 172, boulevard St-Germain 75006 hosts a philosophy discussion the first Wednesday of every month from 7 pm to 9 pm. The discussion at **Meccano** at 99, rue Oberkampf 75011 is on the third Wednesday of the month.

GAY AND LESBIAN LIFE

Said to account for just under 5 percent of the Paris population, the gay and lesbian community is one of the most accepted in Europe, and it hosts the biggest EuroPride march on the conti-nent. The positive impact of Gay Pride is being recognized, as the French government is currently considering legislation to legalize a "contract of social union," giving unmarried cohabiting couples, straight or gay, the same social and financial rights as married couples. In Paris, there are scores of gay hotels, restaurants, bars, discotheques, saunas, and shops. Nonetheless, gays continue to protest against police harassment and discrimination. The Marais and nearby Les Halles are a focus for gay life; look also near the Bastille, around rue Keller.

A host of publications for the gay community can be found at many book stores and newsstands, especially at **Les Mots à la Bouche** at 6, rue Ste-Croix-de-la-Bretonnerie 75004, which serves as a gay information center (tel: 01.42.78.88.30). **Librairie des Femmes** at 74, rue de Seine 75006 is a prominent feminist bookshop which sells the *Annuaire de Lieux, Groupes et Activités Lesbiennes, Feministes et Homosexuelles*; they also have some information on events (tel: 01.43.29.50.75). Lesbians should look for the monthly magazine *Lesbia*.

- 11e — **Centre Gai et Lesbien**: 3, rue Keller (tel: 01.43.57.21.47). Information about the community and ongoing events, publishing *3 Keller*. Meeting place for activities of various groups.
- 4e — **SNEG (Syndicat National des Enterprises Gaies):** 44, rue du Temple (tel: 01.44.59.81.01; fax: 01.44.59.81.03). Business organization for gays and lesbians.
- 12e — **Maison des Femmes**: 163, rue de Charenton (tel: 01.43.43.41.13). *Archives, Recherches, Cultures Lesbiennes (ARCL)*. Feminist organization hosting some women's groups. Publishes an annual directory of addresses and events of interest to lesbians and feminists, plus other documentation in various media.

It would be impossible to list here all the places for entertainment and meeting people, but resources abound, including tourist guides, such as *Time Out Paris*. The annual, bilingual *Guide Gai* is comprehensive in its listings. Look for Frommer's *Paris by Night* and for *L'Introuvable Nights*, a bilingual guide to nighttime

Photo: Zeny Cieslikowski

A famous cabaret in Montmartre.

Paris that has a section on gay venues. *Paris Scene* is in English.
Illico, in French, has articles and ads, and *Double Face* is a lifestyle
magazine. Brentano's stocks the English-language *Out* and *The
Advocate*. Ask also at Les Mots à La Bouche, and try the 24-hour
gay radio station, Radio FG, on 98.2FM or the Minitel: 3615GAY.

NATIONAL HOLIDAYS/ANNUAL EVENTS

Below is a list of annual public holidays, festivals, and events in
Paris, although some festival dates vary from year to year. National holidays (*jours fériés*) are printed in boldface type. If a national holiday falls on a Tuesday or Thursday, some businesses,
including banks, *font le pont* (make a bridge) to a long weekend by
closing on the previous Monday or following Friday. The Paris
Tourist Office should have *Saisons de Paris*, listing all festivals.

291

January
- **1: Jour de l'an (New Year's Day) — National Holiday**
- 6: *Epiphanie*: *La Fête des Rois*. Pastry (*la galette des rois*) embedded with a little porcelain figurine or disk (*la fève*), and the winner becomes king/queen for the day.
- Two weeks in January: *La Mairie de Paris Vous Invite au Concert*: two concert tickets for the price of one.

February
- Early in month: Chinese New Year, with festivals, especially in the 13*e*.
- Second week: *18 heures-18 francs:* reduced prices at cinemas around 6 pm.
- End of month: *Foire à la Ferraille de Paris*: amusing fair in Bois de Vincennes. Antiques and knickknacks.

March
- Beginning of month: *Salon International de l'Agriculture*: World's largest agriculture exposition at Parc des Expositions. Food and wine from French provinces, prizewinning livestock, farm equipment, etc.
- Mid-month: *Salon de Mars*: antique fair in Place Joffre, in front of Ecole Militaire.
- Mid-month: *Musicora*: international salon of classical music at the Porte de Versailles.
- End of month: *Banlieues Bleues*: suburban jazz festival with internationally famous musicians.
- Palm Sunday: *Prix du Président de la République*. Horse race at Auteuil Racetrack, Bois de Boulogne.
- March/April: *Foire du Trône:* amusement park/fun fair on the Reuilly lawn in the Bois de Vincennes.
- March/April: *Paris Festival of Sacred Art*: Easter concerts at churches around Paris.

April

- 1: *April Fool's Day:* pastries and chocolates in the shape of fish. Practical jokes called *poisson d'avril.*
- *Pâques*: Easter Sunday
- **Lundi de Pâques:** Easter Monday — **National Holiday**
- Mid-month: *Paris Marathon*
- End of month*: Salon du Livre:* book fair and exhibitions at the Porte de Versailles
- End of April/May: *La Foire Internationale de Paris*, at the Parc des Expositions. Everything from furniture to food, wine tasting, gardening equipment, etc. Fun to browse through and good food.
- End of April/Early May: *La Mairie de Paris Vous Invite au Théâtre*: two theater tickets for the price of one.

May

- **1: Fête du Travail (May Day) — National Holiday.** Workers' holiday; parade near the Bastille. People give each other sprigs of Lily of the Valley.
- **8: Victoire 1945 — National Holiday**. Celebrating the World War II Victory in Europe.
- *Salon de Montrouge*: annual art show.
- *Les Cinq Jours de l'Objet Extraordinaire*: many antique shops on the Left Bank hold open houses.
- **Sixth Thursday after Easter: Ascension Day — National Holiday**
- **Second Monday after Ascension Day: Pentecost — National Holiday**. Pilgrimages to Sacré-Coeur.
- End of month: *French Open Tennis Championships*: Stade Roland-Garros.
- End of month: *Festival de Paris*: dance, theater, and music at various locations.

293

June

- Mid-June/July: *Festival du Marais*: music, dance, and theater in the historic *hôtels particuliers* in the Marais.
- Mid-month: *Grand Steeplechase de Paris*: annual steeplechase at Auteuil Racetrack.
- 21: *Fête de la Musique*: vibrant welcome to summer with music played in many outdoor venues.
- End of month: *Course des Garçons de Café*: waiters run an 8-km course around the Hôtel de Ville, carrying trays with full glasses of beer.
- *Salon International de l'Aéronautique et de l'Espace*: Parc des Expositions du Bourget. Paris Air Show, held in odd numbered years only; displays of aircraft and air shows.
- End of month: *Grand Prix de Paris*: horse race at Longchamp.
- End of month: *La Marche Homosexuelle* (Gay Pride March).

July

- Early month: *Festival de Saint-Denis*: several weeks of arts events at Saint-Denis.
- Early month: *Foire Internationale d'Art au Grand Palais*: international art exhibition at the Grand Palais.
- 13: Bastille Day Eve: Festivities to open Bastille Day. *Les Bals des Pompiers* are firemen's balls in the streets, lasting until all hours.
- **14: Le 14 Juillet — National Holiday**. Parade on the Champs-Elysées. Fireworks at the Trocadéro.
- Mid-month/Mid-August: *Paris, Quartier d'Eté*: music and dance festival in various venues.
- July–August: *Musique en l'Ile*: concerts in the Eglise St-Louis, on the Ile St-Louis.
- Mid-July/Mid-September: *Festival Estival de Paris*: classical music in churches and museums.
- End of month: *Arrivée du Tour de France Cycliste*: the end of the Tour de France on the Champs-Elysées.

August
- **15: Assumption Day — National Holiday**

September
- Mid-month: *Les Journées du Patrimoine* (Heritage Days): open house at historic landmarks.
- Mid-month: Opera season opens.
- Mid-month: *Fête de l'Humanité*: lively Communist-party-sponsored festival at La Courneuve, to the north.
- Mid-month to December: *Festival d'Automne*: major performing arts festival.

October
- First Sunday: *Prix de l'Arc de Triomphe*. Horse race at Longchamp.
- Mid to end of month: *Festival de Jazz de Paris:* jazz concerts throughout the city.
- Mid-month: *Foire Internationale d'Art Contemporain* (*FIAC*): international fair of contemporary art.

November
- **1: Toussaint — National Holiday**: All Saints Day.
- 1: *Cimetière du Calvaire*: open one day a year to visitors. Oldest in Paris, dating from the 13th century.
- 1–7: *Paris Open*: tennis championships at the Palais Omnisports de Paris-Bercy.
- *Salon d'Automne*: art salon in the Grand Palais.
- **11: Armistice 1918 — National Holiday**: World War I Armistice celebration.
- Mid-month: *Trophée Lalique de Patinage Artistique*: figure-skating competition at the Palais Omnisports de-Bercy.
- Third Thursday: *Beaujolais Nouveau* officially distributed.

December

- All month: Christmas in Paris. Animated *crèche* (nativity scene) outside the Hôtel de Ville. Main shopping streets illuminated. Store windows in the department stores beautifully decorated, often with lovely *crèches*.
- Early month: *Salon Nautique International*: international boat show.
- Early month: Nocturne des Boutiques du Comité Vendôme. Some of the expensive boutiques around Place Vendôme stay open late to encourage Christmas shopping.
- 24: Feast of *Réveillon* at midnight. Oysters and *foie gras*. Midnight mass at city churches.
- **25: Noël — National Holiday.** Christmas. Turkey with chestnuts is a specialty.
- 31: Midnight festivities on New Year's Eve.

Chapter Eighteen

RELIGION IN PARIS

CHURCH AND STATE

Although some 90 percent of the French population claims Catholicism as its religion, it is said that only about 12 percent are active worshipers. Since 1905, there has been an official separation of church and state. In 1996, secular groups objected when President Jacques Chirac took communion at the funeral of his predecessor François Mitterrand and when he knelt to the Pope in Rome. They also protested against the spending of public monies to help pay for the Pope's visit to France in September 1996. Yet in France the lines between church and state remain blurred. State subsidies to Catholic private schools, for instance, continue to be a cause of protest by defenders of secularism. Yet whether one worships or not, the histories of Christianity and of Paris are inextricably entwined, and this is most evident in the

297

city's hundreds of churches, some of which are among the most architecturally impressive in the world.

Only Rome has a history of Christianity as long and as rich as that of Paris. When the Christian martyr Saint Denis was decapitated in about A.D. 250, it is said that he picked up his head and carried it to the top of what came to be called the Mount of the Martyrs (Montmartre) and finally died at what is now the northern suburb of Saint-Denis. A chapel was built, and Christian pilgrims began to come. In the twelfth century, the Basilica of Saint-Denis was built in its present Gothic style. But it was the patron saint of Paris, Sainte Geneviève, who in the sixth century delivered Paris to Christianity, having first impressed Parisians by thwarting an imminent invasion by Attila the Hun through her Christian faith and then by converting the Frankish King Clovis to Christianity.

Like Saint-Denis, the Cathedral of Notre-Dame was built in the Gothic style. Here in itself is the history of Paris. Begun in the twelfth century and taking more than 100 years to complete, the cathedral was built on the ruins of a church dating back to the Merovingians. By descending into the crypt in front of the cathedral a visitor can see some of its foundations and, even older, some city fortifications from ancient Lutetia.

During the French Revolution, Notre-Dame was confiscated along with other churches and transformed into a secular Temple of Reason, at which time its statues were destroyed and the cathedral itself fell into great disrepair. During the restoration of the monarchy, however, Louis-Philippe undertook to restore the cathedral to its former glory. During World War II, the exquisite stained glass windows were removed and stored to keep them intact. And today, despite ongoing renovations, millions of visitors and worshipers come each year to see Notre-Dame and to witness Paris' history at *kilomètre zéro* of France.

CATHOLICISM

The city's more than 200 Catholic churches, including the stately Cathédrale de Notre-Dame, the flashy Sacré-Coeur, the gentle Saint-Sulpice, and the ordinary neighborhood churches, offer regular masses and confessions. Churches open about 8 am and generally hold three masses daily; on Sunday there are more. Masses and confession in English can be heard at **St. Joseph's Church** at 50, avenue Hoche 75008 (tel: 01.42.27.28.56). The **Catholic Information Center** is at 8, rue de la Ville-l'Evêque 75008 (tel: 01.49.24.11.44). Catholic radio is on 102.7FM, Radio Montmartre.

ISLAM

Since the 1960s there has been a large immigration into France of Muslims from North Africa. Currently there are about three million Muslims in France, accounting for about 5 percent of the population, with just under one million in the Paris area. Dating from the 1920s, **La Mosquée** at Place du Puits-de-l'Ermite 75005 is the religious nucleus of Parisian Muslims; call for information about worship times and for information about other mosques (tel: 01.45.35.97.33). Inside its walls, the mosque has a tea room, a *hammam*, and gardens. Guided tours are available every day except Friday. Inquire also at the community's central point, the beautiful **Institut du Monde Arabe** at 1, rue des Fossés St-Bernard 75005 (tel: 01.40.51.38.38).

JUDAISM

Although Jews in France date back to A.D. 39, French Jewry's greatest impact was in the Middle Ages, between the tenth and thirteenth centuries, when rabbinical academies and writings were world-renowned and Jewish poets flowered. In 1394, however, under Charles VI, they were expelled, an official exile that lasted, with some exceptions, until 1784. Under Napoleon, Jews were

299

given full civil rights, although a lingering anti-Semitism continued to exist. This culminated in the Dreyfus Affair at the turn of this century, when a Jewish army officer was unjustly convicted of treason.

Under the Nazi occupation during World War II, about 80,000 Jews were deported. Since the war there has been an influx into France of Sephardic Jews from North Africa. Currently some 750,000 Jews live in France, accounting for just under 2 percent of the population. About three-quarters live in Paris, primarily in the Marais, which is their historical center, and in the suburbs of Créteil to the south and Sarcelles to the north.

Judaism in France is divided into *Non-Consistoire* (ultra-Orthodox), *Consistoire* (Orthodox), *Massorti* (traditionally Conservative), and *Libérale* (between Conservative and Reform). The Orthodox communities maintain strong social distinctions between *Ashkenaz* and *Sepharad*.

Within Paris there are some 80 synagogues. Despite their official names, they are commonly called by their street names, so the Rothschild Synagogue (or Great Synagogue) in rue de la Victoire is known as "La Victoire." This may seem incongruous when, for instance, Paris' oldest synagogue, in rue Notre-Dame de Nazareth, is known at "La Nazareth."

Kehilat Gesher, the French-Anglophone Jewish congregation at 10, rue de Pologne 78100 St-Germain-en-Laye, is a *libérale* community with Shabbat services in Hebrew, French, and English (tel: 01.39.21.97.19). Services are held in St-Germain-en-Laye and in Paris.

For information on the Orthodox community, inquire at the **Association Consistoriale Israélite de Paris** at 17, rue St-Georges 75009 (tel: 01.40.82.26.26) or at the **Centre Rachi** at 39, rue Broca 75008 (tel: 01.42.17.10.10). The Jewish radio station is 94.8FM. *Actualité Juive* and *Information Juive* are two of the community's newspapers. See *Culte Israélite* in the Yellow Pages.

- 9e—**Rothschild (Great) Synagogue**: 44, rue de la Victoire (tel: 01.40.82.26.26). *Consistoire.*
- 16e—**Synagogue Union Libérale Israélite de France** 24, rue Copernic (tel: 01.47.04.37.27). *Libérale.*
- 16e—**Synagogue Montevideo**: 31, rue Montevideo (tel: 01.45.04.66.73). *Non-Consistoire.*
- 16e—**Adath Shalom**: 22 bis, rue des Belles-Feuilles (tel: 01.45.53.84.09). *Massorti.*
- 18e—**Communauté Juive Libérale Ile-de-France**: 6, rue Pierre-Ginier (tel: 01.42.93.03.44). *Libérale.* Pauline Bebe, only woman rabbi in France.

PROTESTANT RELIGIONS

From their beginnings, *Huguenots* (French Protestants) were persecuted in France, culminating in the infamous 1572 Saint Bartholomew's Day Massacre in Paris, when three thousand Protestants and Protestant sympathizers were killed. When Henri III was assassinated two years later, his heir Henri de Navarre, a Protestant, sustained a four-year protest by his subjects until he finally converted to Catholicism in 1593, saying the famous words: *"Paris vaut bien une messe"* ("Paris is well worth a mass"). Although he continued to protect Protestants, their civil rights lasted fewer than 100 years, when the Counter-Reformation finally drove many out. Yet Protestantism has persisted, and today the French Protestant community is said to account for just above 1 percent of the population. The influx of foreign Protestants into Paris, however, has made available many opportunities for Anglophone worship. Call the **Fédération Protestante de France** at 47, rue de Clichy 75009 for information (tel: 01.44.53.47.00).

The churches below offer services in English, and many have social activities for parishioners. The American Church plays a prominent role in Christian Anglophone activities, offering family events, cultural and social activities, and support groups. The

Christian Women's Club of Paris is a French organization that hosts lunches, meetings, and Bible classes (tel: 01.39.46.37.13).

For more specific information on all churches, call the **Centre d'Information et de Documentation Religieuse** at 8, rue Massillon 75004 (tel: 01.46.33.01.01). The Protestant radio frequency is 100.7FM, Radio Notre-Dame. See the Yellow Pages under *Cultes divers* and *Eglises*.

- Anglican/Episcopal — **American Cathedral of the Holy Trinity**: 23, avenue George-V 75008 (tel: 01.53.23.84.00)
- Anglican — **St. George's Anglican Church**: 7, rue Auguste-Vacquerie 75016 (tel: 01.47.20.22.51)
- Anglican — **St. Michael's English Church**: 5, rue d'Aguesseau 75008 (tel: 01.47.42.70.88)
- Baptist — **Emmanuel Baptist Church of Paris**: 56, rue des Bons-Raisins 92500 Rueil-Malmaison (tel: 01.47.51.29.63)
- Christian Science — **First Church of Christ, Scientist**: 36, boulevard St-Jacques 75014 (tel: 01.47.07.26.60); 58, boulevard Flandrin 75116 (tel: 01.45.04.48.93); 30, rue de Penthièvre 75008 (tel: 01.45.62.19.85)
- Church of Christ — **Church of Christ**: 4, rue Déodat-de-Séverac 75017 (tel: 01.42.27.50.86)
- Lutheran — **Lutheran Church**: 16, rue Chauchat 75009 (tel: 01.47.70.80.30)
- Mormon — **Church of Jesus Christ of Latter Day Saints**: 64, rue de Romainville 75019 (tel: 01.42.45.28.57)
- Presbyterian Church of Scotland — **Scots Kirk**: 17, rue Bayard 75008 (tel: 01.48.78.47.94)
- Protestant — **The American Church in Paris**: 65, quai d'Orsay 75007 (tel: 01.40.62.05.00)
- Quaker — **Religious Society of Friends**: 114 bis, rue de Vaugirard 75006 (tel: 01.45.48.74.23)

THE AUTHOR

Frances Gendlin has held leadership positions in both magazine and book publishing. She was editor and publisher of *Sierra*, the magazine of the Sierra Club, a worldwide environmental organization, and was the association's director of public affairs. As executive director of the Association of American University Presses, she represented the 100-member publishing houses to the public and fostered scholarly publishing interests. In 1997, she wrote *Living & Working Abroad: Rome*, a widely read guide to understanding and living in that city.

While she was growing up, her family moved several times to different areas of the United States, each with its own characteristics and culture, climate and cuisine. This has led her to appreciate new cultures, to wonder about their differences and similarities to her own, and to try and understand them. All her life she has enjoyed travel and new adventures, meeting interesting people and making new friends.

Frances Gendlin now lives in San Francisco and owns a free-lance editorial business, *The Right Word*. She evaluates manuscripts and guides, helps writers with their projects, and teaches English and business writing to foreign professionals, both in the United States and abroad. Thanks to the advent of the modem and fax, she can work virtually anywhere in the world. She has thus been able to arrange her professional life to accommodate her love of travel. Currently, she spends part of each year in Rome and Paris.

INDEX